Teaching Children with Learning Problems

Gerald Wallace
University of Virginia

James M. Kauffman
University of Virginia

Charles E. Merrill Publishing Co.
A Bell & Howell Co.
Columbus, Ohio

To Marti and Myrna

Published by
Charles E. Merrill Publishing Co.
A Bell & Howell Co.
Columbus, Ohio

International Standard Book Number: 0-675-08998-0

Library of Congress Catalog Card Number: 72-92777

2 3 4 5 6 7 8 9 10—77 76 75 74 73

Printed in the United States of America

Preface

This book is a guide to remediating learning problems. It is intended for special and regular classroom teachers in training or in service. Our experience in schools and universities indicates that it is possible for most classroom teachers to become proficient in the remediation of learning problems when appropriate instruction and guidance are provided.

Part I of this volume provides a practical approach to remediation. Learning problems are defined in terms of specific behavioral deficits rather than in terms of nonfunctional categories or traditional special education labels. Principles of behavior management and academic remediation are described in understandable language and illustrated with examples drawn from the classroom. Early detection and good teaching are discussed as primary facets of prevention of learning problems. The material presented in Part I serves as a foundation for the development of Part II.

Part II operationalizes the principles presented in Part I. Teaching competencies which have application across curriculum areas are outlined in Chapter 5. Chapters 6 through 11 contain many specific teaching activities in the area of classroom management, visual-motor skills, reading, written language, oral language, and arithmetic. The beginning teacher will find many proven teaching suggestions and the more experienced teacher will be able to adapt the suggested activities to the unique requirements of particularly difficult problems. A list of additional readings at the end of each chapter provides a guide to further study.

This book could not have been completed without the assistance and support of many individuals. Colleagues in the Department of Special Education at the University of Virginia were constant in their encouragement of our efforts. We are especially indebted to Dr. William Lowry for reviewing Chapter 11 and to Dr. Ralph Stoudt for reviewing Chapter 10. Judy Hallahan gave us expert editorial assistance for Chapter 1. T. R. Scranton contributed valuable suggestions for Chapter 6. Former students at both the University of Utah and the University of Virginia provided many ideas for the teaching activities in Part II. Wanda Evans, Bette Scranton, and Linda Wilberger were highly proficient in typing the manuscript. Sandy Smith, our production editor, gave us valuable advice. Our wives and children provided endless encouragement throughout the preparation of the manuscript.

Gerald Wallace

James M. Kauffman

Contents

I

A Practical Approach to Remediation

Most children in our schools do not experience major learning problems. Their behavior is generally acceptable to the teacher, and their academic achievement is within the expected range for their abilities. A significant proportion of school children do, however, exhibit social-emotional problems or academic difficulties. Children with learning problems are becoming more apparent as the forces of educational technology and humanistic values shape American schools.

Present educational efforts to meet the needs of children with school learning problems have not been successful. The preparation of special teachers and the

1

establishment of special classes have not resulted in
adequate educational opportunities for all children.
Nor have personnel designated as "resource," "crisis,"
"prescriptive," or "consultant" teachers resolved the
problem of remedial education. It is becoming
increasingly clear that if the educational needs of all
children are to be met, all teachers must become
skillful in the instruction of children with learning
problems.

All teachers experience the pleasure of teaching
children who learn quickly and easily. The frustration
and anxiety produced by children who learn slowly
and with great difficulty are also felt by all teachers.
We have observed that frustration, anxiety, depression,
and anger can be replaced by an extra measure of joy
and satisfaction for both the teacher and the child
when learning problems are successfully remediated. A
working knowledge of the principles presented in Part
I will increase the probability that the teacher will
develop the technical skill necessary to remediate
learning problems successfully.

Humanistic education highlights the development of
awareness and sensitivity of the teacher to his own
needs and the needs of individual children.
Self-awareness, self-actualization, and sensitivity to
others as persons are prerequisites for good teaching,
but they must be accompanied by a high degree of
technical knowledge and skill or children will not be
helped. Self-realization, awareness, and human concern
for his patients as persons can enhance but cannot
replace the physician's technical knowledge and skill
in the practice of medicine. Likewise, sensitivity and
humanistic goals can supplement but cannot supplant

the understanding and application of learning principles in teaching. Technical mastery allows the practitioner to give form and substance to humanistic values.

Teachers often unknowingly fail to help children with learning problems because they lack technical skill. Consequently, our emphasis is on the knowledge and application of sound learning principles and instructional strategies.

Part I provides a foundation for the development of specific teaching techniques. Chapter 1 is an overview of characteristics, etiologies, and educational services for children with learning problems. Chapter 2 introduces basic principles of classroom management from a behavior-modification point of view. Chapter 3 presents principles of remediating academic deficits which apply to all curriculum areas. Chapter 4 points the way to prevention of learning problems through early detection and good teaching.

I

Dimensions
of
Learning
Problems

A goal of American public education is equal educational opportunity for every child. Although this goal may be attainable, it has remained elusive for decades. The concept of instructional methods matched to the learning characteristics of each child is familiar to teachers, but individualized instruction has not been the hallmark of this nation's schools. It has taken court decisions, federal legislation, mobilization of parents, and new methods in special education to bring the dream of maximum learning for all children closer to reality.

The pragmatic spirit of America is reflected in educational policies and procedures aimed at modal learning patterns. But for a significant number of children, education designed for the "average" child precipitates confusion, academic failure, feelings of inadequacy, disparagement by teachers and peers, and, finally, despair or disgust for school. These children, commonly identified as having school learning problems, have been designated by a wide variety of labels, all of them pejorative: emotionally disturbed, educationally inadequate, brain damaged, educationally handicapped, culturally disadvantaged, learning disabled, educable mentally retarded, slow learning, perceptually handicapped, behavior disordered, maladjusted, hyperactive, and many more.

Our concern in this book is not with labels by which children can be called but with the specific learning difficulties preventing their success in school. Our assumption is that it makes very little difference how a child is labeled or defined for administrative purposes, but that precise definition of his learning problem is the first essential step in remediation. Specifically, it is what the child does and does not do in response to an educational program that is the focus of our concern.

Children defy meaningful classification—the learning problems which they experience do not. The history of systems of classification shows that attempting to fit persons into psychological and educational categories is futile (Linder, 1965; Menninger, 1963). On the other hand, precise definition of the individual's learning difficulties and strengths, which points toward specific treatment procedures, pays enormous dividends in successful remediation (Schiefelbusch, 1967). Since they are essential to acceptable performance, the dimensions of learning necessary for school progress provide the most logical framework for definition of learning problems.

Social-Emotional
Learning

When a child enters school, his progress depends not only on learning academic responses but also on building a repertoire of adequate emotional and social behavior. He must adopt behavior patterns which indicate self-acceptance as well as self-realization. The child most likely to succeed at school is one who is both productive and happy. His behavior reflects confidence, organization, initiative, persistence, self-control, and pride in accomplishment. The successful child relates well to others. Among his peers, he is usually outgoing, friendly, popular, and able to take a leadership role among children. His relationship to adults and authority figures is characterized by confidence, respect, and cooperation.

Children who have difficulty in learning social and emotional responses which would contribute to success at school exhibit a wide variety of maladaptive behaviors. Those most likely to attract the attention of the teacher include talking out of turn, moving about the room without permission, hitting other children, tantruming, and crying (Bergen & Caldwell, 1967). Such inappropriate behavior in schoolchildren may be understood within a three-dimensional framework which includes conduct problems, inadequacy-immaturity, and personality problems (McCarthy & Paraskevopoulos, 1969; Paraskevopoulos & McCarthy, 1969; Peterson, 1961; Quay, Morse, & Cutler, 1966). Conduct problems are characterized by overt aggression, hostility, defiance, boisterousness, hyperactivity, destructiveness, tantrums, and other behaviors associated with striking out at one's environment. The inadequacy-immaturity dimension includes behaviors such as inattention, sluggishness, lack of interest, laziness, daydreaming, and dislike for school. Personality problems are typified by hypersensitivity, self-consciousness, feelings of inferiority, lack of self-confidence, fearfulness, and anxiety.

Individual children often show deficits in social-emotional learning along more than one dimension of problem behavior. A child's conduct problem does not preclude his exhibiting behaviors characteristic of personality deviations. Multi-dimensional social-emotional learning deficits are exhibited in the following cases of Johnny and Fred.

Johnny

An only child, Johnny lived with his mother, stepfather, and grandmother. At the age of 2, he began having petit mal seizures. Although he had an abnormal EEG, his seizures were brought under control with medication, and did not recur after his enrollment in school.

Appearing to be of normal intelligence, Johnny nevertheless experienced academic and social difficulties in the school setting. His kindergarten and first-grade teachers reported that he vomited frequently and spent most of his time crying. In the second grade, Johnny stopped vomiting when the teacher began having him help clean up the vomitus. His crying continued, however, and he was referred to a mental health clinic for psychiatric counseling.

From Johnny's first day in the third grade, he had frequent hysterical fits of crying which seemed to be precipitated by any event causing the slightest discomfort or anxiety, such as the teacher's request that he complete his work, perspiring on the playground, or the occurrence of a fire drill. These displays varied in duration from 5 minutes to 2 hours. His teacher recorded an average of 16 crying fits per day over a 2 week period. Sometimes she attempted to control his crying by giving him soothing attention when he was upset. She also tried shaking him angrily, asking him to leave the room, and ignoring him. All these management techniques were unsuccessful.

Johnny's family situation doubtless had an impact on his behavior. Even when he was in the third grade, he was still accompanied by his grandmother both to and from school, although he lived only two blocks away. The grandmother also dressed him and tied his shoes. Johnny slept with his mother until he was 7 years old, and his mother still bathed him at age 8. He called his mother by her first name and, according to a home-school liaison worker, he showed contempt for his natural father and fear of his stepfather.

Johnny became known throughout the school as a problem child. No one was able to remedy his home situation or enlist the cooperation of his mother and grandmother. He was finally referred to a resource room for emotionally disturbed children.

Fred

Fred was born to an unwed mother in Mexico. The pregnancy and birth were unremarkable. Developmentally, Fred apparently was somewhat slow, standing at 9 months, walking at 13 months, and speaking his first word at 25 months. Until the age of three, when his adoptive American father married his mother, Fred lived in Mexico with his mother, his grandmother, and three aunts. During these early years of his life, Fred was said to be undisciplined and hyperactive.

Because his father's vocation required frequent moving about the country Fred's early education was often disrupted. He attended kindergarten in Miami and Los Angeles and first grade in New York and Kansas City. His mother and father encouraged him to speak Spanish at home. Consequently, he spoke little English until he entered kindergarten. He also developed speech problems in both languages.

During his first-grade experience in Kansas City, Fred was given a battery of psychological tests, the results of which indicated borderline intellectual capacity and perceptual deficiencies in eye-motor coordination, figure-ground relationships, spatial relationships, and laterality. Several months after testing he was placed in a special class for the educable mentally retarded; but because of severe behavior problems, he was removed from the special class and placed on homebound instruction for the last few weeks of the school year.

In the summer following Fred's homebound instruction, he was referred to a psychoeducational clinic for evaluation of his learning and behavior problems. The investigating social worker reported observation of the following behavior problems: running around the room, hitting, drooling, poor motor coordination, frequent falls, nail biting, occasional bed-wetting, fitful sleep, destructive behavior, preference for play with younger children, general hyperactivity, and lack of response to discipline. It was the social worker's impression that Fred's father was authoritative, aggressive, intelligent, informed about his son's problems, and willing to help. Fred's mother appeared to be submissive and possibly resentful of her husband but also eager to cooperate.

Subsequent to his evaluation at the psychoeducational clinic, Fred was enrolled in a special class for children with learning disabilities.

Academic
Learning

There is no task within our schools bringing greater pressure to bear upon a child than academic achievement (Heilman, 1972). From the first day in school, children are made aware that the key to success is effective academic performance. No one knows this more than the child who experiences academic difficulties. The frustrating and agonizing aspects of school failures are all too readily apparent in the child who encounters difficulties in learning to read, write, or calculate.

For some children, school problems are limited to specific skill deficiencies in particular academic tasks. Large numbers of other children, however, experience severe problems in more than one area. Problems almost invariably overlap among all school-related tasks, including listening, thinking, talking, reading, writing, spelling, and arithmetic. It is, therefore, impossible to list all of the many different types of academic difficulties that children may encounter in school.

Children who experience learning problems frequently are considered a homogeneous group. Many of their specific difficulties are obscured, however, by the blanket classification of "academic learning problems." All children are not hampered by identical deficiencies. In addition to extending across academic tasks, learning problems are complicated by varying degrees of difficulty, by the age of the child, and by the child's attitude toward his disabilities. As the following cases illustrate, children having "academic difficulties" may exhibit very different characteristics.

Skip
An eighth-grade student of average intelligence, Skip was referred to a clinic for testing. The boy's small stature made him appear about the size of an average fifth grader, and his general maturity level was also more like that of a fifth grader than that of a junior high school student. In the classroom, for example, he

enjoyed having the teacher read to him, especially from animal stories, tales of adventure, and other types of stories typically found in elementary readers. Socially, he was easy prey for several peers who delighted in ordering him about. In fact, he was virtually friendless.

Skip seemed to have only the vaguest notion of what was occurring in his classroom, even though he made every effort to appear to be doing the right thing. Although he caused very little problem to his teacher, his refraining from class discussion and his negligible contact with other students when they were allowed to work together became a source of concern. Actually, his academic skills were too meager to permit him to be an active student. When tested, he read on the first-grade level, with many mispronunciations, omissions, and repetitions. His word-attack skills amounted to little more than guessing. He was unable to use cursive writing; and his printing, barely legible, was marked by reversals and omissions of letters.

Skip had been sporadically provided with remedial help. At the time of referral he was being seen by a resource teacher for 30-minute periods 3 days a week. This teacher felt, however, that his severe academic problems could not be remediated in such short sessions. Skip was essentially a cipher in the classroom.[1]

Jessie

A slim, soft-spoken 8-year-old third grader, Jessie was referred for help because of academic problems. He professed interests in eating, football, coloring, and stories, especially *The Three Little Pigs.* He was also able to relate and act out varied stories about his activities with his family.

Jessie had a very limited sight vocabulary and no observable word-attack skills. He did not understand the distinction between letter names, the sounds letters make, and words used to illustrate the sounds of letters. He also found it hard to comprehend that a letter could have more than one form, even though he knew the upper- and lowercase forms of a few letters.

In arithmetic, Jessie could count to 16. He could read *30, 40, 50,* etc., but he had little understanding of the one's place beyond *19.* He knew the meaning of addition and subtraction and could perform those operations adequately with single-digit combinations, but he was unsure of two-digit numbers. Completely unfamiliar with fractions, he was stymied by the *meaning* of "half." He had but a rudimentary understanding of telling time, knowing only that there was a "big hand" and a "short one."

Although Jessie was aware of his academic difficulties, his learning problems seemed not to affect his self-confidence and verbal ability. At the time of testing, he expressed a desire to learn how to read. Also, his interaction with his peers was reported as excellent. In fact, the teacher commented that he was probably one of the best-liked members of the class. She also expressed a sincere interest in trying to help Jessie overcome his learning problems.

Why School
Learning Problems Develop

Children experience learning problems for many complex reasons. Single causes of difficulty are seldom, if ever, found. Some causal factors, such as genetics, operate over a long period of time and reach far into the individual's history to create a *predisposition* for learning problems. Other factors, such as a traumatic event or inadequate teaching, are more immediate in their effect and serve to *precipitate* a learning difficulty. Most learning problems stem from an interaction of multiple predisposing and precipitating factors (McCarthy & McCarthy, 1969; Thomas, Chess, & Birch, 1968).

Even if an exhaustive catalog of specific causes of learning problems could be compiled, such a list would be instructive only if each cause implied a specific remedy and the remedy were available to the reader. At present, few specific remedies are implied by known or suspected etiologies of learning difficulties, and fewer still are useable by teachers. Nevertheless, it is useful for educators to be aware of the major factors which may be implicated in the development of school learning problems so that proper referral can be made when remediation by other professionals is possible.

Bio-physical Factors

A child's genetic endowment and physical status obviously have a profound effect on his behavior (McClearn, 1964; Williams, 1967). Birth trauma, oxygen deprivation, infectious disease, drug intoxication, malnutrition, and congenital defects are only a few of the biological events which may influence a child's ability to learn. Attempts to pinpoint specific biological correlates of individual learning problems, however, have not been successful (Cawley, 1967; Clark, 1968; Reed, Rabe, & ManKinen, 1971). Certainly the teacher must be aware of possible bio-physical factors contributing to the development of a school learning problem and should refer the child to appropriate medical personnel for evaluation. But most medical diagnoses clearly have few implications for remediation by the teacher, who is not able to give genetic counseling, prescribe drugs, perform surgery, or administer other forms of medical treatment.

Socio-cultural Factors

The social and cultural contexts in which the child lives undeniably shape his learning also. Family relationships, social class, the expectations of educational systems, and membership in subcultural groups are known to be determining variables in the child's development (Clausen, 1966; Rubin & Balow, 1971; Short, 1966; White & Charry, 1966). There is little doubt that deteriorating family units, poverty, racial discrimination, manipulation by the media, rigid school policies, cultural fetishes and taboos, and other social and cultural factors influence the child's behavior in school (Webster, 1966).

Although the teacher should be concerned with the social and cultural conditions which contribute to children's learning problems, he cannot make socio-cultural intervention the focus of his professional activity.

> Educational objectives must be demonstrably consistent with the priorities of skills valued in our society. Educators must recognize that they are not policymakers. They cannot make up objectives that are inconsistent with society's general commitment to make children competent in the academic arena (Engelmann, 1969, p. 30).*

Psycho-developmental Factors

It has often been suggested that learning problems arise from an underlying psychological disturbance or developmental delay (Berkowitz & Rothman, 1960; Bettelheim, 1961; Ephron, 1953; Erickson, 1963; Freud, 1965; Pearson, 1954). Undoubtedly, anxiety about growing up, separation from one's parents, establishing one's own identity, experiencing traumatic events, learning to express one's emotions appropriately, building trusting relationships, and many other developmental tasks and psychological processes are related to school learning. There is no reason to question the assumption that normal psychological development smooths the way for learning or to doubt that removal of emotional problems makes the remediation of learning difficulties easier. As in the case of bio-physical factors, however, psychological diagnoses seldom point to specific remedia-

---

*From *Preventing Failure in the Primary Grades* by Siegfried Engelmann. © 1969, Science Research Associates, Inc. Reproduced by permission.

tion (Stuart, 1970). Furthermore, when specific remediation is suggested, the teacher is not able to provide appropriate treatment—he is not trained as a psychotherapist.

Educational Factors

It is axiomatic that learning problems may occur because of inadequate or inappropriate instruction. The child may not learn because the teacher fails to teach. The specific deficits in teaching which account for the child's failure to learn *can* be found. When they are found, it is the teacher's responsibility to correct them, for he is trained to control the instructional variables that govern learning. Thus, the teacher must take responsibility for the learning of *all* children. This does not mean that when the teacher has failed to teach a child, despite his best efforts, he has failed as a person or as a professional. It does mean that the teacher will be primarily concerned with educational reasons for children's learning problems and that he will continue to examine and improve his techniques of teaching rather than blame the child or some etiological factor over which he has no control (Engelmann, 1969).

**Provisions for
School Learning Problems**

Educational provisions for children experiencing learning difficulties in school traditionally have been assigned to educators who operate outside the realm of the regular classroom. These supportive personnel, teaching in special classes or resource rooms, have had major responsibility for ameliorating school learning problems. In terms of actual numbers, however, remedial specialists have had little effect in reducing the prevalence of academic difficulties among school-age children. The task has been too overwhelming for specialists alone to handle. Under these circumstances, the concentration of effort outside the regular classroom has proven to be a monumental and unrealistic task.

Nevertheless, only in the past few years has it been widely suggested that working within the regular classroom and allowing classroom teachers the opportunity of remediating learning difficulties may provide a possible alternative approach to remediation (Long, Morse, & Newman, 1971; Ross, DeYoung, & Cohen, 1971). In a short period of time, this approach has proven to be a most feasible and effective means of remediating school learning problems. At the same time, special education arrangements have come to be considered more appropriate for the child with severe learning problems. Two of these special administrative arrangements are summarized below.

Resource Room

In this arrangement, children are enrolled with their peers in a regular classroom, and, depending upon the nature of their difficulty, they are seen by a specially trained teacher for various lengths of time to work on specific problems. Some children may be seen individually by the resource teacher for fifteen to forty-five minutes daily while others may be seen twice weekly in small groups. The extensiveness of contact with the resource teacher will largely depend upon the severity of the child's difficulty. Normally, the resource teacher is housed in a classroom especially equipped with various materials and educational equipment particularly suited to the needs of the children.

The resource room has been used successfully both with academically retarded and with behaviorally disordered children. However, the limited number of children who can be seen by one resource teacher represents a disadvantage of this arrangement. It is often an impossible task to see all the children who need help. In addition, because resource teachers must often divide their time among two or more schools, their time for communication with regular classroom teachers may be confined to brief conversations in the hallway or the lunchroom. A number of school districts have attempted to overcome some of these problems by varying the role of the resource teacher. One such plan involves the utilization of the resource teacher as a curriculum specialist or instructional consultant to the classroom teacher (Blessing, 1969). This approach makes more efficient use of the resource teacher's talents and provides direct help to classroom teachers. The plan also offers additional advantages not apparent in the traditional resource room model, such as keeping the child with his peers and upgrading the instructional skills of the regular classroom teacher.

Special Classes

One of the oldest special education arrangements is the segregated special class for specific types of handicapped children. In terms of actual numbers, classes for the mentally retarded have been most common (Simon & Grant, 1968), but special classes for the learning disabled and behaviorally disordered have increased substantially in the past few years (Kirk, 1972). Children enrolled in special classes usually spend the entire day in the class with other similarly handicapped children. Since maximum enrollment per class is usually dictated by state law, the special class often contains fewer students than does the regular classroom.

Most critics of special classes argue that their segregated nature detrimentally affects the overall development of children (Dunn, 1968). Isolation from normal peers and poor academic achievement are often cited as disadvantages of special class placement (Stanton & Cassidy, 1964; Goldstein, Moss, & Jordan, 1965). On the other hand, the superior social and emotional adjustment achieved by special class pupils frequently provides an argument for their continuation (Cassidy & Stanton, 1959; Jordan & DeCharms, 1959; Kern & Pfaeffle, 1962). However, because of the legal questions involved in placement, the very survival of special classes is decidedly threatened (Cruickshank, 1972; Ross, DeYoung, & Cohen, 1971).

Regular Class Remediation

The current trend in American education toward more personalized instruction has provided a means for handling school learning problems in the regular classroom. Teachers and administrators alike have become more aware of individual differences among children. With this increased awareness, particular attention has been given to means for meeting individual differences. Teachers' aides, team teaching, departmentalization, and lay volunteers have provided classroom teachers with both the time and resources needed to meet the instructional goals for children with individual learning needs. The teacher with thirty students, for example, is now often afforded the opportunity of working alone with a single child while another individual works with the larger group of children.

The wide availability of personalized instructional tools, such as programmed materials and individual study carrels, also makes it possible to remediate learning problems in the regular class. All these changes have helped to make it possible for teachers to teach *all* children within the class. Nothing, however, has been of more help than the recognition by many educators of the necessity of planning for individual instructional needs. This alone has served as an impetus for working with all types of school learning problems within the confines of the regular classroom.

A Prescription
For Change

The principles of behavior management, academic remediation, and prevention discussed in the next three chapters are intended to provide *all* teachers with a practical guide for remediating school learning problems. Although the role of regular classroom teachers is slowly emerging as the most crucial component of the remediation process (Tompkins, 1971), special education teachers can also profit from carefully re-examining their teaching procedures and techniques. The principles and teaching techniques that follow may be used in any type of administrative arrangement. Successful remediation of school learning problems is not dependent upon types of classes, appropriate labels, or detailed etiological studies. *The teacher is the key to effective remediation.*

NOTES

[1]We are indebted to Dr. Maurice Derbyshire for his observations of Skip.

2

Principles
of
Behavior
Management

Every teacher is faced with the task of classroom management of problem behavior. Children who have school learning problems often increase the difficulty of this task (Graubard, 1971; McCarthy & Paraskevopoulos, 1969; Paraskevopoulos & McCarthy, 1969). It is unlikely that a teacher will be successful in remediating academic deficits if he is not skillful in the management of classroom behavior. Consequently, it is essential for him to know many practical and effective techniques for managing specific behavior problems.

Behavior modification has been found to be effective for many types of children in a wide variety of classroom settings (Cruickshank, Bentzen, Ratzeburg, & Tannhauser, 1961; Fargo, Behrns, & Nolen, 1970; Haring & Lovitt, 1967; Haring & Phillips, 1962, 1972; Hewett, 1968). Abundant scientific evidence and an accumulation of classroom experience suggest that it is most fruitful for the teacher to view *all* behavior as learned (Bandura, 1969; Becker, 1971b; Benson, 1969; Ferster & Perrott, 1968; Madsen & Madsen, 1970; Phillips, 1967). The child's acquisition of appropriate classroom behavior is viewed as a learning problem for which the teacher is responsible.

This point of view makes it possible for the teacher to integrate classroom-management techniques with the teaching of academic skills.

Alternative approaches to the management of problem behavior emphasize intrapsychic conflict, biophysical defects, and interpersonal relationships as the causes of inappropriate behavior. These approaches tend to stress intervention as the primary responsibility of the psychotherapist (Bettelheim, 1970), the physician (Bakwin & Bakwin, 1960), or special school personnel (Morse, 1965). Although these approaches have undoubtedly made contributions to the education of children with learning problems, they do not enhance the role of the teacher as the primary agent of positive behavioral change in the classroom (Hewett, 1968; Stuart, 1970; Tharp & Wetzel, 1969). Consequently, we have chosen to stress a behavioral approach to classroom management which: (*a*) has been shown by extensive research and practice to be effective, (*b*) emphasizes the teaching-learning process, and (*c*) is understandable and practical for the classroom teacher.

Definition of
Behavior Modification

Within the past decade, many techniques for changing classroom behavior have been developed by behavioral scientists. These techniques were derived primarily from laboratory studies of behavior by B. F. Skinner and his associates (cf. Skinner, 1953) and from the clinical practice of psychologists (Ullmann & Krasner, 1965). The array of techniques developed in the laboratory, clinic, and classroom is often referred to as behavior modification. *Behavior modification refers to any systematic arrangement of environmental events which produces a specific change in observable behavior.* This definition emphasizes *systematic* procedures and *observable* behavioral change which can be attributed to *specific* teaching techniques. Behavior-management techniques which are used haphazardly or produce unobservable changes in children are not included in our definition.

The aspects of behavior management with which we are most concerned may be represented schematically as shown in Table 2.1.* Table 2-1 illustrates that our analysis of behavior management includes:

---

*We are indebted to Ogden R. Lindsley, "Direct Measurement and Prosthesis of Retarded Behavior," *Journal of Education* 147 (1964): 62-81, for suggesting the basic elements of this schematic.

TABLE 2-1 Schematic Representation of Behavior Management

Program →	Stimulus →	Behavior →	Arrangement →	Consequence
(the system which programs the presentation of the cue or task; the daily sequence of activities)	(antecedent event: what happens just before the child's behavior; the cue or task presented to the child; the setting in which the behavior is likely to occur)	(action: what the child does that can be observed, counted and repeated; a response)	(the system which arranges the consequence of the child's behavior; the contingency of reinforcement)	(subsequent event; what happens just afterward; what the child's activity produces; a reinforcing or punishing event)
(Example: during daily arithmetic period 9:00-9:30)	(Example: teacher gives child 10 arithmetic problems to work)	(Example: child writes answers to 10 problems)	(Example: when all answers are written correctly)	(Example: child may engage in quiet activity of his choice for remainder of arithmetic period)
(Example: during weekly P.E. instruction 1:00-1:15)	(Example: when asked by teacher, to do jumping jacks with class)	(Example: child runs crying from P.E. area)	(Example: each time child runs crying from P.E. area)	(Example: teacher leaves class, runs after child, and returns him to the classroom)
(Example: whenever during school day)	(Example: child is given seatwork)	(Example: child leaves desk and walks around room)	(Example: occasionally while child is walking around room during seatwork)	(Example: teacher or peer remind child to sit down and do his work)

(*a*) The child's behavior
(*b*) Events preceding the child's behavior
(*c*) Events following the child's behavior

Definition of Behavior

Effective control of the classroom requires precise definition of the child's behavior. *Behavior must be defined as an observable, countable, and repeatable action of the child.* The teacher must pinpoint exactly what the child does or does not do rather than how the child feels or how he makes others feel. Interpretation of behavior must not be confused with the behavior itself.

Observability

A behavior is observable when someone can see and/or hear it occur. For example, "out-of-seat" and "talking out" are observable behaviors. Likewise, behavior is observable when a child screams, hits another child, writes the correct answer to an arithmetic problem, eats an eraser, sits in his chair, kicks the wastebasket, runs from the room, or says "thank you." Self-concept, feelings of humiliation, desire to excel, anger, and pleasure are not actions that can be observed. Therefore, they are not acceptably defined behaviors.

Countability

An observable behavior is countable when it can be recorded accurately and reliably by any competent observer. Human error is eliminated in laboratory research by electromechanical devices, but automatic recording is seldom possible in the classroom. Consequently, it is necessary to define behavior so that any impartial and competent individual can count the frequency of its occurrence. For example, "hits another child," "percent of arithmetic problems completed correctly," "words read correctly per minute," "shows the 'naughty finger'," "number of words written in experience story," "drops tray in cafeteria," and "throws books on floor" are countable behaviors. It would not be difficult for observers to agree on the number of such behaviors occurring in a given period of time. "Irritating comments," "hyperactive," and "distractible," however, are not countable because they are interpretations of behavior which will vary from one observer to another. Countable behaviors are specific, overt actions which occur as discrete units with definite beginning and ending points.

Repeatability

A repeatable behavior must be able to occur more than once. "Ruining her new blouse," "disrupting the Christmas assembly," and "breaking out Richard's two front teeth" can be accomplished only once. These behaviors may be repeatable, however, if they are considered instances of a larger class of behaviors, such as "destroying clothing," "disrupting groups," or "hitting other children." It is important to work with behaviors which are repeated frequently. Behaviors which occur infrequently are difficult to modify because the child has relatively little opportunity to experience the consequences. Attempting to change a behavior occurring less than once each day is usually unwise.

Once the behavior is precisely defined, the teacher must devise a plan for monitoring the childs behavior.

Monitoring
Behavior

Behavioral laws operate regardless of a person's failure to recognize their validity or measure the results of their application. When one wishes to make practical use of a behavioral law, it is helpful to monitor the effects of its application by careful measurement. The teacher who does not objectively and accurately measure the results of his instruction must proceed by intuition and guesswork. Research has shown that subjective judgments of how often problem behaviors occur and to what extent behavior has changed are very unreliable. As a result, behavior modification stresses the importance of an objective record of the child's behavior which provides the basis for judging whether or not the desired change has occurred.

Children's behavior can be monitored effectively by making daily observations and recording the results on a graph. For classroom applications, a simple graphing convention is followed. As shown in Figure 2-1, the horizontal axis of the graph represents successive days on which the behavior was recorded and the vertical axis represents the number of times the behavior was observed each day. It is also possible to let the vertical axis represent:

(a) percent of responses correct (e.g., arithmetic computation or reading comprehension),

Definition of Behavior: _____   Name of Child: _____

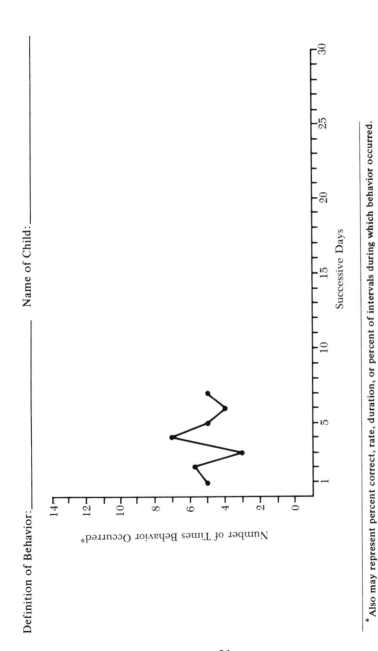

* Also may represent percent correct, rate, duration, or percent of intervals during which behavior occurred.

FIGURE 2-1 Typical Graph Used to Monitor Behavioral Change

21

(b) rate of behavior (e.g., reading rate or speed of computation),
(c) duration of the behavior (e.g., the number of minutes a child is out of his seat),
(d) percent of intervals during which the behavior was observed (e.g., the teacher glances at a child every fifteen minutes and records whether he does or does not have his shoes on his feet).

There are several effective and efficient ways of making daily observations of behavior. The particular method of observing and recording must be tailored to the situation. It is essential to record the behavior immediately after it occurs so that accuracy is maintained. It is also highly desirable to occasionally have a second observer (e.g., teacher aide, another teacher, or a responsible student) record the behavior simultaneously. The record of behavior may be assumed to be highly reliable when there is nearly perfect agreement between the two observers.

Continuous Recording

When the behavior being recorded is easily observed, occurs in a variety of settings, and typically occurs less than twenty-five times per day, it is usually wise to record each instance of the behavior. The teacher should begin observing the child at the beginning of the school day and continue to record occurrences of the behavior until the child leaves school. The number of occurrences each day can then be plotted on the vertical axis of the graph.

Time Sample Recording

When the behavior being recorded occurs only in a specific setting (such as reading instruction or the playground), is difficult to observe, or usually occurs more than twenty-five times per day, a time sample recording technique is usually advisable. The teacher may record occurrences of the behavior only during a specific activity, or he may record the behavior only during a specified time interval. It is usually wise to keep the time interval during which the behavior is recorded consistent from day-to-day. When the observation interval remains the same from day-to-day, the behavior may be plotted on the vertical axis of the graph as frequency per day.

If the observation interval varies in length from day-to-day (e.g., Monday fifteen minutes, Tuesday twenty-five minutes, Wednesday forty minutes, Thursday ten minutes, etc.) the behavior should be plotted on the vertical axis of the graph as *rate,* or number of behaviors observed divided by the number of minutes of observation. If, on the days referred to above, the behavior occurred ten, twelve, twenty, and fifteen times respectively, the rate for each day would be: Monday .67, Tuesday .48, Wednesday .50, and Thursday 1.5. When observation periods vary in length, rate has the advantage of giving directly comparable estimates of how frequently the behavior is occurring.

Occasionally, a teacher may wish to make a single, quick observation of a child at regular intervals to see whether the child is exhibiting a certain behavior. For example, he may make a point of glancing at the child every fifteen minutes (or every five, ten, or twenty minutes) to notice whether or not he is wearing his hat, chewing his pencil, or engaged in some other specified behavior. The intervals should be as frequent as possible, and consistent both in length and number each day. Percent of intervals during which the behavior occurred may then be plotted on the vertical axis of the graph.

Duration Recording

Some behaviors are of concern to teachers not because of their frequency but because of their duration. For example, in the early stages of learning to read, it may be desirable to increase, not the number of books looked at by the child, nor the number of pages turned, but the cumulative amount of time the child spends sitting quietly at his desk looking at a book. A simple recording technique in such cases consists of observing the child when he is given a book to "read" and recording the number of seconds or minutes he spends actually perusing the book during a period of three to ten minutes. A stopwatch is essential for accurate recording, and it is necessary to observe the child continuously for a brief time period. When duration of behavior is recorded, the number of minutes or seconds may be plotted on the vertical axis of the graph.

Work Records

For some children, the behavior of greatest concern to the teacher may be percent of assigned work completed, percent of work completed correctly, or rate (speed) of work. When productivity or accuracy are the behaviors in question, recording the behavior is simply a matter of computing the appropriate percentage or rate and plotting it on the vertical axis of the graph. Care should be taken to record work in each academic subject separately, to keep the number of possible responses approximately equal on successive days, and to make sure that the assigned work requires discrete responses.

Mechanics of Monitoring Behavior

It is essential that behavior be recorded at the time of its occurrence. If a teacher or other observer relies on his memory of how often the behavior occurred, even for a short period of time, it is unlikely that the record will be accurate. Furthermore, it is unnecessary for a teacher to attempt to remember each occurrence of a behavior while conducting classroom activities. A number of prosthetic aids to memory can be purchased at a low cost or improvised from classroom supplies. Many teachers have found inexpensive golf counters (the wrist-worn type is particularly convenient) and grocery counters ideal for recording behavior. It is also convenient to tally each occurrence of the behavior by making a mark on a strip of masking tape placed on the wrist or on a slip of paper. An inexpensive kitchen timer can be used to cue observations at regular intervals. When work completion and work accuracy are recorded, it is necessary to compute percent completed or percent correct after each work period.

In addition to recording the behavior immediately after it occurs, the teacher should enter his observations on a record form. This provides for the orderly accumulation of data before it is plotted on the graph. A useful record form for nearly any behavior is shown in Table 2-2. For any given behavior, only those parts of the form appropriate for the recording technique should be used.

It is not always necessary for the teacher to record the child's behavior himself. In many cases the child himself, a peer, or a teacher's aide can do the recording (Hall, Fox, Willard, Goldsmith, Emerson, Owen, Davis, & Porcia, 1971). Care must be taken to maintain reliability of the record and avoid unethical or unprofessional practices. The problem of reliability can be minimized by careful training and occasional checks of the recorder's performance. Ethical and professional questions are likely to be raised only when a peer is asked to record the child's behavior. These questions nearly always can be avoided by informing both the child and his peer of the purpose of the record.

Recording techniques may themselves be used as a technique for the modification of behavior. Not infrequently, the child's knowledge that his behavior is being recorded changes his behavior to a significant degree. Consequently, it is often appropriate to keep the

TABLE 2-2 Record Form for Monitoring Behavioral Change

Behavior Recorded: _____   Name of Child: _____

Day	Date	Behavior Recorded from:	Tot. Time Behavior Recorded	# of Behaviors Observed	Rate Per Min.	Duration in min. and sec.	Behavior Recorded Each ___ Min.: # of ___ Recordings	# of Times Behavior Observed	% of Intervals Behavior Observed	% of work completed	% of work correct	Comments
1.		__ to __										
2.		__ to __										
3.		__ to __										
4.		__ to __										
5.		__ to __										
6.		__ to __										
7.		__ to __										
8.		__ to __										
9.		__ to __										
10.		__ to __										

(Continue in this manner)

25

act of recording hidden from the child during the first phase of an attempt to use behavior modification procedures.

Phases in Monitoring Behavioral Change

After a behavior has been defined appropriately and a technique for systematically recording it has been devised, it is necessary to assess behavioral change which may be the result of a teaching procedure. It is customary to record the behavior during three distinct phases of this assessment: (*a*) *before* the teaching technique is employed, (*b*) *during* its use, and (*c*) *after* the teaching procedure is modified or discontinued. These phases are referred to in technical terminology as *baseline, intervention,* and *follow-up* periods. The reason for recording behavior before any intervention or specific teaching procedure is attempted is to obtain an accurate estimate of its occurrence under present conditions.

For purposes of comparison, it is frequently helpful to record data on a second child who is not considered a problem. Often, teachers find that their subjective estimate of the behavior is very different from the objective record and that they must either revise their expectation for the child or select a different behavior for modification. Baseline observation may indicate that the child does not differ significantly from his classmates in terms of the recorded behavior or that the behavior chosen for modification is not the most important problem.

The "before" period or baseline also provides an objective basis for assessing the effectiveness of the teaching procedure. If the teaching procedure is effective, there will be a dramatic change in the behavior graph when the procedure is instituted. Failure of the graph to indicate a marked change in the behavior when the teaching or intervention procedure is introduced is an indication that another procedure should be attempted. The "after" or follow-up phase provides an objective indication of the permanence of any behavioral change observed during intervention. When a behavior is taught, it is usually hoped that it will be maintained without the continued use of the teaching procedure. Measurement of the behavior after intervention provides an indication of the necessity for further teaching.

The baseline condition is usually continued for a minimum of five to ten days before intervention is begun. It is sometimes necessary to continue the baseline period for a longer time to allow the behavior to stabilize. When the behavior has stabilized the *trend* of the data plotted on the graph will approximate a horizontal line, as shown in Figure 2-1.

Behavior is generally recorded during the intervention phase until the desired effect is achieved. Although a dramatic change in the behavior should be expected during the intervention phase, it may take several days for the change to become obvious. If the expected change has not been achieved after ten days, a second teaching procedure should be tried.

Follow-up may be continued as long as necessary to indicate whether the behavioral change is being maintained. Generally, it is advisable to continue follow-up for at least as long as the behavior was recorded during baseline.

There are exceptions to the general pattern of recording behavior during the phases discussed here. At times a child's behavior is so disturbing to the teacher that baseline recording is omitted and an intervention procedure is introduced immediately. Occasionally a teacher is so gratified by the behavioral change achieved during intervention that he is reluctant to discontinue use of the teaching technique during follow-up.

The case of Lester illustrates the use of techniques for monitoring behavioral change:

A second-grade teacher, Ms. A, was concerned because Lester was out of his seat too frequently during a ten-minute seatwork period. She defined out-of-seat behavior as leaving the chair without permission for any length of time. Ms. A recorded each out-of-seat by making a tally mark on a slip of paper which she kept at her desk. Each day, she plotted on a graph the total number of times Lester was out of his seat, as shown in Figure 2-2. During baseline, when Lester did not know that Ms. A was recording his behavior, he was out of his seat without permission an average of five times during each seatwork period. On days two and six, the teacher's aide recorded Lester's behavior simultaneously as a reliability check. The aide's observations are shown on the graph by an X. There was close agreement between the two observers. After recording baseline data for seven days, Ms. A tried an intervention technique. On the eighth day, she showed Lester the graph of his behavior and told him that if the graph was at zero for a particular day, he could pass out the seatwork materials on the following day. She tried this for eight days but was not satisfied with the results. Although Lester's inappropriate behavior decreased, it was zero on only two days and the average out-of-seat behaviors was still about three per day. Consequently, Ms. A decided to try a different intervention. She had noted that Lester was fascinated by the graph and that he especially liked to work with felt-tipped pens. On the sixteenth day she talked to Lester again and suggested that they

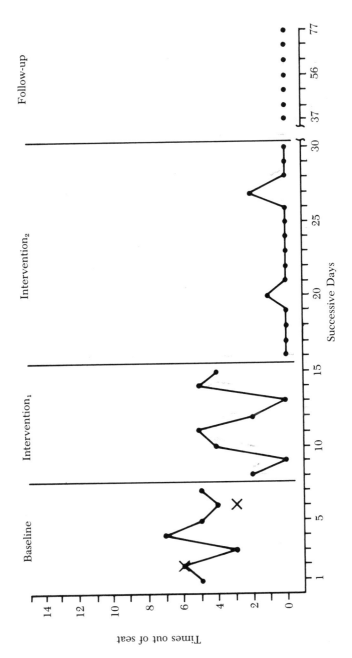

FIGURE 2-2 Graph of Lester's Out-of-Seat Behavior

tape a small card to his desk at the beginning of the seatwork period. Lester would be given a felt-tipped pen which he would use to make a tally mark on the card each time he got out of his seat without permission. If he was not out-of-seat during the seatwork period, he could use the pen to write or draw anything he chose on the card after his work was finished. He would also be allowed to plot his behavior on the graph if he had not been out-of-seat. Ms. A continued to record Lester's behavior during the second intervention and also began to praise him frequently for staying in his seat. The graph shows that these procedures were highly successful. After using the second intervention for fifteen days, Ms. A discontinued the procedure but recorded Lester's out-of-seat behavior once each week. The follow-up data shown on the graph indicate that Lester had learned to stay in his seat without rewards other than praise.

Controlling Function
of Consequences

All behaviors are followed by certain environmental events. These subsequent environmental events have a profound effect on the person's future behavior. Behavioral scientists have clearly shown that behavior is controlled to a great degree by its immediate *consequences.* For example, when a child touches a hot iron he immediately experiences a painful consequence which decreases the likelihood that he will touch a hot iron in the future. If a child is immediately recognized by the teacher when he raises his hand, the likelihood that he will raise his hand in the future is increased.

A reinforcer is an event which controls behavior. Consequences or reinforcers may be positive (things a person will try to get or retain) or negative (things a person will try to avoid or escape). Reinforcers may be used to increase (reinforce) or decrease (punish) a behavior. A reinforcer may be either presented or withdrawn to influence the strength of behavior. Thus, there are four distinct methods of influencing a behavior by presenting or withdrawing positive or negative reinforcers, as shown in Table 2-3. *The process of reinforcement always results in an increase or strengthening of behavior. Punishment always results in a decrease or weakening of behavior.* Negative reinforcement should not be confused with punishment. *Negative reinforcement,* withdrawing something unpleasant after a behavior, has the effect of *increasing or accelerating* the behavior it follows. *Punishment,* withdrawing something pleasant or presenting something unpleasant after a behavior, has the opposite effect of *decreasing or decelerating* the behavior it follows.

TABLE 2-3 Methods of Influencing Behavior

	Positive Reinforcer (a pleasurable or desirable event)	Negative Reinforcer (an unpleasurable or aversive event)
Present Reinforcer	*Positive Reinforcement* Effect: increase or strengthen behavior which produces reinforcer; acceleration of behavior. Example behavior: child begins assigned seatwork consequence: teacher smiles at child and remarks, "Good, I see you've started!" If the child's initial effort at doing his assigned work is consistently given immediate attention and praise by the teacher, the promptness with which he begins his work will likely increase.	*Punishment* Effect: decrease or weaken behavior which results in loss of reinforcer; deceleration of behavior. Example behavior: child "tattles" to teacher consequence: teacher turns away from child (withdraws attention completely) If the teacher consistently and totally withdraws his attention from the child immediately after he begins to "tattle", tattling will likely decrease.
Withdraw Reinforcer	*Punishment* Effect: decrease or weaken behavior which produces reinforcer; deceleration of behavior. Example behavior: child destroys paper of other children. consequence: teacher points at child and shouts "NO!" If the teacher is generally positive, controlled, and soft-spoken in his interaction with the child, but consistently points at child and shouts "NO!" when he begins to destroy another child's paper, his destruction of papers will likely decrease.	*Negative Reinforcement* Effect: increase or strengthen behavior which avoids or escapes the reinforcer; acceleration of behavior. Example behavior: child runs out of the classroom when teased by other children. consequence: teasing stops. If the child can escape from the teasing by running out of the room, running out is likely to increase when teasing occurs.

A nearly infinite number of environmental events occur subsequent to any behavior, not all of which have a controlling function. In many cases it is difficult to identify precisely the events which do control behavior. In the classroom, positive reinforcers for maladaptive behavior often go unidentified because inappropriate assumptions are made concerning the definition of reinforcers. *Reinforcers are defined by their effect on the behavior which they follow, not on the basis of how one thinks they should function.* Although it is possible to make general statements regarding the classification of events, the reinforcing property of a subsequent event may vary for a *specific* individual or group under certain circumstances. Teachers often assume that their reprimands and "desist" signals, (e.g., "sit down," "don't interrupt when someone else is talking," "I don't want to have to tell you again," finger-snapping, etc.) are negative reinforcers; i.e., that presenting them following undesirable behaviors will weaken the behavior. Unfortunately, reprimands and signals assumed to be aversive often serve to strengthen rather than weaken the undesirable behavior (Becker, Thomas, & Carnine, 1969).

Schedules of Reinforcement

Effective control of behavior is largely a result of the arrangement of consequences. In any behavior-management situation there are rules, either explicitly stated or implicit in the sequence of events, which determine the arrangement of rewards and punishments. These *rules which arrange the relationship between the occurrence of behavior and its consequences are called contingencies or schedules of reinforcement.* A contingency states the conditions under which reinforcement will occur. For example, the child may be required to do a certain *number* of specified behaviors to obtain reinforcement, or he may be expected to complete a task during a certain *time* interval in order to get a reward.

Although there are many very complicated reinforcement schedules which scientists use in research, they are derived from combinations and modifications of a few basic schedules which may be used in the classroom. Several of these basic schedules are described in Table 2-4. There are two classes of reinforcement schedules; continuous, in which every response is reinforced, and intermittent in which not all of the child's appropriate responses are reinforced.

Continuous Reinforcement. It is advantageous to reinforce every occurrence of a desirable behavior when it is first being taught. Otherwise, the behavior may not be learned at all or may be learned very slowly. Continuous reinforcement should be offered when a new skill or behavior is being learned, but after it has become firmly estab-

TABLE 2-4 An Outline of Basic Schedules of Reinforcement

I. *Continuous Reinforcement*

Every time the behavior occurs, it is reinforced.

Example: Each time the child completes an arithmetic problem correctly he is given a point for his progress chart.

II. *Intermittent Reinforcement*

A. *Ratio Schedules*

Reinforcement is given for every *n*th behavior and depends on the number of behaviors the child performs regardless of time.

1. *Fixed Ratio*

A fixed number of behaviors must occur for each reinforcement.

Example: Every 10th sight word read correctly is rewarded with an M&M candy.

2. *Variable Ratio*

An average number of behaviors must occur for each reinforcement. The number of behaviors required varies around a mean.

Example: On the average, every 5th time the child raises his hand he is called on by the teacher. The actual number of times he raises his hand before being called on varies.

B. *Interval Schedules*

Reinforcement depends on the passage of time *and* the occurrence of a behavior.

1. *Fixed Interval*

A fixed amount of time must pass, after which the next appropriate behavior will be reinforced.

Example: Every three minutes during recess the teacher observes the child to see whether or not he is talking to another child. The next time he approaches another child and speaks to him the teacher pats him on the shoulder and praises him for being friendly.

2. *Variable Interval*

A variable amount of time must pass, after which the next correct response will result in reinforcement. The amount of time required varies around a mean.

Example: On the average, every five minutes the teacher observes whether or not the child is writing another correct answer to the questions covering the geography lesson. When he answers the next question correctly, a smiling face is drawn on his paper. The actual number of minutes which elapse before she checks his behavior varies.

lished, other schedules may be more effective and efficient. For example, when a child is being taught a new computational skill, it is best to reward him for each problem completed correctly in order to maintain his interest in the task and allow him to observe his progress. However, after the child has mastered the new computational skill, continued reinforcement of every correct response is unnecessary, inefficient, and impractical. Continuous reinforcement after the skill has been learned may result in disinterest in the reward and a decline in appropriate behavior. Continued interest in the reward and a high rate of appropriate behavior can be maintained by using intermittent reinforcement.

Intermittent Reinforcement. Behavior that has been learned can be efficiently maintained by arranging consequences for only a portion of the child's appropriate responses. Reinforcement may be based on the number of responses or on a response completed after the passage of an interval of time, as shown in Table 2-4. When a change is made from continuous to intermittent reinforcement, the requirement for reinforcement must not be increased too quickly or the behavior may be lost. A gradual increase in the requirements will insure a smooth transition without loss of the newly learned response. If the child who has learned a new computational skill for the reward of a star for every problem completed correctly is suddenly expected to complete fifty or one-hundred problems before earning a star, he may not continue to work for the reward. He will probably continue to work industriously, however, if he is expected to complete first two, then three, then five, and finally ten such problems. Eventually he may be willing to complete one-hundred problems before receiving his reward. It is likely, in this case, that other natural consequences in his environment are providing intermittent reinforcement for his behavior.

Each specific schedule of reinforcement generally produces a characteristic pattern of response.[1] Reinforcement given on a variable schedule, in which the child cannot predict when the next reward will be available, will usually produce faster and more persistent responding than a fixed ratio or fixed-interval schedule, where the child can anticipate when he will be given the next reinforcer.

Timing of Consequences. Reinforcers are most effective when they follow the desired behavior immediately. Adults can often work for distant rewards, as in the case of the prospective teacher working to obtain a teaching certificate. Children, particularly those with learning problems, usually work diligently for more immediate consequences. Praise given immediately after performance of a desirable behavior will be more likely to have the desired effect than a delayed reward. For example, grade cards given daily are more effective in controlling academic responses than grades given every six to eight weeks. As a child's behavior improves, it may be possible to gradually extend the delay between his behavior and its consequences. The temptation to move too quickly to delayed reinforcement must be resisted. In the analysis of many behavior-management problems, it is found that immediate rather than delayed consequences are controlling behavior. Arranging immediate consequences for behavior improves performance.

Shaping Behavior

In teaching children to behave appropriately, the teacher must carefully define the terminal goal or behavioral objective. He must describe in objective and measurable terms how he wants the child to behave after he is taught. He must also consider in objective and measurable terms how the child presently behaves. This means analyzing the behavioral goal in relation to the child's present behavior and arranging a sequence of ordered steps or tasks. The teacher must begin by reinforcing a behavior that the child already emits and gradually increasing the requirement for reinforcement. The sequence of steps arranged by the teacher must be *successive approximations* of the ultimate goal. If the approximations are too large, the child is unlikely to learn the behavior or the teaching procedure will be inefficient. The teacher who fails to reward increments of improvement in behavior is not likely to be successful in using behavior-modification techniques (Kuypers, Becker, & O'Leary, 1968).

The process of ordered teaching of prerequisite behaviors which are successive approximations of the final goal is called *behavior shaping*. The child who cannot walk cannot be expected to do so until he learns certain prerequisite skills, one of which is standing. Usually, a child must learn to associate letters with sounds before he can learn to read. It would be foolish to expect most children to speak in sentences before they can name objects.

Several examples of behavior shaping in the classroom are presented in Table 2-5. The size of the steps in learning must be adjusted to the learning characteristics of the child. Highly gifted children may be able to make great leaps in learning, omitting successive approximations. Children with special learning problems, on the other hand, may need to take more than the ordinary sequence of steps in learning. The more severe the child's learning difficulty, the smaller the successive approximations of the final goal must be.

TABLE 2-5 Examples of Behavior Shaping in the Classroom

Behavioral Goal	*Successive Approximations*
Child will sit at his desk continuously for twenty minutes	Standing near his desk for a few seconds; touching desk or chair; sitting, leaning or kneeling on his desk or chair; sitting in his chair for a few seconds; sitting in his chair for three minutes; sitting for five minutes. . . .
Child will complete seatwork assignments	Looking at assignment, picking up pencil, putting pencil on paper, completing one answer, completing two answers. . . .
Child will participate fully with class in softball game	Watching game from a distance, standing behind backstop, keeping score, serving as bat boy, playing a position for ½ inning, playing a full inning. . . .
Child will be able to write the letter *H*	Writing a vertical line, writing a horizontal line, combining the two lines, making an additional vertical line.
Child will be able to color within the lines	Holding a crayon, coloring in large areas, gradually decreasing the size of the area until the child completes the desired size.
Child will be able to name his body parts	Knowledge of parts making up the body, naming gross features of a stick figure, naming and relating stick figure features to one's own body, gradually introducing specific features of human figures and relating to his own body.

Individual Determination of Consequences

The effective use of consequences to control classroom behavior must be individualized for the child, the teacher, and the situation. Since a reinforcer is defined by its effect on behavior, an event which is reinforcing for one child may be punishing for another. It is the task of the teacher to find and use those events which are reinforcing for a specific child. This can be done by: (*a*) observing what the child does or seems to enjoy when given a free choice, (*b*) asking the child what he would be willing to work for, or (*c*) systematically arranging a consequence for the child and observing its effect on his behavior.

For example, if the child spends most of his free time working puzzles, it is highly probable that working puzzles will serve as a reinforcer for him. Also, it is a simple procedure to ask the child, "What would you like to do when you finish your writing?"

The Premack Principle. A very practical behavior management principle was formulated by Premack (1959). The Premack Principle states that anything a child likes to do more can be used to reinforce any behavior he likes to do less. The implication of this principle is that by observing children's preferences for certain events and activities, the teacher can use more preferred activities to reinforce less preferred behaviors. The greater the difference in preference between two activities, the greater the reinforcing power of the preferred event. This makes it possible to use certain academic and play activities, as well as more "artificial" or contrived reinforcers, as consequences for appropriate behavior. Examples of the application of the Premack Principle are given in Table 2-6. The child's preference for an activity must be established through observation, as guesswork may result in providing a less preferred event contingent upon a more preferred activity. This arrangement would punish desirable behavior.

TABLE 2-6 Application of the Premack Principle

Child's Preference	*Reinforcement Arrangement*
child prefers drawing to reading	make drawing contingent upon reading
"helping the teacher" is preferred to going outside for recess	allow going outside for recess to earn the privilege of "helping the teacher"
child likes to eat candy kisses more than he likes to do arithmetic	make eating candy kisses contingent upon doing arithmetic
given the choice of doing writing or reading, the child always does reading	require writing just before allowing reading
writing on the chalkboard is something the child relishes, while writing on paper is something he detests	allow writing on the chalkboard only after a writing assignment has been satisfactorily completed on paper
child would rather put together a model than spell words	arrange to have spelling words written correctly produce permission to work on model
child spends every spare moment reading but rarely speaks to anyone	make access to reading material contingent upon a specific amount of verbal interaction

Contingency Contracting. Contingencies of reinforcement may be stated in the form of an agreement or contract. Children benefit by an explicit statement of the relationship between their behavior and its consequences. Negotiating a contingency contract involves reaching an agreement that after the child has done something the teacher wants him to do (e.g., spell twenty words correctly) the teacher will provide something the child wants (e.g., permission to go to the listening station for ten minutes).[2] An effective contingency contract must meet the requirements of any good business contract, i.e., it must be fair for both parties, be clear in its statement of terms, offer a positive incentive, and be adhered to systematically and honestly (Homme, 1969).

Token Reinforcement. Behavior-management transactions can often be conducted by arranging reinforcing events to follow appropriate behavior immediately. In other situations, it is practical to allow the child to engage in the reinforcing activity only during a specified time period which follows his appropriate behavior by several hours, days, or weeks. For example, a teacher may be able to arrange for a grade of A on a science test to be followed by the privilege of playing a game of ping-pong with the school principal. He may also be able to arrange working with the school janitor, earning small toys or packages of candy, helping in the cafeteria, taking a field trip, visiting his home, watching a cartoon movie, and many other activities as reinforcing events for a child or children in his class. The logistics of making these events contingent upon specific behaviors and allowing them to occur immediately following appropriate behaviors is a very difficult problem. But, if the reinforcing event does not follow appropriate behavior immediately, its effectiveness in increasing the desired behavior is likely to be lost. One method of solving the logistics and timing problems is to establish a system of token reinforcement or a token economy in the classroom. Points marked on cards or other tokens can be given immediately after an appropriate behavior occurs and exchanged during a specific time period for reinforcing activities. Tokens serve as reinforcers because they can be used to "buy" reinforcing events. Before implementing a token reinforcement system in his classroom, the teacher should read extensively concerning the mechanics of establishing and operating such a system. The details which must be considered in the use of token reinforcement include the problems of supply, demand, inflation, recession, distribution, theft, extortion, and other problems observed in any monetary system. The benefits of a properly functioning token reinforcement program are many, but the pitfalls are equally numerous.[3]

Use of Group Contingencies. The classroom teacher will often find it advantageous to manage contingencies of reinforcement for groups of children as well as for individuals. The teacher who excuses rows of children only when each child is seated quietly is employing a group contingency-management technique. In this example, each member of the group must exhibit appropriate behavior for the group to obtain the reinforcing consequence. When such a contingency is applied, there is considerable group pressure to conform to the expectancy of the teacher.

It is also possible to make a reinforcing event for the entire class dependent upon the behavior of a single individual. For example, a special treat for each member of the class could be made contingent upon a single child's completion of his work. In this example also, the operation of group pressure is likely. Peers may give encouragement to the child whose behavior regulates their reward and distract him as little as possible. When using this group contingency technique, the task must be within the child's capability and positive consequences of his performance must be stressed. Failure of the problem student to perform should never result in punishment for the class.

Finally, it is possible to arrange a contingent reward which can be earned by each member of the class individually. For example, any member of the class completing an assignment may be allowed to go to recess two minutes early. Care must be taken to provide an appropriate task for each child. With this type of group contingency, group pressure will not operate to increase the probability of appropriate behavior.[4]

Specific consequences for behavior must also be determined by individual teachers. Certain teachers find it difficult or impossible to administer consequences which other teachers consider appropriate. Some teachers can provide visits to their homes, special activities after school, small toys, or treats for children while others feel that some or all of these events cannot be appropriately offered as rewards. However, unless the teacher is willing to provide *some* effective reward on a contingent basis, it can be predicted that he will be ineffective in classroom management.

Other variables also require individualization in the selection of consequences. The constraints of school administrators, parents, other teachers, or the physical limitations of the school may prohibit the use of consequences which the teacher could otherwise employ very effectively. Principals who are unsympathetic, parents who demand strict adherence to traditional methods, fellow teachers who are cynical, and school buildings designed for the past are realities faced by many teachers who wish to implement creative contingency-management ideas (Kauffman & Vicente, 1972). On the other hand, principals, colleagues, and parents are often invaluable allies in successful modification of children's inappropriate behaviors, and antique features of school buildings can provide opportunities for innovation. The assessment of these situational variables demands no less attention than the consideration of one's own feelings and the careful evaluation of the individual child.

Controlling Function
of Antecedent Events

Thus far we have stressed the use of subsequent events or consequences in classroom management. Although behavior will be shaped and maintained only if it is followed by effective reinforcers, teaching also involves setting the stage for behavior. The teacher must establish appropriate instructional goals, acquire instructional materials, provide a model for the student, schedule a sequence of activities, and give unambiguous signals that behavior should occur. Each of these classes of antecedent events has a significant controlling function in classroom management.

Antecedent events have the effect of increasing the likelihood that a specific instance of a behavior will occur. For example, when a second grader is presented with the stimulus $2 + 2 = $ ____, the probability that he will give the response 4 rather than another response is greatly increased.[5] The presentation of the antecedent event, $2 + 2 = $ ____, does not *reinforce* the response 4; it is what occurs *after* the response is given that provides reinforcement. If the teacher informs the child that his answer is correct or offers some other reward for his performance, the probability that the child will give the response 4 is increased.

When reinforcement is consistently paired with a stimulus, the stimulus signals the child that reinforcement is likely to occur. Similar responses which lead to the same consequences will also be increased in probability. Thus, the child may respond to $2 + 2 = $ ____ by writing 4, saying "four," tapping four times with his pencil, pointing to the numeral 4, etc. This tendency to give similar but not identical responses in the presence of a stimulus, all of which lead to reinforcement, is called *response generalization.* It is often necessary to specifically teach response generalizations. Children who have been successful learners tend to be able to respond appropriately in many different ways to an instructional task. Children with school learning problems, on the other hand, may need to be taught a variety of appropriate responses.

When stimuli differ perceptibly along a significant dimension or combination of features, a similar response is not considered appropriate and will not be reinforced. The task $2 + 2 =$ _____ calls for a completely different response than $2 \times 2 =$ _____ or $2 + \_\_ = 4$. The process of learning to respond differentially to different stimuli is called *stimulus discrimination.* When a child consistently makes a differential response to a stimulus (e.g., when he consistently responds "cat" to c-a-t) he has learned a discrimination. A basic problem in remedial education is teaching appropriate discriminations. Learning to read and to do simple arithmetic computations involves learning many discriminations. Learning to behave appropriately in the classroom means that the child must learn to discriminate the stimuli which signal that he will be reinforced for sitting down, for listening, for following directions, and for other behaviors that facilitate academic learning. *Discriminations are learned only when behavior is differentially reinforced in the presence of specific stimuli.* For example, the child will learn not to talk out if he is consistently ignored for doing so and reinforced for talking when appropriate.

Determination of Tasks

The teacher can determine specific instructional tasks for a child only after he has formulated a behavioral goal.[6] He must define the behavior he wants the child to perform in observable, countable, and repeatable terms. The conditions under which the teacher wants the child to perform the behavior and the criterion for satisfactory performance must also be stated. When adequate goals have been established, instructional tasks for the child logically follow. It is essential that the task presented to a child be clearly stated in terms of beginning and ending points. It is of utmost importance that the child know what he is to *do* and what constitutes completion of the task. The directive, "study your spelling" is not a task which specifies exactly what the child is to do, nor does the task have an unambiguous beginning or end. "Write each of your spelling words five times," on the other hand, is a task which specifies the behavior which the child is to emit.

Clarity in the presentation of tasks allows both the child and the teacher to discriminate the occasions for reinforcement. If the child does not know what to *do* to obtain reinforcement he is likely to exhibit maladaptive behavior. Analysis of many behavior-management problems suggests that the child is uncertain about what specific behavior the teacher considers desirable at the moment. If the teacher does not know exactly what he wants the child to do, he will not be able to determine when to provide a reinforcer for appropriate behavior.

Ambiguity concerning what behavior is desired by the teacher is often encountered by children during nonacademic activities and between the completion of one academic task and the beginning of another. During these times, the teacher must set clear expectations for nonacademic tasks. The explicit statement of positive rules for behavior is an essential feature of efficient classroom control (Madsen, Becker, & Thomas, 1968). To avoid confusion, the number of rules should be kept small. To be effective, the rules must be stated positively and specify behaviors which are incompatible with misconduct. Rules which state what a child should *not* do allow the child to demand another rule to cover each example of misconduct. They are not a guide to reinforcement for the child or the teacher. "Work quietly at your desk" is preferable to "Don't bother others" because it specifies for the child how he is expected to behave and tells the teacher what behavior to reinforce. When rules are stated positively and explicitly, communication with the child concerning his behavior is simplified.

Use of Models

Direct presentation of tasks and rules is one method of communicating with children. Children also constantly observe the behavior of the teacher and their peers. The behavior of others provides a model or example which the child will tend to follow. Observing the reinforcement of other children who are behaving appropriately tends to induce similar behavior in the observing child.[7] Consequently, modeling and vicarious reinforcement, *i.e.,* demonstration of appropriate behavior and its reinforcement, can significantly decrease the amount of time for a child to learn desirable behavior.

Modeling or demonstration of appropriate behavior is commonly used by teachers in presenting academic tasks. Teachers characteristically demonstrate the solution of an arithmetic problem before expecting the child to solve a similar problem. It is less common, however, for teachers to provide models and vicarious reinforcement for nonacademic behavior. Ignoring the miscreant and focusing praise and attention on the children who are behaving well is a highly effective management technique.

The teacher who sets a poor behavioral model for his students will be less effective in controlling misbehavior than the teacher whose behavior should be emulated by his students. Teachers may also provide an academic model for students. Reading for pleasure, searching for information, writing, and applying computational skills to the solution of everyday problems are behaviors every teacher may exhibit in the classroom.

Providing Cues for Behavior

Teachers must give students signals that indicate *when* they are to emit a behavior. Hand signals, special visual or auditory stimuli, facial expressions, touching, and single words can be used to cue performance. Cues will serve a discriminative function for specific behaviors only when they are systematically followed by consequences. To be effective, cues must be made especially clear and consistent.

Teachers tend to emphasize the development of cues which indicate to a child that he should stop a maladaptive behavior. Nearly every teacher has a well developed repertoire of "desist signals," such as finger-snapping, bell-ringing, ruler-tapping, frowning, ear-tugging, finger-pointing, shushing, "boys and girls!," etc. These signals are used *after* children have begun to exhibit undesirable behaviors such as noise-making, conversation with peers, movement about the classroom, and talking out of turn. They are often either ineffective or have only a temporary restraining effect on misbehavior because: (*a*) they are mildly aversive events that children can easily learn to escape or avoid by temporarily behaving well, *(b)* the child's immediate cessation of behavior, which is aversive for the teacher, provides negative reinforcement for him, and *(c)* the attention of the teacher, although intended as punishment, serves to reinforce the child's disturbing behavior. Although desist cues can be used effectively and should be part of every teacher's repertoire, effectiveness will deteriorate if they constitute a majority of the teacher's signals to children.

Few teachers have developed an extensive set of cues which can be used to signal that desired behaviors should occur. Learning to use many such signals, however, is an important skill in behavior management. When the teacher emphasizes cues for performance of desired behavior rather than desist signals, he is likely to observe an increase in reinforcable behavior. For example, cueing children to speak in a discussion is more likely to achieve the desired result than reprimanding children who speak out of turn.

Programs of Activities

Although schedules of reinforcement have been studied in detail (Ferster & Skinner, 1957), little attention has been given to the controlling function of programs or schedules of antecedent events. The controlling effects of specific antecedent events themselves have been studied in classroom situations only recently (Lovitt & Curtiss, 1968; Lovitt & Smith, 1972). The program of tasks presented to a child may have a significant effect on his academic and social behavior (Gallagher, 1970). Because many children with school learning problems have experienced inconsistency and unpredictability in their environment, it is helpful to follow an invariant daily schedule of activities. The child should be able to predict from day-to-day the sequence of tasks which will be presented to him. As his academic and social responses improve, the routine can be made more flexible and the child can take a greater part in the determination of his work schedule.

The principles discussed previously provide a guide for programming specific tasks in sequence. Generally, the daily schedule should consist of a series of short work periods followed by brief periods of reward. As behavior improves, reward periods can be decreased in length and scheduled to occur at less frequent intervals. Work which can be done individually and without movement about the classroom should be emphasized until appropriate patterns of response are established. Subsequently, academic activities requiring social interaction, free movement about the classroom, and group participation can be increased gradually. The child's least preferred work should be scheduled early in the day and his most preferred work, late in the day. A child should not be allowed to go on to the next activity until he has successfully completed the task preceding it. Both the first and last activities of the day should be easily accomplished tasks which are pleasant for the child and encourage him to return to school.[8] These programming suggestions are based on the observation that arrangement of antecedent events builds reinforcement into the schedule and makes the occurrence of reinforceable behavior more likely.

General Behavior-Management Techniques

The behavior principles discussed in this chapter have led to the development of thousands of specific techniques for the management of individuals and groups. The principles can be applied to the unique requirements of each problem situation. Classroom teachers and researchers are constantly devising new techniques for behavior-management problems. A number of specific procedures which have been found useful in resolving common behavior problems are listed in Chapter 6. Teachers may find some of the techniques listed in Part II directly applicable to their classrooms, but it cannot be emphasized too strongly that knowledge of the general principles of behavior will give the teacher added flexibility in improvising specific management methods which are most effective for pupils.

Behavior principles have also led to the development of a number of general methods and procedures. These procedures emphasize a highly structured environment in which clarity of directions, firmness in expectations of performance, and consistency of follow-through are of primary importance.[9] Teacher interaction with the child is kept task centered and the child is given many success experiences through individualized assignments and behavioral expectations. Unnecessary verbalizations to the child are kept at a minimum. Academic work is evaluated immediately to provide feedback to the child regarding his performance. Improvement in behavior is an indication that teaching has been successful, while failure to improve is regarded as a signal to try different procedures. Punishment is deemphasized as a behavior control technique, and shaping appropriate responses by successive approximations is stressed. Emotions are evaluated as by-products of behavior rather than as causes of behavior, and it is assumed that as behavior improves the child's feelings about himself and his attitudes toward others will also improve.

These newer methods of behavior management, which have been tested empirically in the classroom, provide powerful techniques for positive control of behavior problems. There is no guarantee that the teacher using these techniques will be successful in his first attempt to change behavior. As in the acquisition of any set of skills or the solution of problems in any field of human endeavor, repeated trials may be necessary. The teacher who at first is not successful must try to determine the reasons for failure and try again. Teachers expect no less of children.

General Techniques for Decreasing Unwanted Behavior

The most common classroom-management problems involve talking without permission, getting out of seat without permission, refusing academic work, failing to complete assignments, hitting other children, tantruming, and crying. Although the management problem may involve the entire class, one or two pupils frequently account for most of the troublesome behavior.

It is self-defeating for the teacher to try to change many troublesome behaviors at once. Concentrating on the one or two most serious problems is much more likely to be a successful strategy. When the targets for behavior change have been selected, it is helpful to collect baseline data so that a valid assessment of change can be made. Then, one or more of several general procedures for decreasing the unwanted behavior can be employed.

Extinction. As a procedure, extinction refers to removing the reinforcers for a behavior. As a process, it means that behavior which is not reinforced will decrease in strength and eventually cease. When observing maladaptive behavior, the teacher must also observe what happens immediately after the behavior occurs which may serve to reinforce it. If the reinforcer can be removed, the behavior will be extinguished. A very common reinforcer for inappropriate behavior is the attention of another person. Often, the child's misbehavior produces attention from the teacher or his peers, usually in the form of reprimands or reminders to behave appropriately. Frequently, his misbehavior is followed by attention on an intermittent schedule, which has the effect of maintaining his unwanted responses at a high rate. When using an extinction procedure it is necessary to make sure that the reinforcer is removed completely so that occasional reinforcement does not occur.

Most troublesome classroom behavior does not result in permanent damage to persons or property and, consequently, can be ignored. Ignoring misbehavior completely can be an effective extinction procedure. However, extinction will not be maximally effective unless other adaptive behaviors are strengthened.

When using an extinction procedure, the teacher must be prepared for a temporary increase in the behavior before its strength begins to drop. When the usual reinforcer for a response is not forthcoming the child will at first attempt to produce the expected consequence by escalating his misbehavior.

Reinforcing Incompatible Behaviors. Incompatible behaviors are behaviors that cannot occur at the same time. Sitting is incompatible with walking about the room. Reading is incompatible with sleeping. Sitting in a chair is *not* incompatible with talking. Neither is writing incompatible with standing. A more powerful procedure for decreasing unwanted behavior than merely removing the reinforcer (extinction) is to reinforce a behavior incompatible with the maladaptive response. For example, the child may not only be ignored whenever he is out of his seat without permission but be reinforced for sitting in his chair.

Changing Antecedent Events. Maladaptive behavior sometimes occurs primarily in certain settings which predispose the child to misbehave. A change in the situation in which the behavior is likely to occur may produce marked improvement. For example, being in close proximity to a certain classmate may be the setting in which a child tends to make distracting noises. Changing the seating arrangement so that the two children are distant from each other may decrease the inappropriate behavior significantly. Keeping objects such as dolls, balls, small rubber animals, or other objects in their desks may provide the occasion for children's desk-searching behaviors, unwanted noise-making, or arguments. Removal of these objects from children's desks may resolve the management problem.

Some children's academic responses can be greatly increased by simple changes in the way in which tasks are presented to them. Presenting fewer problems per worksheet, presenting single pages cut from a workbook, heightening the stimulus value of the materials with color cues, amplification, or tactile stimuli may accelerate response rate and decrease dawdling, daydreaming, and other behaviors which interfere with instruction.

The effectiveness of reinforcers is determined in part by events antecedent to the behaviors they follow. The probability that a behavior will occur, and its power as a reinforcing event for other behaviors, is constantly changing (Homme, 1966). One factor affecting these changes is the passage of time. For example, immediately after a full meal, eating food is a less reinforcing event than after several hours with no food. The child who has been deprived of candy is more likely to work to obtain candy as a reward than one who has continuous access to sweets. Thus, the probability that a behavior will occur can sometimes be decreased by allowing it to occur freely or requiring that it occur frequently, a technique which produces *satiation.* For example, the tendency of children to tire quickly of a formerly prohibited activity once restrictions are removed is well known.

Unpleasant emotional responses usually accompany forcing a child to behave in a given manner. Allowing the behavior to occur freely is usually preferable to forcing repetition of the undesirable response. For example, the child prone to write socially unacceptable four-letter words on the walls may be permitted (not forced) to write them freely on a special sheet of paper. Prudent businessmen have occasionally controlled defacement of their restroom walls by providing a chalkboard convenient for graffiti.

Differential Reinforcement of Other Behavior. When complete elimination of a behavior is desired it is possible to arrange for the child to obtain reinforcement only if a specific behavior has *not* been emitted during a given time interval. For example, the child may be allowed to work on a special project only if he does not leave the room without permission at any time during the school day. It is impossible to reinforce the absence of behavior; *some* behavior will be reinforced, and it will likely be the behavior occurring just prior to the reinforcing consequence. Therefore, the reinforcer must *never* be given immediately after an inappropriate behavior.

Differential Reinforcement of Low Rate. Differential reinforcement of low rate is useful for maintaining a manageable level of behavior when too frequent occurrence of the behavior is the basic problem. Behaviors related to biological functions, such as eating, are likely to be appropriate targets for this technique. When the technique is employed, the contingency explicitly states the *maximum* number of behaviors that may be emitted during a specified time interval to obtain reinforcement. For example, the problem with the child who bolts his food is not that he eats, but that his rate of eating is too high. A useful contingency for this child may be that he will obtain a reward by finishing his lunch in no less than fifteen minutes or that his reward will depend on his taking less than five bites per minute while eating his lunch.

Punishment. Historically, American public education has stressed the use of punishment to suppress undesirable behavior, including the use of ridicule and, sometimes, the infliction of physical pain. A behavior-modification approach focuses on positive rather than punitive control (Skinner, 1971). Nearly all classroom behavior problems can be solved without the use of punishment. Excepting cases in which the maladaptive behavior is a serious threat to the health and safety of another person or the child himself, other means of reducing behavior problems should always be tried first. In the few cases in which punishment is necessary, it is important to recognize that "punishment is not synonymous with physical pain or bodily harm and does not necessarily result in emotional responses" (Hall, Axelrod, Foundopoulos, Shellman, Campbell, & Cranston, 1971, p. 25).

As will be recalled from previous discussion, punishment is defined as the systematic use of consequences to decrease the strength of a behavior. This may involve presenting an aversive consequence (negative reinforcer) or removing a rewarding consequence (positive reinforcer) contingent upon the behavior. Thus the removal of teacher attention is an effective punishment technique for many children. The removal of earned rewards or token reinforcers can also be effective punishment, but this technique must be used with caution in order to avoid unfair treatment or resentment. In some cases, rewards are presented on a noncontingent basis and then removed contingent upon inappropriate behavior. For example, the child may be given ten token reinforcers at the beginning of a period and one may be taken away each time the child talks out during the class. Restriction of activity or removal of privileges (being first in line, choosing the game for the day, permission to visit the library, etc.) may also serve as punishment. Frequently, public recording of the maladaptive behavior is sufficient to reduce the problem. "NO!" spoken in a loud, firm voice contingent upon the behavior will often decrease its frequency.

A procedure which combines the features of both types of punishment (withdrawal of rewarding stimuli and presentation of aversive conditions) is commonly referred to as *time-out.* Time-out refers to a time when reinforcement is not available on any terms; it does *not* mean merely time out of the classroom or time out of the teacher's sight. Unless there is an established, on-going program of positive reinforcement it is impossible to use a time-out procedure effectively. When used correctly, time-out involves removing the child from a positively reinforcing situation, such as simply turning away from the child and avoiding any contact with him for a specified time period (usually thirty to sixty seconds). When the child is being managed in a group rather than on a one-to-one basis, other uncomplicated time-out techniques can be used. For example, if a token reinforcement system is being used, time-out may mean that the child cannot earn tokens for a specified time period (e.g., five to fifteen minutes). If the child is engaged in a pleasurable play activity when the maladaptive behavior occurs, an effective time-out procedure may be to require the child to stop the activity or "sit out" for a specific length of time (usually three to five minutes).

Occasionally it is helpful to isolate the child from the teacher and his peers for a brief interval. Ideally, the time-out area to which the child is restricted should be a small, lighted room containing only a chair. The room should not contain objects or other stimuli which might be interesting to the child. Spending more than one or two minutes in such a room is aversive for most children due to the lack of stimulation. When isolation in such a room is employed, time-out involves not only removal from a reinforcing environment (the classroom) but presentation of an aversive environment. Special care must be taken to avoid placing the child in a frightening or dangerous situation. Unlighted, frightening, or dangerous isolation rooms cannot be defended ethically, and their use increases the teacher's liability.[10]

When an ideal time-out room is not available, one may be improvised by screening off a corner of the classroom. The temptation to place a child in the hallway or send him to the principal's office must be resisted, as these places are likely to provide many interesting and reinforcing events. If the child encounters interesting stimuli during time-out, the value of isolation as an aversive technique is lost.

When punishment is used to suppress undesirable behavior, it will be most effective if its use is restricted to occurrences of a specific behavior. Some teachers tolerate misbehavior until their patience wears so thin that they explode with punitive action for a variety of behaviors. This is clearly an ineffective method of management. To be maximally effective, punishment should be administered unemotionally and consistently. Immediate action is necessary to prevent reinforcement of the behavior before punishment occurs. Delayed punishment will be as ineffective as delayed reinforcing consequences.

General Techniques for Increasing Good Behavior

A teacher must establish priorities for teaching good behavior as well as for reducing behavior problems. After the teacher has determined the most important things for his students to learn, he must select effective methods for teaching those skills. At least five alternative general techniques for increasing desirable behavior are available to every teacher.

Stating Rules, Praising Good Behavior, and Ignoring Inappropriate Behavior. Efficient behavior management in the classroom seems to consist of at least three basic techniques which must be used in combination to be most effective (Madsen, Becker, & Thomas, 1968). Rules for conduct in the classroom must be clearly and positively stated. Children must know how they *are* to behave. It may be helpful to post rules in a conspicuous place in the classroom and review them periodically. Rules alone, however, are not likely to produce appropriate behavior. They are antecedent events which are of little value without the systematic application of consequences for behavior related to the rules.

Teacher attention and praise for rule-following behavior is a powerful positive consequence for most children. The teacher must seek out those children exemplifying appropriate behavior and praise them. In this way, he calls attention to appropriate models and offers vicarious reinforcement for other class members. Teacher attention may consist of nearness or proximity to the child, a touch on the

shoulder, assistance with academic work, a wink, or any other sign
of recognition. Praise can be given by a smile, a nod of approval, a
"happy face" drawn on the child's paper, other nonverbal signals of
approval, and a variety of verbal statements. When verbal praise is
given, it is best to indicate specifically what the child is doing that is
praiseworthy. "I'm glad you've started your work already" is preferable as a praise statement to "You're being a good boy this morning,"
or "Agnes, you're a doll."

In addition to establishing rules and "catching the children being
good," ignoring inappropriate behavior will be likely to increase
classroom control. The fallacy of attempting to control misbehavior
primarily by criticism or "talking it through" has already been discussed. The more skillful the teacher becomes at totally withdrawing
attention from misbehaving children the more likely he will achieve
efficient classroom management.

Criticizing, nagging, rebuking, punishing, and other negative interactions are more tiring than positive interactions such as praising,
complimenting, approving, and thanking. This is true whether one
is on the giving side or on the receiving end of the transaction. At
the same time, negative interactions seem more likely to occur when
an individual's energy is depleted. Consequently, the teacher who
does not waste his energy, and the energy of his students, by attending to misbehavior may successfully avoid a dangerous spiral of unpleasant behavior.

Successful use of this technique depends on the application of the
three elements: rules, praise, and ignoring. Without rules, children
will not know how to behave. Without teacher attention and praise
for good behavior, they will not learn to follow the rules. But without
teacher attention as a consequence, misbehavior will likely subside.

Rewarding Approximations. Few complex behaviors are learned in a
day. Acquisition of a complex skill requires repeated trials over a
period of days, weeks, months, or even years. The child whose expectation turns to disappointment when he does not learn to read a book
the first day of school exemplifies lack of knowledge about how learning takes place. The teacher who expects a disturbing child to
become a model of perfection immediately will be disappointed
because he has lost sight of the principle of behavior shaping. Looking for and rewarding small improvements in behavior is one key to
successful teaching. If the teacher waits for perfection, he will probably never have an opportunity to reinforce the child's behavior. If he
identifies and reinforces successive approximations of his goal for the
child, he will likely see gradual but steady improvement in behavior.

Before embarking on a behavior-management program, the teacher should be able to state what actions of the child will constitute improvement.

Strengthening Reinforcers. Children vary greatly in their behavioral responsiveness to reinforcers. Traditional social reinforcers, such as attention and praise, are sufficient to control the classroom behavior of most children. For others it is necessary to provide more effective consequences. This may mean the use of food, money, toys, personal-care items, special privileges, or special activities as reinforcers (see Chapter 6 for a list of possible reinforcers). A subsequent event which is not a reinforcer is of no value in teaching appropriate behavior. *It is essential that the teacher find what the child will work for and employ those things as reinforcers.* Consequences that are more natural should always be preferred to those which are more contrived or artificial. If the teacher must employ more extrinsic or primitive rewards than are necessary for most children, little is to be gained by appealing to the child's "love of learning," lamenting his lack of "maturity," or disparaging his acquisitiveness. Whenever a teacher is unsuccessful in obtaining the responses he wants a child to emit, he should consider the possibility of increasing the strength of the reward. The strength of reinforcers may be determined by observing what children prefer, asking them what they would like to work for, or providing a consequence for behavior and observing its effect. In addition to strengthening the reinforcers themselves, it is often helpful to make the consequences of behavior more explicit by using a contingency contract or establishing a system of token reinforcement.

Making Reinforcement More Immediate. Delayed rewards are effective only for indiviuals who have achieved a high level of self-control. Children with school learning problems seldom have learned the self-control necessary to work for distant reinforcers. They must be taught the self-control which brings their behavior under the control of future consequences. Until the complex task of self-control is taught, their behavior will remain almost exclusively under the control of immediate environmental consequences. Therefore, a technique for increasing appropriate behavior is to move the reinforcers closer in time to occurrence of the behavior. In general, the sooner a child is allowed to have his reward after behaving appropriately, the more successful the teacher will be. A token reinforcement system helps to reduce the tactical problems of delivering immediate rewards. Tokens can be given immediately after an appropriate behavior without interrupting classroom routine.

Varying the Schedule of Reinforcement. Schedules of reinforcement appear to be as important a factor in behavioral change as the reinforcers themselves. The schedule by which a reinforcer is administered often determines its power. Although some behaviors apparently are acquired with intermittent reinforcement, learning is more likely to occur when every response is reinforced. Continuous reinforcement is not, however, an efficient schedule for maintaining behavior. Furthermore, change to an intermittent schedule may produce marked acceleration in response rates. Reinforcement on a variable ratio or variable interval schedule will maintain a steadier rate of behavior than reinforcement on a fixed ratio or fixed interval. Consequently, the teacher must always choose a schedule of reinforcement which fits his teaching objectives and the child's level of learning. When the child is not responding to a behavior-modification procedure, an appropriate change in the schedule of reinforcement may produce the desired results. It is not uncommon to find that learning has not been acquired because reinforcement has been too infrequent or that learning has not been maintained because of failure to shift gradually to an intermittent schedule.

Changing Antecedent Events. Antecedent events which may be modified to produce behavioral change include rules, tasks, cues, models, and setting events. Establishing positive rules for behavior has already been discussed. The tasks presented to children must be carefully prepared and presented if other elements of behavior management are to be effective. For children with school learning problems this may mean an individualized instructional program. Chapter 3 provides principles of academic remediation.

Cues and models may be presented for social-emotional as well as academic behavior. The performance of many behaviors can be regulated by appropriate prompts or cues. Normal adults program cues for their own behavior by using watches, notes, hand signals, grocery lists, flashing lights, metronomes, bells, and a wide variety of other devices. Children's classroom behavior and academic performance often fall short of teacher expectation because unambiguous cues indicating how, when, or where the child is to behave are not provided. The child who talks out may do so because the teacher has not developed clear, consistent signals for permission to speak. Children with auditory learning difficulties may have difficulty understanding the verbal prompts of the teacher, especially if the teacher ououtverbalizes instructions. Sometimes children have difficulty reading the teacher's cues because the postural, gestural, intonational, and verbal signals given by the teacher are not consistent. For example, a teacher may call a child's name, indicating that he is to make a verbal response but fail to look at the child or turn away. For the child with a history of acting-out behavior or learning deficits, the teacher may need to use more dramatic and abbreviated prompts. Withdrawn children, on the other hand, may respond more readily to subtle prompts.

A behavioral model is invaluable in teaching. When a teacher is attempting to help a child acquire a new skill, he must provide many demonstrations of the final performance. Otherwise, he risks inefficient teaching or needless attention to detail in shaping behavior. The child who consistently hears a good language model is much more easily taught appropriate language patterns than one who is exposed frequently to models of poor language.

Changes in antecedent events can be used to decrease unwanted behavior. Providing a quiet, uncluttered place to work, attractive and interesting materials, and individualized tasks at which the child can be highly successful will increase learning. Study booths or "offices" in which a child may work without the distraction of other classroom activity may increase the child's attention to the task at hand.

Deprivation of reinforcers, the inverse of satiation, may be used to increase the reinforcing potential of consequences for good behavior. When the child has been deprived of a reinforcer for a period of time he is more likely to work to obtain it. For example, a child is more likely to work for the privilege of writing on the chalkboard if it is offered as a consequence for good behavior when he has not had the opportunity for several hours. Reinforcement should be offered frequently, but it should be given in relatively small amounts so that satiation does not occur.

Changing the program or schedule of antecedent events may be used as a technique for increasing good behavior. The teacher who would like the child to talk only when called on in class discussions must remember to cue his behavior by calling on him frequently. The child who has completed an academic task can make more responses only when additional tasks are presented. Making certain that ample opportunities to respond appropriately are provided is an essential element of behavior management.

General Techniques for Maintaining Behavioral Gains

Behaviors learned are not necessarily skills retained. Reinforcement is necessary for the maintenance of behavior as well as for its acquisition. Teaching a child a new behavior only to see it forgotten or not applied is both inefficient and disheartening. The ultimate goal of classroom management should be self-controlled, highly motivated learners. When artificial or obvious contingencies of reinforcement are necessary to control an individual's behavior, he lacks self-control. If consequences native to the individual's environment produce appropriate behavior, he is in control of himself. When frequent reinforcement is necessary to maintain behavior, the child is thought to lack motivation. If he continues to behave as desired under contingencies which result in a low frequency of reinforcement, he is considered highly motivated. Maintenance of appropriate behavior by infrequently occurring reinforcement in the natural environment of the child should be sought by every teacher. At least four general techniques for achieving this goal are available.

Gradually Reducing Reinforcement. The frequency and amount of reinforcement may be varied to increase good behavior. After a behavior is learned, reinforcement should be intermittent rather than continuous to make the behavior more resistant to extinction. The shift to intermittent reinforcement must be gradual, and occasional reinforcement of the behavior must continue if extinction of the response is to be avoided. Gradual reduction of the frequency of reinforcement will increase the likelihood that the child will adopt a "normal" motivational pattern.

Gradually Delaying Reinforcement. Immediate reinforcement is essential for effective modification of behavior. Although delayed reinforcement can exercise a significant degree of control over behavior during maintenance, it is necessary to provide feedback to the child regarding his progress in earning the reinforcer. A child is not likely to continue working toward a long-term goal without recognition of intermediate accomplishments. Token reinforcement is particularly well-suited to the successful use of delayed reinforcement because the child can observe the accumulation of tokens as an immediate consequence. As the child is able to work for rewards which are delayed for a longer time, he will approximate more closely the motivational model of the teacher.

Gradually Fading Artificial to Natural Reinforcers. Natural reinforcers are those which can be viewed as native to the environment of the child, assuming that his environment is not pathological. Thus, tokens, toys, money, candy, and other reinforcers contrived for therapeutic ends may be considered artificial because they are not ordinarily used as consequences for most children. Teacher attention, praise, grades, records of progress, special activities, etc., are natural reinforcers in that good teachers ordinarily provide such consequences. Natural reinforcers have two distinct advantages over artificial reinforcers: *(a)* they occur in a wider range of environments, and *(b)* they are less obvious to the casual observer. As remediation of the child's behavioral deficits progresses, a gradual shift should also occur from artificial, material rewards to natural, social rewards. It must be remembered, however, that reinforcers are natural or artificial in terms of specific behaviors and situations. The successful teacher continues in his profession for both material and social rewards. If either is lacking, i.e., if the teacher never receives social reinforcement from his pupils or if his pay is terminated, he will not continue to teach. Material rewards for children's appropriate behavior are sometimes essential (Green & Stachnik, 1968), but the emphasis should be on social rewards.

Reinforcing Self-Control Behaviors. Response to natural reinforcers is not the only characteristic of self-control. Haring and Whelan (1965) have detailed the stages through which a child passes in remediation of maladaptive behaviors. The final stage is one of integration, in which the child not only observes the relationship between his behavior and its consequences but also begins to control his own reinforcers to further improve his behavior. Children can be taught to manage their own behavior through systematic development and reinforcement of the behaviors which constitute self-control (Homme, 1966, 1970). The child who selects an appropriate task for himself, makes a realistic and positive statement about himself or his performance, or establishes his own contingency of reinforcement offers the teacher a clear opportunity for reinforcement of self-control. Failure to respond to such behavior with a positive social consequence is a costly omission for everyone concerned with the child's success as a learner.

Beyond the Classroom

The teacher does not control all of the consequences for children's behavior. Parents, siblings, other teachers, the school principal, peers, or acquaintances in the community may be able to provide very powerful reinforcers for the child. The teacher will increase his effectiveness as a modifier of behavior if he is able to enlist the aid of other individuals who control the child's rewards. The coach, the industrial arts teacher, the principal, the janitor, or the cook often can offer powerful school-related incentives for the child. If they agree to assist in providing contingent rewards, they can contribute significantly to modification of the child's behavior.

Other than the classroom teacher, the principal has the greatest potential effect on children's behavior in school. He is responsible for the emotional climate of the school, whether it emphasizes punitive control or the positive control of rewards. His support of the teacher's efforts to establish a climate of positive control may make the difference between success and failure in the implementation of behavior-modification techniques. The principal who responds primarily to misbehavior seems doomed to an ever-widening spiral of unpleasant interactions. The teacher who arranges to send children to the principal for compliments rather than criticism, pats on the back rather than spanks, rewards rather than punishment, can help the principal focus on positive control and increase his own options for the use of positive consequences.

Behavior-modification techniques can easily be taught to parents and other persons outside the school environment (Becker, 1971a; Deibert & Harmon, 1970; Tharp & Wetzel, 1969). There is little empirical evidence, however, that behavioral improvement at school will necessarily result in positive changes outside the classroom, or vice versa (Wahler, 1969). Remediation should be a joint effort of parents and teachers. Parental use of behavior-modification techniques can contribute significantly to the acquisition and maintenance of learning.[11]

Levels of Application of
Behavior Principles

Like a craftsman selecting his tools, the teacher must select techniques for changing behavior. However, just as the tool does not determine the skill of the craftsman, the behavior-management technique does not make a good teacher. Behavior-modification techniques must be viewed as precision instruments—useless in the hands of the incompetent and invaluable in the hands of a master. The behavior principles discussed in this chapter have produced numerous techniques which can be applied with varying degrees of precision and sophistication. At least three levels of application can be defined.

Structured Classroom

Good teachers have used behavior principles for centuries. It is not uncommon for the experienced teacher to remark, "but I've been doing that for years!" when introduced to behavior modification. When an experienced teacher is experiencing classroom-management problems despite his knowledge of basic principles, it is often because he has not applied them consistently and systematically.

The principles of work before play, contingent rewards for good behavior, consistency, firmness, fairness, clarity of instructions, and individualization of expectations seem to be minimum requirements for successful teaching. When these underlying principles of behavior management are employed systematically, a high degree of "structure" is introduced into the classroom. This structure or predictability of the classroom environment has been found to have a therapeutic effect on children's social-emotional and academic behavior (Cruickshank, Bentzen, Ratzeburg, & Tannhauser, 1961; Haring and Phillips, 1962; Phillips, 1967; Phillips, Wiener, & Haring, 1960; Whelan, 1960). The structured classroom makes systematic use of most of the behavior principles discussed in this chapter but is a more intuitive, less technological level of application than methods currently being researched. A major difference between the structured classroom and more sophisticated levels of application is its lack of emphasis on daily recording of specific behaviors.

Behavior Technology

At a second level of application, greater precision is employed in manipulating environmental variables and monitoring behavioral change. The structured classroom concept is extended to include more explicit contingencies of reinforcement and daily recording of behaviors (Deibert & Harmon, 1970; Haring, 1968; Haring & Phillips, 1972; Whelan, 1966). Teachers applying behavior principles at this level are interested in precise measurement of the effects of their teaching procedures on children's behavior (Zimmerman, Zimmerman, Rider, Smith, & Dinn, 1971). Although it is possible to use behavior principles successfully at a less sophisticated level, teachers should strive to be as precise as possible in teaching and evaluating learning. The application of behavior principles at this level may not be as simple as it first appears (Birnbrauer, Burchard, & Burchard, 1970), but the competent teacher is not likely to find it extremely difficult to learn the use of behavior technology.

Research Designs

Some teachers will want to develop skills in the scientific analysis of behavior change. Many teachers are capable of using basic research designs to explore the extent of their control over the variables influencing learning (Hall, 1971a, 1971b; Hall, Cristler, Cranston, & Tucker, 1970). Research designs allow the teacher to state with greater confidence whether teaching techniques are responsible for changes in their pupils' behavior. The efficacy of various teaching procedures can also be compared by using research methods. Discussion of specific research designs is beyond the scope of this chapter, but it is expected that the teacher who has mastered the basic elements of behavior technology will want to extend his use of behavior principles to more scientific applications.[12]

Limitations of
Behavior Modification

It would be presumptuous to assert that a behavior-modification approach to classroom management represents a limitless solution to educational problems (Hewett, 1968; Kauffman, in press; MacMillan & Forness, 1970; Whelan, 1966). Likewise, it would be incredibly naive to assume that all intervention approaches to school learning problems are equally valid or useful. No other approach is supported by the empirical research which undergirds behavior modification. Of the alternatives available to classroom teachers, we believe that a behavior-modification strategy is the best point of departure.

Summary

Behavior modification involves the systematic manipulation of environmental events to produce specific change in observable behavior. The teacher may control events which occur before, during, and after a problem behavior to modify its occurrence. The teacher confronted with a classroom-management problem must first define the problem behavior as an observable, countable, repeatable action of the child. An objective and reliable baseline record of occurrences of the behavior should be obtained and plotted on a graph. After a baseline has been established, a wide variety of intervention techniques designed to increase or decrease the behavior may be employed. The behavior should be monitored during baseline, intervention, and follow-up phases. General procedures for decreasing undesirable behavior include extinction, reinforcement of incompatible behaviors, changing stimuli which precede the behavior, differential reinforcement of other behavior, differential reinforcement of low rate, and punishment. Some general techniques for increasing good behavior include stating rules, praising good behavior, ignoring misbehavior, rewarding approximations, strengthening reinforcers, making reinforcement more immediate, varying the schedule of reinforcement, and changing tasks, cues, and models presented to the child. Behavioral gains can be maintained by gradually reducing the frequency of reinforcement, delaying reinforcement, fading from artificial to natural reinforcers, and reinforcing self-control behaviors. To be most effective, behavior modification should be extended to the home and other settings outside the classroom. Although behavior modification is not a panacea, its effectiveness is supported by more scientific research in the laboratory and classroom than any other approach to behavior management.

NOTES

[1]For a more complete discussion of the effects of various schedules of reinforcement see: Ferster & Perrott (1968); Lovitt & Esveldt (1970); Reynolds (1968); and Whaley & Malott (1971).

[2]For a more detailed discussion of contingency contracting see: Cantrell, Cantrell, Huddleston, & Woolridge (1969); Homme (1969); Tharp & Wetzel (1969); and Zifferblatt (1970).

[3]For additional information regarding the establishment and operation of token systems see: Axelrod (1971); Kuypers, Becker, & O'Leary (1968); Neisworth, Deno, & Jenkins (1969); O'Leary, Becker, Evans, & Saudargas (1969); Phillips, Phillips, Fixen, & Wolf (1971); Stainback, Payne, Stainback, & Payne (1973); and Wolf, Giles, & Hall (1968).

[4]For further examples of the use of group consequences see: Barrett, Saunders, & Wolf (1969); Patterson (1965); and Wolf, Hanley, King, Lachowicz, & Giles (1970).

[5]In our approach to behavior modification we have chosen to use an *operant* conditioning model exclusively. The term "stimulus" should not be confused with the meaning of the term in classical or respondent conditioning. In respondent conditioning a stimulus *elicits* a reflexive response. In operant conditioning a response is never elicited by a stimulus, but antecedent stimuli may increase the probability that a specific response will be emitted. For a more complete explanation of the differences between respondent and operant conditioning see: Bandura (1969); Becker, Engelmann, & Thomas (1971); Bijou & Baer (1961); Ferster & Perrott (1968); and Reynolds (1968).

[6]For further discussion of behavioral goals see: Hernandez (1971); Mager (1962, 1968); and Popham & Baker (1970).

[7]For more detailed discussion of imitation and modeling see: Bandura (1969); Bandura & Walters (1963); and Peterson & Whitehurst (1971).

[8]For additional discussion of the scheduling of activities in behavior management see: Cruickshank, Bentzen, Ratzeburg, & Tannhauser (1961); Haring & Phillips (1962); Hewett (1968); and Phillips, (1967).

[9]For discussion of general procedures for classroom management following a behavioral model see: Ackerman (1972); Blackham & Silberman (1971); Clarizio (1972); Gallagher (1970, 1971); Hall (1971a); Haring (1968); Haring & Whelan (1965); Hewett (1968); Phillips (1967); Phillips, Wiener, & Haring (1960); Sulzer & Mayer (1972); and Whelan (1966).

[10]Theoretical, ethical, and moral issues in behavior modification are discussed in: Bandura (1969); Bradfield (1970); Fargo, Behrns, & Nolen (1970); Harris (1972); Krasner (1969); Skinner (1971); Stuart (1970); Tharp & Wetzel (1969); and Ullmann (1969).

[11]For suggested behavioral methods for parents see: Becker (1971a); Buckley & Walker (1970); Deibert & Harmon (1970); Patterson (1971); Patterson & Gullion (1968); Sluyter & Hawkins (1972); Smith & Smith (1966); Tharp & Wetzel (1969); Vallett (1969); and Zifferblatt (1970).

[12]For description of research methods for teachers see: Baer, Wolf, & Risley (1968); Hall (1971a); Hall, Cristler, Cranston, & Tucker (1970); Miller (1969); Sherman & Baer (1969); Staats (1970); and Tharp & Wetzel (1969).

3

Principles
of
Academic
Remediation

The remediation of school learning problems often requires personalized instruction and the use of specialized materials and techniques. Special teachers, rather than regular classroom teachers, have commonly been assigned the task of remediation (Kirk, 1972). However, many of the instructional methods employed by remedial specialists can be used in the regular classroom. Furthermore, the principles that apply to the remediation of academic problems are not limited to the special class. The principles discussed in this chapter, and the teaching suggestions outlined in Part II, are intended for use in both the regular classroom and in specialized remedial situations.

Eight Principles
of Remediation

I. Proper Remediation is Dependent upon Evaluation of the Child's Weaknesses, Needs, and Strengths.

This principle is of primary importance to the success of any remedial process. Attempting to help a child overcome academic problems without first determining what special strengths the child has and what specific problems he is encountering will be fruitless. We often have seen children struggling through various academic programs with little evaluation or understanding of their specific difficulties. In many situations, lower grade-level materials are selected because the child is experiencing difficulty with the material normally used in his class. The only consideration has often been one of finding "comfortable" or easy instructional materials for the child, not one of evaluation of individual needs or deficits.

It is unfortunate that the concept of evaluation as it pertains to a child's strengths and weaknesses has been misunderstood and inappropriately implemented. An evaluation procedure has often been viewed as a structured, formal situation where the child is administered three or four highly specialized tests (Lovitt, 1967). These tests usually have been given to the child by an individual other than the person who will be actually teaching the child (Perry & Morris, 1969). This situation, however, necessitates the additional step of interpretation of test results to the person who will be working with the child.

Evaluation is an on-going teaching procedure, one in which the teacher has the responsibile role. Instruments need not be so highly specialized that teachers are excluded from evaluation (Hammill, 1971). The primary concern of the evaluation procedure should be one of assessing individual needs. This objective can be attained without the traditional emphasis on test scores.

Teacher Observation. Many of the clues that will be utilized in planning an instructional program can be easily detected in everyday classroom behavior. The only diagnostic tool that is required for this level of evaluation is a keen observational eye. Teacher observation of a child's behavior while attacking a word in a reading passage, for example, provides information which can be used in assessing instructional needs. The teacher who reads daily with a child is the logical person to obtain this information. He is the one who regularly views the learning strategies that the child brings to the printed page. Similar information is obtainable through the administration of diagnostic tests; however, these tests are unnecessary if the teacher can provide identical information through his daily interactions with the child. During the observation stage of evaluation, the teacher must be aware of specific behaviors exhibited by the child (Langstaff & Volkmor, 1969). Specific behaviors to be considered in observations are listed by Wilson (1967).

For example, in reading instruction the teacher should initially ask himself the question, "What does the child do when he is reading and is confronted with a word that he does not know?" Responses to this question could include:

1. "Usually stops and refuses to respond"
2. "Looks at the initial consonant and guesses at the rest of the word"
3. "Tries to break the word into syllables"
4. "Slowly sounds out the whole word"
5. "Tries to figure out the word from its configuration"

Similar questions which may be asked for difficulties in arithmetic, written language, etc., are outlined in Part II. The responses lead to further questions, many of which can be answered by the teacher without the administration of standardized tests. Questions that teachers ask of themselves provide crucial evaluative data which become the basis for remediation. Once the academic problem is identified in general terms (e.g., difficulties in the analysis of unfamiliar words), careful observation may provide the answer to pertinent questions regarding more specific learning difficulties, as discussed in Chapter 5.

Informal Tests. In addition to the observational data obtained through daily interactions with the child, it is often necessary to administer informal teacher-made tests (Lerner, 1971). These specific task-oriented tests provide additional evaluative teaching data, many times exceeding the value of information obtained through more formalized testing procedures. Informal measures may be given by the teacher in the classroom. Although some of these tests may be individualized, they must be considered a part of the regular instructional program (Smith, 1969a).

Instruments that are included at this level of evaluation include: (a) seatwork exercises emphasizing *one* specific task; (b) orally administered exercises; (c) informal teaching lessons assessing various skills; and (d) individually administered written assignments. Teacher-made evaluative instruments are informal and designed to assess one particular skill (e.g., knowledge of a certain blend, knowledge of a specific letter sound, etc.). An illustration of an informal test evaluating the child's knowledge of the names of the letters of the alphabet follows:

INSTRUCTIONS: Prepare a worksheet with the alphabet in random order, as shown below. Ask the child to read the letters to you aloud. Note specific difficulties by circling the letters not known or writing in letters called incorrectly. Following the administration, look for particular clues, such as reversals (e.g., "d" for "b") and inversions (e.g., "b" for "p").

f	k	z	a	u	r	i	v	g
b	m	j	x	s	d	h	l	y
o	c	w	n	e	q	t	p	

A number of alternatives to this informal test can be constructed by adapting the format to the particular skill to be evaluated. Specific chapters in Part II list additional informal tests that may be used in different curriculum areas. The instruments are not intended to be complicated, expensive, or time-consuming. They are teacher-made and teacher-administered, and the information obtained provides the teacher with data in planning for the specific needs of an individual student.

Formal Tests. In addition to observational data and informal testing procedures, teachers may need supportive data provided by standardized diagnostic tests. If formal testing is indicated there are a number of very comprehensive tests currently available for this purpose. However, formalized tests will often provide the teacher with little more than he already knows, especially if informal procedures have been accurately administered (Kaluger & Kolson, 1969). There is little reason to assume that most diagnostic tests need to be administered by someone other than the teacher. Because this level of evaluation is more likely to involve direct individual interaction with the child, teachers sometimes find it difficult to schedule the time for formal pupil assessment. Consequently, formal testing is often left to someone other than the teacher. However, the teacher should attempt to schedule the evaluation during a quiet time in the class, before or after school or during recess. The teacher should administer all aspects of the evaluation that are within his capabilities.

The selection of a standardized test involves careful planning on the part of the teacher. Prior to the actual selection, the teacher must decide what questions should be answered by the evaluative instrument. Questions should pertain specifically to the child's instructional needs. Strang (1969) provides a number of questions which should be considered in selecting a standardized test. It is frustrating and a waste of time for both the teacher and the child to administer instruments which provide little in the way of specific information. The standardized test that is selected should be based upon the unique aspects of each child's academic difficulties. If the test that is chosen is composed of a number of specific subtests, only those subtests that are necessary should be administered. Much time and energy could be saved if careful planning and analysis preceded the actual administration.

A final note involves the administration of more exacting tests that require specific training in interpretation and analysis. It may be necessary to obtain the services of a qualified examiner who is trained in the areas of personality or intelligence testing. When this type of service is warranted, the results of these tests should be viewed in conjunction with the data previously obtained by the teacher. Too often, the information accumulated by others is not used by the teacher because of the indirect implications for instructional programs (Hewett, 1968). There should be closer coordination between informal teacher evaluations and formal test results. Individuals working together should be able to evaluate more accurately the specific instructional needs of children experiencing learning problems in school.

Remediation is likely to be successful only when it is based upon adequate evaluation of the child. Clearly, the best evaluation is ineffectual if the results are not used in planning instructional programs.

II. Evaluative Results Should be Directly Utilized in Planning Remedial Programs.

In many schools, testing seems to have become an end in itself rather than a means to planning an instructional program. The emphasis upon exact scores *without considering the information behind each score* (cf. Stephens, 1970) has been one factor contributing to the incorrect usage of test results. The basic purpose of remediation seems to have been lost because of the unnecessary importance placed upon IQ scores, percentiles, and grade-equivalent scores. Few teachers seem to remember that the purpose of evaluation is to provide data which will be used in developing an instructional program for individual children. The important information which led to the *formulation* of the score(s) is overlooked. In addition, the behavior exhibited by a child during testing should be included in test reports. Unfortunately, it often is not.

Obtaining Teaching Information from Tests. One solution for handling the problem of test scores is to consider what the child can and cannot do in terms of actual academic behaviors. Information pertaining to *specific skill deficiencies and strengths* is provided by informal tests. For example, it is useful to know that John knows the names of all the letters of the alphabet, except *c* and *g,* and that he knows only the sounds of the letters /*a*/ and /*m*/. In contrast, to know that he reads at the 1.2 grade level is of little value. The descriptive information provides the teacher with basic data for planning an instructional program (Stephens, 1970). On the basis of descriptive information, the teacher can decide *what* needs to be taught, and eventually, with additional information, *how* it should be taught.

"Teachable" Tests. The teaching information that is provided by informal evaluative devices can also be obtained from more formal standardized tests (Woolbright, 1971). A number of standardized tests provide excellent "teachable" information. The *Gates-McKillop Reading Diagnostic Test* (Gates & McKillop, 1962) serves as a good illustration. This test consists of eight major sections and a number of subsections. Grade-equivalent scores are provided for most subtest raw scores. However, the information obtained from subtests can easily be translated into instructional tasks.

David, a ten-year-old youngster, was administered the *Gates-McKillop.* The results of the testing were summarized as follows:

> David knew all of the letter sounds except the short *o.* With regard to the names of the letters, David said *P* for the capital *B.* For the lowercase letters, he called *l* for *i,* and *p* for *q.* He was particularly weak on discriminating final letter sounds, calling *f* for *v, l* for *k, p* for *b, n* for *b.*
>
> On the Oral Reading subtest, he tended to omit and mispronounce words. He read slowly with poor phrasing and emphasis in a low, often indistinct voice. He appeared to depend mainly on a combination of initial letter sounds plus general configuration to attack a word, frequently skipping unfamiliar words. Infrequently, he would name the letters in attacking a word. Finally, on the Spelling subtest, David usually guessed at the remainder of the word after correctly saying the initial sound.

Based upon additional observational data and a number of informal tests, David's teacher knew that his oral language exceeded his written language development. It was also noted that David needed to learn attending and listening skills.

The results of the informal measures and the *Gates-McKillop* provided the teacher with a basis for initiating an instructional program. In David's case, the teacher utilized a language-experience approach to develop sight vocabulary, word analysis skills, and writing ability. Telephone conversations aided in developing his attending and listening skills. The teacher also used the Language Master[1] to develop a sight vocabulary and work on medial and final letter combinations. Some of the teaching activities listed in Chapter 8 under initial and final letters, were utilized to teach this particular skill.[2]

The *Gates-McKillop Reading Diagnostic Test* is one example of a standardized test that provides the user with "teachable" information. Many other standardized tests (as listed in Part II) can also be used if the administrator is willing to carefully analyze a test for the needed instructional information. Very often, the teacher himself must translate test information into instructional processes, since most tests provide few guidelines. However, this fact certainly does not preclude the usability of test results for planning a program of remediation. The teacher must know and obtain what information is important to him in planning for an individual child.

Utilizing All of the Information. An important but often overlooked facet of evaluation is the information that clearly points to a child's strengths. What a child *can* do is as important in planning a program as what a child cannot do or does poorly. Learning strengths that are exhibited both in the classroom and in informal and formal tests will many times provide the teacher with the basis for a teaching program.

For example, when John was administered the *Gates-McKillop* he knew all the names of the letters, but only one letter sound. Although he had been in school for a total of three years, John had a sight vocabulary of just sixty words. The teacher made use of John's knowledge of letter names in planning his program of remediation. Eventually, he worked on his letter sound deficiencies, but only after the visual strengths in basic sight vocabulary were utilized as a foundation for beginning the remediation.

It is important to evaluate *all* available information and use that which will be most helpful in planning for individual children. Some of the information that is obtained will be more directly applicable in initial program planning. However, no information should be considered totally useless in helping a child overcome his learning problems.

Data obtained through both informal and formal evaluations serve as a guideline in planning remedial programs. Some of the information (e.g., knowledge that the child reverses letters) can be used directly in the teaching process. Other information (e.g., observation that the child learns motor skills quickly) will be used for total program planning. Wherever the evaluative data are utilized, they serve as a foundation upon which future successes can be built.

III. Remediation Is a Process of Continuous Evaluation which Is Periodically Altered to Meet the Changing Needs of the Individual.

In planning a program of remediation, the initial evaluation of a youngster should be viewed as a starting point for continuous evaluation (Meyen, 1972). Those children who succeed will eventually outgrow specific materials and methods and there will be a need to alter the instructional program. Other children will experience particular difficulties as they proceed in learning. These situations require constant evaluation. Often, teachers are able to improvise a teaching procedure in order to clarify a concept for a particular child. In other cases, a more detailed analysis of the situation is needed before the teacher can instruct the child successfully. These situations will sometimes require formal testing or consideration of alternatives to the presently used materials or techniques.

Continuous evaluation is also necessary in the case of the child with difficulties in more than one academic area. Once the child experiences success in analyzing unfamiliar words, for example, it might be wise to consider his difficulties in arithmetic. The emphasis in the remedial setting will then be transferred from one subject area to another. *Teachers should be extremely careful not to abandon successful work in one area to initiate remediation of another academic problem. Children need continued success so that they do not lose their original gains.*

Flexibility of instructional materials is one particular problem that is often neglected in the on-going evaluation of children experiencing learning problems. Individual children who are finding success in a remedial program will complete materials at a very rapid rate. This necessitates the availability of numerous sequential materials. Unfortunately, teachers tend to select materials at random. The teacher's awareness that a child has outgrown a specific material is a part of the evaluation process which might necessitate instructional change.

Sequential Learning. The sequential nature of learning is primary to the effectiveness of a remedial program. The teacher must be aware that the child changes as he learns. The teacher should evaluate the mastery of a particular skill through informal procedures. For the child who has learned the sound of *s,* the teacher may evaluate the skill by asking him to sound out a number of words that contain the /s/ sound. Likewise, the sequential nature of learning dictates that the /s/ sound needs to be known *before* a child is introduced to consonant blends containing the *s* sound. *The teacher should not expect a child to learn more advanced skills unless the prerequisites for that particular skill have been learned.* (See Chapter 5 for discussion of task analysis.) Closely related to the process of sequential learning is the principle of continuous evaluation. The evaluation process will enable the teacher to recognize when particular skills have been mastered to insure continuous success.

Program Evaluation. In the majority of cases, teachers will be able to informally evaluate the effectiveness of the remediation program through observational techniques and teaching procedures. When a child is not succeeding, it might be necessary for the teacher to change the method, give additional supportive teaching, or reevaluate the effectiveness of the entire remedial process. In the latter case, the teacher will be required to reassess his remedial goals and look for possible explanations for a program's failure. When supportive teaching is required, it might be a matter of prolonging the exposure to a particular skill that is being taught or changing the medium of presentation so that the child is exposed to an additional sensory modality. This requires creativity and originality on the part of the teacher. He must analyze the situation and then decide what might be done to clarify the concept for the child. Evaluation is viewed as a part of the teaching process (Stephens, 1970). The teacher must evaluate the effectiveness of his teaching and the learning taking place in his class. Ultimately, the success of the remedial program will depend upon this phase of the teaching process.

One technique that has been used successfully by a number of teachers is the "end-of-the-period" evaluation. Immediately following a teaching period, a teacher writes down his observations and thoughts concerning the effectiveness of the preceding lesson. Immediate recall is an important ingredient, and the written part of the process lends itself to periodic review and analysis for developing trends (Capobianco, 1964). This technique resembles a daily log that can be added to lesson plans. The style is unimportant, but the concept inherent in the technique serves as a tool for evaluating effectiveness, both on the part of the teacher and the student. It is often possible, for example, to notice a relationship between "good" days and the use of certain materials or rewards with specific children.

IV. Successful Remediation Is Dependent upon Use of a Wide Variety of Materials, Techniques, and Methods.

There is no one best instructional material or method for academic remediation. Likewise, what will work to one child's advantage may possibly work to another's disadvantage. Teachers should be able to handle any number of different learning problems by utilizing what will work for a particular child (Frostig & Horne, 1965). Heilman (1972) has suggested that if there are significant individual differences in the way children learn, it follows that different approaches are advisable in helping children who are experiencing failure in learning. Lack of flexibility in teaching approaches is often a source of learning problems in children. We consider such inflexibility to be an inappropriate teaching method for particular children. It is frustrating to observe a child struggling with a specific approach to reading instruction, later realizing that a different method would be successful. Often, a change in procedure may be the very key required for successful learning.

Flexibility of Instructional Materials. One of the challenges of teaching is adjusting to individual differences among normal children. Even more challenging are the differences presented by children experiencing difficulties in school. *Probably the most complex problem confronting the teacher is that of adjusting instruction to individual differences.* The ability to adjust instruction requires that teachers have a working knowledge of a wide variety of materials and techniques. Nothing is more convincing than to view a child reach academic success because of a change in instructional methods or materials.

Articulate arguments, and occasionally empirical evidence, can be cited in support of certain materials or techniques. Children with specific skill deficiencies may *require* a specific teaching method. For example, the child with severe auditory discrimination difficulties is likely to achieve initial success with a sight-word approach to reading. The concern, however, is the number of children in a class who might be experiencing *individual* problems requiring different approaches. The more children with learning problems seen by a teacher each day, the greater the likelihood of the need for differing methods and materials. The evidence supporting a specific approach to remediation loses some of its impact when a teacher is faced with twenty-five children exhibiting ten different patterns of learning.

Successful remediation is based upon teaching versatility. This is not considered to be an easy task. On the contrary, it requires detailed planning, conscientious study, and hard work. One difficult aspect of this process involves experimentation with differing methods and materials for particular children until a successful approach is found. The child will continue to fail and lack motivation until a successful teaching technique is found. The teacher will also be frustrated during this stage. Some teachers hesitate to experiment with new teaching methods and materials for fear of another failure. When a particular approach is successful with a specific child, remediation is only a matter of conscientiously attending to the teaching task and continually reinforcing the child's success. The material or approach itself may serve as a reinforcer when teaching is highly successful.

Teacher Flexibility. It is difficult for some teachers to use more than one teaching method. It is equally difficult to convince the teacher of the merits of a specific approach for a particular child if the teacher is already convinced of the "advantages" of using a certain material with all children. Nevertheless, the teaching process is less frustrating when alternative approaches to instruction are used with specific children. For example, individuals who have experienced continual failure in learning how to read with a strong phonics emphasis will often achieve success with a more visually oriented approach. Frustration is lessened and learning is enhanced when the teacher is flexible in his approach to instruction.

The difficulty involved in individualizing a program for a few children is frequently mentioned by the teacher as an argument against employing a variety of instructional approaches. The ease of using one method with all children is viewed as the corresponding advantage. The obvious flaw in the argument is rarely considered, that being the amount of extra work entailed in trying to fit a child to a specific material or technique not suited to his needs. The burden is very often lightened when teachers try to match an approach to the learning style of individual children. The planning for individual children suddenly seems to be much less work when youngsters are learning.

Many teachers have found that a change of approach for one child will sometimes indicate a change of materials for other children in the class. Methods and materials selected for children with learning difficulties often may be utilized successfully with children who have not experienced severe learning problems.

V. Remediation Materials Must Be Carefully Selected and Tailored to Individual Needs.

Many teachers are convinced that successful remediation is dependent upon the use of a variety of materials and methods but find it difficult to select materials and determine their effectiveness for particular learning problems (Adamson & VanEtten, 1970). The selection of materials for remediation is one of the most important tasks that a teacher must perform. Successful remediation is often dependent upon the instructional material or approach that is used. The teacher should consider the following questions when selecting materials for specific children:

1. What are the child's strengths? Through which modalities does he seem to learn best?
2. What are the child's weaknesses? Through which sensory modalities does he seem to have the most difficulty?
3. Is the child immature for his age? Does he become frustrated easily? How long does he attend to a task?
4. What is the child's interest level? What are his special interests?
5. What methods and materials have been used in the past? Which have been successful and which have been unsuccessful?
6. Does the child have any physical handicaps that necessitate specialized equipment?[3]

Factors to Be Considered in Selecting Instructional Materials. Responses to the questions listed above may be obtained through informal and formal evaluations of the child. Decisions concerning which material or approach to use with individual children will be based upon responses to these questions.

If the child has already experienced success with a specific instructional material, it is probably wise to continue with its use. Children experiencing learning problems often have used materials not directly suited to their specific learning styles. Equally debilitating are the situations in which children have been switched from material to material without any consistency from year to year. It is always discouraging to examine such a child's cumulative folder. In addition to the thickness of the folder, one is always amazed by the number of different programs, approaches, and materials to which the child has been exposed. Changes in instructional materials were apparently of no avail, since the child continues to experience academic difficulties. Any number of reasons may have caused the continual difficulty, not the least of which may be the lack of appropriate planning for selection of instructional materials.

The process of determining which material to use with particular children should begin with the questions listed above. Patterns usually develop whereby certain types of materials or methods are eliminated because of specific difficulties. For example, a sight word approach to reading instruction would not be an effective choice for a child experiencing visual memory problems. Likewise, a child who has spent two years with the *Sullivan Programmed Readers* (Buchanan, 1968) with little academic improvement, may profit from using an alternative reading series.

Following an analysis of all available information (test results, informal observations, prior use of certain materials, and individual interests), the teacher should be able to list a number of alternative instructional approaches. Based upon individual teacher judgment, one approach should be chosen and implemented. No magical formula is available at this stage, although Weinthaler and Rotberg (1970) have attempted to specify particular variables that require consideration during material selection (see also Chapter 5). A number of possible factors complicate the final material selection. The availability of certain materials, the financial status of the school district, administrative policies of the school district, and teacher preference are all factors which ultimately affect which material can and will be used with a particular child. Nonetheless, once all these factors have been considered, the final decision rests with each individual teacher.

Evaluation of Material Selection. The selection of a specific instructional material is not the completion of the remediation process. As the teacher progresses with his instruction he will sometimes find that the material is not meeting the needs of the child. The immediate tendency is to consider another method. However, this is not always the best procedure to follow. Children who have experienced academic difficulties over a long period of time will need some time to adjust to new methods and materials. For the child who has continually failed, it can not be expected that the difficulties will disappear immediately. Some period of adjustment to the new approach is required. Flexibility in the use of materials is encouraged, but an instructional approach must be given time to succeed. *Alternating the approach should be considered only after the teacher has given the method ample opportunity to succeed.* Individual differences preclude rigid guidelines, but two weeks may be a reasonable minimum for experimenting with a new material. Little can be assumed before this amount of time has been allowed for success.

Once a teacher has decided that a specific approach is not working, he should refer to his original list of possible materials. In no way should a teacher consider the situation hopeless. Seldom is success immediately found. Some teachers hesitate to experiment with a variety of methods for fear of further confusion on the part of the child. This should not be a deterrent to finding the right approach for each child.

In many cases, one approach will not be sufficient. The more effective formula for success may include using a variety of materials with one child. The severity of a child's difficulties might indicate the use of a specific exercise in learning the mechanics of reading and another type of material in applying the mechanics to textual reading. Similarly, the child with severe written language and reading difficulties might require a number of different materials.

Evaluation of Materials. The proliferation of commercially prepared instructional materials has added to the teacher's material-selection dilemma (Ensminger, 1970). The hard-sell and the creative packaging of materials has placed the teacher in the position of questioning the effectiveness of the materials he is presently using. Much can be said concerning the number of excellent materials currently available. On the other hand, volumes could be written about the hundreds of ineffective and poorly conceived materials. It is unfortunate that many advertising gimmicks have helped to sell basically inferior materials. Teachers must be aware of packaging and advertising deception (Lazarus, 1971) and judge a material on its intrinsic value and appropriateness to their particular situation.

The many outstanding newer materials that are finding their way into remedial programs should be both well received and widely used. Many of these materials have been expressly designed for children experiencing specific learning problems. There is an acute need for good materials, since children with learning problems often have failed to respond to programs designed to meet the instructional needs and characteristics of normal children. Specialized approaches and materials which are uniquely designed for handicapped children serve a very useful purpose in education. They provide the teacher with precise tools which help in remediating academic problems. The material that is matched to specific difficulties enables the teacher to spend additional time on other aspects of remediation.

Teachers should evaluate the effectiveness of specific instructional materials. Easily applied evaluation models have been provided by Armstrong (1971), Ensminger (1970), and McIntyre (1970).

VI. Remedial Instruction Must be Concisely Organized.

Following the selection and evaluation of appropriate materials, the equally difficult task of implementing and organizing the remedial instruction is required of the teacher. Children experiencing academic problems will usually respond positively to an organized and structured classroom situation (Bradfield, 1965). These children also require more systematic instruction than children who are not experiencing learning difficulties.

The unstructured classroom is often the place that causes the greatest difficulty for the child with academic problems. Situations where these children do not know what is expected of them will reinforce the behaviors that originally contributed to the learning deficits (Haring & Phillips, 1962). A specific program of organization is, therefore, a primary consideration in planning for remediation.

Program Organization As a first step, the program being used with a particular child should be written down. Our earlier suggestion for the "end-of-the-day" evaluation can be easily incorporated into this type of daily plan. A format that includes the following information is both functional and less time-consuming than the detailed lesson plans that often have been suggested:

Date	Skill(s) to be worked on	Method and Material to be used	Lesson Outcome

This type of planning can be continued throughout the remediation program. It serves as a concise chronology of what a teacher has done with a particular child At the same time, it provides the teacher with a means to on-going evaluation of both materials and achievement. Teachers have also used this format in reporting pupil progress to parents. If the format is continued over some period of time, it serves as a type of "remediation diary." The written outline of remediation provides the teacher with a plan for organization that lends itself to sequential program planning.

Other considerations that need to be taken into account in planning a remedial program for children with academic difficulties include:

1. Children should be aware of the day's plan in terms of what they are expected to do and what they should complete (Cruickshank, Bentzen, Ratzeburg, & Tannhauser, 1961; Phillips, 1967). Periods of remediation are sometimes so haphazard that children have a diffi-

cult time relating what happened yesterday to what will be happening today. The organization of an instructional period and the "why" behind certain teaching materials should be explained to a child who is experiencing learning problems. The child should know what he will be doing during a certain period and how the material at hand relates to the particular skill being developed. Setting clear expectations for completion of the task provides the child with a goal to reach for that day. Reinforcement can be based upon the attainment of specific goals, as suggested in Chapter 2.

2. Children should be assigned a permanent seat. The child who knows where he is to sit is more likely to be task oriented than the child who sits in a different place each day. Permanent seating also provides the child with the stability that may have been previously lacking in his educational experiences. The chances of exhibiting inappropriate behaviors are also lessened when the child is assigned some permanency in a classroom.

3. Children should know where their materials are located. Children who waste minutes looking for particular papers or books and asking procedural questions of the teacher could be greatly helped if their materials were always located in the same place with daily written directions for them to follow, (cf. Phillips, 1967). The teacher who is involved with other children is not interrupted by questions such as "where is my notebook," "what do I do," "what page is the lesson on," etc. A child should also be told the specific activities in which he may participate after he has completed the assigned work. This provides an answer to the inevitable question, "what do I do *now?*"

4. Children should know and see that good work produces appropriate rewards (Peter, 1965). Children who are succeeding after having experienced failure for so long need to know that they are doing well. Many times success is self-evident to children. Nonetheless, it is important that these children attain some type of overt recognition. Reinforcing events associated with learning provide children the motivation to continually try to do their very best. (Chapters 2 and 6 list appropriate reinforcement techniques.)

The teacher working with children experiencing academic difficulties will reap obvious advantages from a well-organized classroom. The individualization of programs for particular children necessitates concise organization if remediation is to be effective. Many failures in this area can be partly attributed to the lack of structured programs. A well-organized classroom serves as a prerequisite for effective instruction in any school. This need is doubly important for the child with learning problems.

VII. The Basic Foundation Upon Which Successful Remediation is Built is Effective Teaching.

Effective remediation is not much more than good teaching (Kaluger & Kolson, 1969). Remediation is only as effective as the teacher. Unfortunately, this principle has been widely misunderstood. Many have suggested that remediation is based upon a set of principles totally different from those adhered to in regular classrooms. Nothing could be more inaccurate. The principles that apply to good teaching are principles that cut across all types of instruction. The child who is experiencing academic difficulties will be taught in basically the same fashion as the child who is succeeding academically in school. The only differences are those of degree. The time that is spent teaching a specific skill, the individualization of instruction, and the variability of materials are procedural differentiations. These differences are brought about only because of the uniqueness of the learning problem. The teaching that occurs during the remedial session differs little from what goes on within a group of "normal" learners.

Remediation is Teaching. Effective remediation necessitates direct teaching. Such a simple statement seems obvious to many. Materials are viewed by some as the teaching agent or the means by which a child will learn a certain skill. *Materials cannot teach.* The teacher must teach a child how, for example, to carry in addition or make the / s / sound in reading. The materials may facilitate teaching, but nothing can replace the teacher (Bradfield, 1965) in actually performing his role as the "change agent" in remediation.

Unique materials, aids, and games that are used in a remedial teaching situation should be viewed as temporary teaching devices. *At no time, should these devices be considered the remedial programs.* They should be considered motivators that help a youngster overcome a particular difficulty in understanding a specific concept (Heilman, 1972). Lengthy dependency upon such devices can serve no useful purpose, and, ultimately, only hamper a child's chances for success. The teacher must not depend on these materials to do the teaching job for him. He must realize that the only way a child will learn to read, or write, or calculate is by his teaching the child to do so. No instructional material will be able to do this for a teacher. Those who oppose this viewpoint are merely seeking excuses for inappropriate teaching. A conscientious and skillful effort on the part of the teacher is the primary factor in successful remediation.

Teaching Directly to the Problem. There is a tendency on the part of some teachers to neglect those aspects of the learning problem that call for direct remedial action. Teachers are often tempted to devote an inordinate amount of time to peripheral skill development and disregard the actual problem. This situation occurs many times in the case of children with reading difficulties complicated by perceptual-motor problems. Teachers can easily spend months perfecting the skill of walking on the balance beam, for example, neglecting the child's deficits in reading. It is our belief that balance-beam-walking is a poor substitute for learning the skills needed for success in reading. This is not to denigrate the teaching of perceptual-motor skills (see Chapter 7), but the development of motor skills separate and apart from the reading process, for a child experiencing difficulties in reading, is considered a travesty of the remediation process. Children will learn to read by reading, or to calculate by calculating, etc.

Obviously, the more time spent in effectively developing any given skill, the greater the chance that the child will learn that skill. In essence, if the objective is to teach a child how to read, then this is where the emphasis should be. Similarly, remediation should also be provided for the child who needs help in the development of gross motor skills. However, a teacher must not assume that once a child has perfected skills in one area (e.g., gross motor skills) his progress automatically generalizes to other areas of difficulty (e.g., reading or arithmetic). On the contrary, children need to be taught the specific skills they are lacking. This is not always an easy task, but it can be successfully accomplished.

VIII. Overcoming Academic Difficulties Is a Complicated Process.

The complexity of remediating individual learning difficulties is understandable when one considers the complicated nature of learning and the variety of pressures that are brought to bear upon the child. All children, at some time, are subjected to the pressures of school. Most children are able to cope with the frustrations, anxieties, and confusion that accompany the learning process and suffer little from the encounter. But for the child with academic problems, the situation is different. The pressures that are brought to bear upon the child reduce his ability to respond appropriately and, in many cases, little if any learning takes place. The child who is permitted to remain in such frustrating situations becomes so educationally handicapped that he often drops out of school at the earliest possible time.

Some children with school learning problems are fortunate enough to be recognized and helped. In some cases, the slightest alteration of instruction may be enough to move the child on his way

Others may require more detailed individualization of instruction over a prolonged period of time. In the process of remediating the problem, the teacher will often find that the task is complicated. The many considerations concerning evaluation, materials, organization, reinforcement, and individualization will be important considerations in the remedial program. The child's progress will sometimes be slow, and often frustrating. However, successful cases of remediation seem to make the entire process very worthwhile. In retrospect, remediation does not seem as difficult once a learning problem has been overcome.

One complicating element of remediation is the orderly sequence of skill presentations. Children with school learning problems require much more systematic instruction than the child who is learning without difficulty. There is a tendency on the part of some to neglect the sequences involved in basic academic areas and to emphasize the development of specific isolated skills. The slower-paced remedial instruction and the difficulties encountered with specific skills seem to account for this inclination in remedial settings. Skills must be taught in an integrated, orderly fashion. Nothing should be omitted or assumed. Our discussion in Chapter 5 provides operationalized principles for sequential skill development.

As we have previously discussed, teachers in regular classrooms have been led to believe for too long that remediation falls entirely within the realm of the specialist. Few classroom teachers have been given the opportunity to exhibit their remedial teaching competencies. However, many children with learning problems can and should be handled in the regular classroom by regular classroom teachers. A substantial number of the suggestions presented in this chapter can be easily adapted to regular class instruction. The principles are also applicable to teachers currently involved in remedial programs. Remediation should be a concern of *all* teachers.

Summary

This chapter serves as a basis for effective remediation in any educational setting. All teachers at some time in their careers are faced with children experiencing academic learning problems. These children often require specialized instruction to overcome their academic retardation. Successful instruction will depend upon a concisely formulated system of remediation. Eight basic principles that all teachers should consider in designing a program of remediation have been outlined.

The initial and on-going instructional needs of the individual child should serve as the focus of a remedial program. Formal and informal diagnostic results must be utilized in planning programs and evaluating program effectiveness. Successful remediation will depend on the selection of a wide variety of materials, techniques, and methods that are tailored to individual needs. Finally, the difficult aspects of overcoming learning problems in children are directly related to the type of instruction provided for the child. The successful remedial program is little more than good teaching.

NOTES

[1]A recording device that can be used to record and play back letter names, words or sentences written on special cards (Bell and Howell, Inc.).

[2]The authors acknowledge Ms. Marty Massey for her skillful evaluation of David.

[3]This list was originally compiled in an unpublished paper by Ms. Margaret Moore.

4

Prevention
of
Learning
Problems

During the past ten years, there has been a surge of public and professional interest in the problems of children in schools. School programs for educationally handicapped, learning disabled, and emotionally disturbed children have proliferated. Compensatory education and related services for culturally different children have received federal support, and proposals for massive child-care programs have been considered. In short, services for children with school learning problems have become a matter of national concern.

Recent research in early childhood education has suggested that many learning problems can be ameliorated or prevented (Kugel & Parsons, 1967; Lichtenberg & Norton, 1970). As the health-related disciplines have discovered that good health practices are the best prevention of disease, educators have observed that good teaching is the best prevention of school learning problems. Many individuals at every level of the educational enterprise are now concerned with the prevention of learning problems.

Prevention of school learning problems has two basic facets. The first entails the development of techniques that preclude or greatly reduce the probability that problems will occur. The second involves therapeutic and prosthetic teaching methods that minimize existing problems, prevent complications, or provide solutions. Although the first facet is the ultimate goal of education, the second has been the focus of most special education and related services. Schools have tended to wait for problems to develop before taking constructive action.

The value of prevention both to individuals and to social institutions seems obvious. The child and his parents are spared considerable psychological suffering when unnecessary difficulties in the child's learning are avoided. Communities and institutions reap benefits in human and economic resources when learning problems are prevented. Nevertheless, the implementation of preventive programs in the schools is not universally lauded, nor are the preventative efforts of an individual always accepted without controversy (Bower, 1969).

That it is a major responsibility of the school to prevent learning problems is not arguable. Furthermore, nearly all educators agree that two fundamental principles of prevention are good teaching and early detection of learning problems. However, there is no consensus among educators regarding what constitutes good teaching or what procedures are most reliable and useful in early identification.

Early Detection
as Prevention

There is no lack of evidence that the precursors of serious school learning difficulties can be identified (Chamberlin & Nader, 1971; Glavin, 1972; Minde, Lewin, Weiss, Lavingueur, Douglas & Sykes, 1971; Robbins, 1966; Thomas, Chess, & Birch, 1968; Westman, Rice, & Berman, 1967). Maladaptive behavior patterns and academic learning deficits at any age are a poor augury for later development. Consequently, it behooves individuals interested in the welfare of children to intervene when learning problems are first observed.

The earlier a child's learning problem is detected the more easily it can be remediated. School systems that are seriously interested in meeting the challenge of prevention should develop strategies and tactics of early identification of learning difficulties. Until very recently, however, few schools have attempted to use any systematic procedures to identify incipient problems because special services have been available only for those children with the most obvious and disturbing learning deficits (Morse, Cutler & Fink, 1964). There is little point in identifying problems for which no services are available. Identification under such circumstances highlights the inadequacy of the schools and tends to create pressure for inappropriate solutions.

Identification of learning problems must be a systematic and continuous effort of all professions dealing with children. Teachers should be involved in the identification process through the administration of effective, efficient screening instruments and careful observation of children. Information obtained through the identification process should lead directly to diagnosis and a prescription for remediation.

Because the primary responsibility for early identification rests with the classroom teacher, he needs to be familiar with available screening instruments and be acutely aware of behaviors which signal potential learning difficulties.

Screening Instruments

Rating scales, checklists, and other types of tests often help teachers to survey the behavior and achievement of their pupils and identify possible learning difficulties. Brief, easily administered tests for which there is some evidence of predictive validity are most useful to classroom teachers. Screening devices are not diagnostic tests but instruments which select children who have a high probability of experiencing difficulty in school. Any child whose performance on a screening instrument indicates a possible learning problem should be evaluated more thoroughly before a diagnosis and prescription are formulated.

The number of rating scales, checklists, and observation schedules available to school personnel is growing. Care must be taken to select a screening device to meet the needs of particular situations. A number of specific criteria for evaluating screening tests have been provided by Bower (1969). Brief descriptions of several screening tests that may be administered by the classroom teacher are provided on the following pages.

Evanston Early-Identification Scale (Landsman & Dillard, 1967). The Evanston scale is intended for group or individual administration to kindergarten children (ages five-six). The test consists of asking the child to draw a person. The drawing is scored by the teacher on a ten-point scale. Teachers rank the children in three groups on the basis of their scores: low risk (will have no problem in school), middle risk (may have some difficulty in school), and high risk (can be expected to have problems in school and need special services.)

First-Grade Screening Test (Pate & Webb, 1969). The FGST is designed to be administered near the end of kindergarten or early in the first grade. It identifies children who will probably not be ready for second grade without special help during their first-grade year. Separate forms are provided for boys and girls, and the test is easy to administer and score. It samples general information, body image, self-perception, perception of parental figures, visual-motor coordination, memory, and ability to follow directions.

Meeting Street School Screening Test (Hainsworth & Siqueland, 1969). The MSSST is designed for individual administration to children in kindergarten and first grade in order to identify those "who do not possess the requisite language and visual-perceptual-motor skills and gross motor control to adequately process the symbolic information of the traditional school curriculum" (p. 1). The test can be administered in fifteen-twenty minutes. The manual provides cut-off scores for high-risk children and a discussion of the use of scores in understanding the skills of a particular child with learning problems, as well as a discussion of the problem of planning and carrying out early-identification programs.

A Psychoeducational Inventory of Basic Learning Abilities (Valett, 1968). Valett's test consists of teacher ratings on a five-point scale of the child's performance on fifty-three tasks grouped into six categories: gross motor, sensory-motor, perceptual-motor, language, conceptual, and social. The rater must have the Inventory workbook and a number of household materials (e.g., teaspoon, jump rope, hand mirror, brick, etc.) to administer the test. The test is designed to identify learning difficulties in children ages five to twelve.

Preschool Inventory (Caldwell, 1967). This screening device is designed for individual administration to children ages three to six. It measures the child's achievement on sixty-four items which sample the following: basic information and vocabulary; number concepts and ordination; concepts of size, shape, motion, and color; concepts of time, object class, and social functions; visual-motor performances; following instructions; and independence and self-help. The test is designed to be administered by the child's teacher. The PSI provides a percentile rank for the child's raw score based on his chronological age.

A Process for In-School Screening of Children with Emotional Hand-icaps (Bower & Lambert, 1962). This screening instrument has separate forms for primary, elementary, and secondary grade levels. At each level, the child's social-emotional learning is evaluated by teacher rating, self-rating, and peer rating. It is designed to identify children with suspected emotional handicaps.

Screening instruments have value in that they formalize the teacher's assessment of each child. However, as adequate informal assessment of learning may preclude the necessity for formal testing, as discussed in Chapter 3, acute awareness of behaviors which indicate learning problems may make the use of screening tests superfluous.

Behavioral Indications of Potential Problems

The potential problem behaviors listed in this section should be viewed from the broad perspective of child development. Every child exhibits *some* maladaptive behaviors. Furthermore, many normal children *temporarily* exhibit a number of behaviors characteristic of children with severe learning problems. Maladaptive behavior and academic deficits should be viewed as pathological only when they are demonstrated to a marked extent and over a period of time (Bower, 1969). This does *not* mean that preventive action should be taken only after the child has shown a severe and chronic learning difficulty. It *does* mean that the child will not be considered to have a serious problem on the basis of an isolated incident or a temporary condition.

Only major categories of problem behaviors have been outlined below.[1] Behaviors relevant to preschool and primary-age children have been stressed because preventive efforts logically are concentrated at that age level.

I. Indications of Low Self-Concept

A child with school learning problems often reveals that he does not feel good about himself, that he feels incompetent, inadequate, and worthless. The teacher may suspect that the child has such negative feelings about himself if he:

A. Speaks disparagingly of self
B. Is unwilling to attempt new or difficult tasks
C. Is fearful of new situations
D. Is excessively shy and withdrawn
E. Lacks self-reliance; often says "I can't"

F. Shows excessive concern over acceptance by others
G. Is usually unhappy or depressed; seldom smiles; cries or frowns often
H. Demonstrates inability to make everyday decisions
I. Demonstrates inability to accept errors or correct mistakes
J. Shows extreme negative reaction to minor failures
K. Has slovenly, unkempt appearance
L. Is unable to evaluate his behavior realistically; brags or denigrates his accomplishments

II. Disturbed Relations with Peers

Often, the child with learning problems is a misfit in the social group of the classroom, a pariah among his classmates. Problems in relating to peers are noted when the child:

A. Has no close friends or "chums" in peer group
B. Is avoided by children in games and activities
C. Hits, bites, kicks, or otherwise physically assaults peers
D. Is incessantly teasing or teased by others
E. Belittles accomplishments of others
F. Seeks company of much older or younger children
G. Withdraws from group activities

III. Inappropriate Relationship to Teachers, Parents, and Other Authority Figures

Constructive relationship to authority is often a special problem for children with school learning difficulties. Adults who are responsible for the child are often in a quandary when he:

A. Refuses reasonable requests
B. Defies direct commands
C. Disobeys classroom rules
D. Encourages peers to disrupt the class or defy adults
E. Strikes, bites, kicks, or otherwise attempts to injure other children or adults
F. Runs away from school or home or leaves the classroom without permission
G. Steals
H. Lies
I. Manipulates adults to his advantage
J. Is overprotected; seldom allowed to enter new age-appropriate situations alone or allowed to take reasonable risks
K. Is overindulged; "spoiled" by being given noncontingent or excessive rewards

IV. Other Signs of Social-Emotional Problems

In addition to maladaptive behaviors related specifically to self, peers, and authority, the child with school learning problems may exhibit a variety of other inappropriate responses. The teacher may observe that the child:

A. Exhibits inappropriate behavior for a given context (e.g., laughs when someone is hurt, interprets figures of speech literally)
B. Is overly suspicious or jealous of others
C. Complains of physical symptoms, pains, or fears in mildly stressful situations; complains of every little hurt
D. Is in constant motion; compulsively manipulates objects, moves about the room excessively
E. Engages in repetitive, stereotyped motor behavior; has tics, bites nails, sucks thumb, rocks, etc.
F. Talks incessantly; frequently talks out without permission or interrupts conversations
G. Explains inappropriate behavior by rationalization or intellectualization
H. Does not seem to learn from experience; behavior does not improve with usual disciplinary methods
I. Is retained in grade or excluded from school
J. Fails to learn when there is no evidence of intellectual, sensory, or health factors
K. Makes meaningless or "animal" noises
L. Acts impulsively and shows poor judgment; does not consider or understand consequences of his behavior
M. Is easily distracted; cannot concentrate or attend for more than a few minutes
N. Has not mastered bowel or bladder control
O. Shows extreme interest in monsters, war, fighting or gruesome events
P. Is overcome frequently by drowsiness or sleep
Q. Places inedible objects in mouth or shows appetite for inedible materials
R. Has violent outbursts of temper
S. Lacks curiosity
T. Daydreams; sits with a vacant expression, doing nothing productive

V. Deficits in Speech and Language

A child's speech and language often betray his emotional status or his intellectual or academic competence in unique ways.

One may suspect that the child is experiencing an emotional or academic problem when he:

A. Does not speak
B. Speaks only when spoken to
C. Speaks with inappropriate pitch; voice too high-pitched or too low-pitched for age and sex
D. Speaks with inappropriate volume; voice too loud or too soft
E. Has irritating vocal quality; voice too harsh, hoarse, nasal, etc.
F. Speaks with marked dysfluency; stutters, clutters, or otherwise interrupts the flow of speech
G. Uses primarily jargon, neologisms, profanity, or other speech inappropriate for a context
H. Misarticulates many words
 I. Has difficulty learning signs and symbols
 J. Cannot interpret directions
K. Lacks ability to describe persons, places and things
L. Cannot identify an object from its description
M. Does not comprehend simple sentences or familiar sequences when a part is missing

VI. Disordered Temporal Relationships

Orientation in time and ability to sequence events are required for adequate social and academic functioning. The child's behavior may be indicative of a learning problem if he:

A. Cannot tell a story in sequence
B. Does not repeat sound patterns in order
C. Cannot remember a sequence of events
D. Is chronically late
E. Is absent-minded; often forgets important events
F. Is unable to plan a sequence of events
G. Refuses to talk about the past
H. Cannot shift readily from one activity to another
 I. Is easily confused by a change in routine
 J. Confuses seasons, months, years, days, and other intervals of time after the age at which most children learn these concepts
K. Cannot acquire basic auditory sequences, such as telephone numbers, alphabet, nursery rhymes, etc.

VII. Difficulties in Auditory and Visual Perception

The ability of the child to integrate what he sees and hears in a meaningful way is essential for progress in school. The child may have a serious problem in interpreting visual and auditory stimuli when he:

A. Attends to irrelevant details
B. Cannot organize materials
C. Loses place frequently when copying
D. Has difficulty cutting, coloring, or pasting
E. Does not discriminate differences in size, shape, color, or perspective
F. Does not discriminate changes in pitch, loudness, or timbre of sounds
G. Has difficulty recognizing common objects when a part is missing
H. Has difficulty recognizing sounds made by common objects
I. Does not understand positional words, such as up, down, above, in, etc.
J. Cannot relate pictures to parts of a story
K. Does not understand the meaning of pictures
L. Has difficulty reproducing simple geometric shapes with pencil and paper (e.g., cannot copy a square, circle, rectangle, etc.)
M. Is unable to recognize rhymes or give rhyming words
N. Makes poorly formed or reversed letters; poor handwriting
O. Has difficulty drawing corners or angles
P. Has difficulty spelling phonetic units or words
Q. Makes facial contortions when doing visual tasks

VIII. Poor Quantitative Reasoning and Computational Skill

Quantitative reasoning and computational skills are considered to be basic components of intelligence. They are a vital part of school learning and necessary for independent functioning in our society. When a child has a learning problem in this area, it is often found that he:

A. Has difficulty with concepts of inequality (e.g., more-less, larger-smaller, heavier-lighter)
B. Does not understand one-to-one correspondence
C. Is unable to count to a number appropriate for age
D. Has marked difficulty learning basic number facts
E. Does not understand the value of coins

  F. Is unable to understand place value (cannot regroup for borrowing and carrying)

  G. Can make necessary computations but is unable to organize information from a "story problem"

  H. Relies excessively on finger or bead counting for simple computations

IX. Deficits in Basic Motor Skills

The child's fine and gross movements are often indicative of his learning characteristics or adjustment to school. A problem in school learning may be suspected when the child:

  A. Is unable to balance on one foot

  B. Has an unsteady, awkward, or unusual gait

  C. Is unable to throw and catch a ball

  D. Does not hold a pencil or scissors normally

  E. Has poor coordination; clumsy and inaccurate in movement, often accidentally breaks things

  F. Cannot tie shoes, button, or zip clothing

  G. Avoids physical activities or sports

Good Teaching
as Prevention

Principles of good teaching are based on the assumption that the teacher is responsible for children's learning. Without this assumption, the onus of failure falls on the child, a burden he should not be required to bear, or on "society" for which no remedy can be expected during the crucial learning years of the child's life. The five principles of good teaching listed below are applicable to all educational situations. Consequently, they serve also as basic principles of prevention.

Principle 1: Good Teaching Means Teaching Specific, Measurable Skills. It is of crucial importance for the teacher to formulate learning goals or instructional objectives for the children he teaches. It is essential that these objectives state what the child will be able to do, the conditions under which he will do it, and the criterion that will be used to judge his performance. Unless specific, measurable skills are taught it is impossible to evaluate the teacher's effectiveness. High-sounding but vague, subjective goals are of no value in teaching because one can never determine whether or not they have been attained. For example, the teacher very likely will never be able to determine whether or not he has "given the child a life-long love of reading for recreation," but he can easily evaluate whether or not the child "reads during at least 20 percent of his free time in the classroom."

Principle 2: Good Teaching Means Continuous Assessment of the Child's Performance. When the teacher has stated adequate performance objectives for the child, each task presented in a teaching program becomes a potential test of the child's learning. Clearly stated behavioral objectives provide the teacher with continuous feedback concerning what has and has not been taught. The teacher is able to modulate his instruction most effectively by taking his cues from the child's responses to the teaching program itself, rather than from irrelevant response requirements of standardized tests.

Principle 3: Good Teaching Means Establishing Priorities. Teaching will not be effective when tasks and concepts are taught in a random order. Effective teaching depends on initially identifying the behaviors which are most important for a child's survival in his environment. It also depends on analyzing specific tasks to determine precisely their response requirements. The effective teacher will waste no time trying to teach tasks for which the child has not learned the prerequisite skills. Neither will he squander his time and effort teaching skills which are of no functional value to the child.

Principle 4: Good Teaching Means Being Directive. Learning may happen spontaneously, randomly, and erratically when children are in the presence of individuals who are not trying to teach. But learning will not be efficient or predictable unless the teacher actively controls specific variables which make learning occur. The teacher teaches by arranging tasks, directing attention, prompting responses, differentially reinforcing behavior, and employing other techniques that change children's behavior (Becker, Engelmann, & Thomas, 1971). "The focus cannot be on techniques if the teacher begins with the idea that the children are responsible for what they learn and that the teacher is simply a supplier of 'learning opportunities'" (Engelmann, 1969, p. 40).* It is the teacher's responsibility to direct the child's behavior, and if a child does not learn it can only be concluded that the teacher has failed to teach that child.

---

*From *Preventing Failure in the Primary Grades* by Siegfried Engelmann. © 1969, Science Research Associates, Inc. Reproduced by permission.

Principle 5: Good Teaching Means Using Positive Methods. Efficiency and effectiveness are necessary but not sufficient criteria for evaluating teaching. Good teaching also involves concern for the happiness and emotional well-being of the child. When the teacher concentrates on positive reinforcement, children are likely to learn more efficiently and happily (Madsen & Madsen, 1970). This does not mean that the child's inappropriate responses will go without correction or that punishment will always be avoided. It does mean that good teaching consists primarily of positive teacher-pupil interactions and that the teacher is genuinely concerned about the feelings and welfare of the child.

It is the thesis of this book that the teacher must be primarily concerned with instructional and behavior-management variables as etiological factors. It follows that our major concern in the area of prevention is adequate teaching. If the teacher is to be an effective preventive agent, he must limit his professional efforts to the teaching process.

Summary

During the past decade, concern for the education of handicapped children has expanded to include interest in the prevention of learning problems. Prevention may entail: (*a*) teaching methods that preclude or reduce the probability of learning problems or (*b*) therapeutic or prosthetic teaching to minimize existing problems and prevent their complication. In most schools the primary responsibility for preventive action is likely to fall on the classroom teacher. Two fundamental principles of prevention are early detection and good teaching. Early detection requires knowledge of available screening instruments and acute sensitivity to behaviors which signal possible problems. Good teaching means teaching specific, measurable skills, continuous assessment of the child's performance, teaching first things first, being directive, and using positive methods.

NOTE

[1]For additional lists of behavioral characteristics see Denhoff and Novack (1967) and Peterson (1967).

II

A
Guide
to
Teaching
Activities

Sound principles are needed to guide teaching practice, but sound practice goes beyond the mere repetition of principles. It is not enough for a teacher to know that behavior that is reinforced is more likely to occur again or that remedial teaching involves continuous assessment of the child's performance. The teacher must know how and when to reinforce appropriate behavior, how to assess the child's performance, and how to present instructional tasks. A major purpose of this book is to provide the teacher with an array.of specific behavior-management and instructional activities which have proven their value in the classroom.

Remedial teaching requires that the teacher examine his instructional behavior as well as the child's learning problem. Chapter 5 provides an outline of competencies which the teacher may use to evaluate his instructional activities in any curriculum area.

Chapter 6 suggests techniques for dealing with classroom-management problems related to specific academic and social behaviors. Chapters 7-11 contain suggested instructional activities for remediating specific learning problems in core curriculum areas, including visual-motor skills, reading, written language, oral language, and arithmetic. Each of the chapters includes a brief statement of the major skills which the child must learn to perform adequately in that curriculum area. This is followed by suggestions for diagnosis of the child's problems, including teacher observation, informal assessment techniques, and formal tests. Subsequently, teaching suggestions are organized under diagnostic questions which are designed to help the teacher identify the child's learning problem. Additional readings at the end of each chapter provide a guide for in-depth study of learning problems and teaching methods.

We have attempted to organize our teaching activities within chapters according to the sequential development of skills. It must be recognized, however, that a full exposition of sequential skill development in any curriculum area goes far beyond the skeletal framework on which our chapters are organized. Hopefully, our outlines of sequential learning will provide a beginning point for further study and analysis.

Many basic skills that children learn are relevant to several academic areas. For example, form discrimination is a skill which is prerequisite for success in reading, written language, and arithmetic. Because of interrelationships among basic academic tasks, many of our teaching suggestions can be adapted for use in curriculum areas other than the one for which they are given.

Most of our teaching activities are intended for use with elementary school children who are deficient in very basic skills. The teacher who works with older children will need to adapt many of our suggestions to meet the needs and interests of children of junior high or high school age.

The source of some of our remedial activities is our own teaching experience. Many of the activities, however, did not originate with us. The sources of those suggestions, or of slight variations of them, have been cited wherever possible. In many cases the original sources of "tried-and-true" activities could not be found.

5

Remedial Teaching Competencies

Effective remedial teaching in the regular or special class situation depends on the teacher's mastery of specific instructional skills which are grounded in the principles discussed in Part I. Specific competencies which operationalize those principles include the teacher's ability to:

1. Use diagnostic information to initiate a remedial program
2. State instructional goals as performance of specific tasks
3. Analyze tasks to pinpoint learning problems
4. Present learning tasks to remediate problems
5. Provide the learner with feedback on task performance
6. Structure the environment in which the task is performed
7. Keep evaluative records of teaching and learning

When a child is experiencing difficulty in school, it is essential that the teacher attempt to diagnose and remediate his behavioral or academic problems. However, the teacher must first analyze his own teaching behavior. Our suggestion in Part I that the teacher is responsible for children's learning implies that remediation of teaching problems must precede remediation of learning problems.

Teaching involves constant reevaluation of instructional behavior as well as constant reassessment of pupil performance. The behaviors which comprise teaching are no less open to scrutiny and diagnosis than the behaviors which constitute learning. Therefore, the teacher must continuously monitor and correct his own behavior in order to be most effective. The remainder of this chapter is an outline of remedial teaching competencies needed by all teachers. It provides a checklist for evaluating teaching problems which may be contributing to the child's learning difficulty.

A Competency
Checklist

I. Use Diagnostic Information to Plan an Initial Remedial Strategy

Diagnostic information should serve one major purpose—that of providing a basis for remediation. Useful diagnostic information comprises two major categories:

Type I—general information which gives an overall picture of the child and suggests a beginning point in remediation.

Type II—specific information which is obtained from the child's responses to remedial teaching and provides the basis for further instruction.

Type I information is the concern of this competency. The use of *Type II* information is discussed under competency VII.

A. *Use all available sources of information*

In order to get as broad and complete a picture of the child's weaknesses and strengths as possible, no source of useful information should be overlooked. All school personnel, both professional and nonprofessional, should be considered and evaluated as sources of observations of the child's academic and social behavior. School records, parents, peers, and community agencies (e.g., church, scouts, family service, welfare, etc.) are also potential sources of useful data. However, it cannot be stressed too strongly that the classroom teacher is the best single source of useful information in teaching the child. By systematically observing the child's behavior, an experienced teacher can accurately formulate an initial remedial program.

B. *Estimate the child's developmental level*

The remedial strategy should be consistent with the child's level of development. It is important to note whether the child's physical development is discrepant from the norm, whether his social behavior is appropriate for his age and sex, whether his academic achievement is within the expected range, and whether the rewards he prefers are characteristic of other children his age. The initial remedial activities should fall within the child's physical capacity, degree of socialization, academic ability, and reward preference.

C. *Eliminate possible health and sensory factors as causes of learning problems*

For maximum learning efficiency, the child must be in good health and all of his senses must be functioning properly. It is particularly important to be aware of indications of a hearing or vision problem which may be contributing to the child's learning difficulty. The child may have a hearing problem if he:

1. Has an articulation (pronunciation) problem
2. Is delayed in language development
3. Is inconsistent in responding to oral directions and questions
4. Is inattentive, hyperactive, or restless
5. Has frequent ear infections or earaches

If there is reason to suspect that the child may have a hearing problem, he should be referred immediately to a speech and hearing clinician for screening. The child may have a vision problem if he:

1. Frequently stumbles, runs into objects, and/or walks cautiously
2. Avoids bright or direct light and/or frequently rubs his eyes
3. Has a tendency to close or cover one eye or shows a divergence of gaze in one eye
4. Complains frequently of dizziness, headaches, or pain in the eyes
5. Has a tendency to hold objects or printed matter very close (less than six inches)

If there is reason to believe that the child may have a vision problem, he should be referred immediately to the school nurse for screening.

Disease, malnutrition, and other physical conditions obviously can contribute to learning problems and should be corrected by appropriate professionals as quickly and completely as possible. Nevertheless, the teacher must not use suspected or real physical or sensory defects as an excuse for failing to develop the best possible remedial teaching program.

D. *Observe the methods through which the child learns best*

Normally, academic learning in any curriculum area involves multisensory stimulation and a variety of response modes. The primary channels through which school learning takes place appear to be auditory-vocal and visual-motor. However, it has been suggested recently that the question of primary concern for the teacher should be what methods work best with a given child regardless of his supposed strengths or weaknesses in modal learning (Birch & Belmont, 1965; Harris, 1969; and Katz, 1967). To know that a child learns spelling words more quickly by tracing them than by hearing them spelled is more useful than to know that he scores high on visual-motor and low on auditory-vocal tasks on a standardized test. From the first moment that he works with the child, the teacher should begin observing the teaching methods that work best for him.

E. *Integrate Type I information into an initial teaching strategy*

Type I information includes test scores, anecdotal observations, physical status, and other data which are useful in formulating an initial teaching strategy. The value of such a beginning strategy is that it allows the teacher to focus quickly on remedial tasks and teaching methods which have a high probability of success. The integration of Type I information into an initial remedial teaching strategy is illustrated by the case of Monroe. The test and observational data were obtained and interpreted by a classroom teacher.[1] Note that the recommendations suggest a beginning point for remedial teaching.

Monroe is a highly verbal nine-year-old fourth grader of average height and weight. He has no apparent physical or sensory defects. Teachers have been concerned about his "lack of academic progress, immaturity, and hyperactivity" since he entered the second grade. He has one sibling, a three-year-old sister. His parents are divorced and he lives with his mother, who has not remarried. His mother reports that her ex-husband visits Monroe weekly and that Monroe "is wild about his father and will do anything to spend extra time with him."

The teacher has observed Monroe's behavior and performance informally and given him several formal tests during two testing sessions. In the classroom he is easily distracted and seldom completes his assigned work. His response to praise as a reward for performance is inconsistent. For candy or trinkets he will work diligently for 20 to 30 minutes. He seldom interacts socially with other children. When he does play with someone else, it is usually with a younger child. His handwriting is neat and legible. His recognition of words in isolation is good, but he is deficient in word recognition and word attack skills in textual reading. He has not fully mastered the basic addition and subtraction facts in arithmetic. When number facts are presented orally he does much better than when they are presented as a paper-and-pencil task.

RESULTS OF TESTING

Observations

In the testing sessions Monroe was constantly squirming in his chair and trying to manipulate the test materials. During the second session he sucked his left thumb most of the time. He was cooperative as long as the test items were easy for him, but when items were difficult he refused to respond. Several times when he could not give the correct answer he closed his eyes and rubbed them profusely, appearing to be near tears. If the teacher dropped back to easier items he appeared relieved and again responded readily. His scores were as follows:

Gates-McKillop Reading Diagnostic Test (Gates & McKillop, 1962).
   Oral Reading—grade score—2.7
   Words: Untimed presentation—grade score—3.8
   Knowledge of Word Parts:
      Giving Letter Sounds—26/26 (normal progress+)
      Naming Capital Letters—25/26 (normal progress)
      Naming Lowercase Letters—26/26 (normal progress)
   Recognizing the Visual Form of Sounds:
      Initial Letters—19/19 (normal progress)
      Final Letters—12/14 (normal progress)
      Vowels—7/10 (normal progress+)

Auditory Blending—12/15 (normal progress)
Supplementary Tests:
Oral Vocabulary—grade score—6.4

Wide Range Achievement Test (Jastak & Jastak, 1965).

	Grade Equivalent	Standard Score	Percentile
Reading Score (word recognition)	4.4	103	58
Spelling Score	3.7	97	42
Arithmetic Score (computation)	1.9	79	8

Wepman Auditory Discrimination Test (Wepman, 1958).
X score 2/30; Y score 0/10—adequate development

Interpretation

Although Monroe seemed to have no difficulty in recognizing letters, sounds, initial and final consonants, or auditory blending, his oral reading score on the *Gates-McKillop* was 2.7, one year below his grade placement. A close analysis of his errors revealed that he was seeing the first one or two letters and guessing at the remainder of the word. He displayed very little effort in trying to sound out unfamiliar words in text.

His arithmetic grade equivalent on the *Wide Range Achievement Test* was 1.9, two years below his grade level. He only tried the simple one-column addition and subtraction problems. He had no knowledge of carrying or borrowing. Monroe also rotated the number "6" ("9") and reversed the number "41" ("14").

Monroe scored 3.7 on the spelling subtest of the *Wide Range Achievement Test*. This score is just slightly below his grade level of 4.0. It was interesting to note the word attack skills he utilized in spelling. Whenever he did not know a word, he spelled it exactly as it sounded, e.g., "sirprise" for "surprise" and "rezalt" for "result". This was not unexpected, since he had an excellent knowledge of letter sounds, letter recognition, and initial and final consonant sounds. Most of his spelling errors involved medial vowels.

Monroe had no major auditory discrimination problem, as evidenced by his score of 2/30 on the *Wepman Auditory Discrimination Test*. Both mistakes were made with the "f" and "th" sounds.

GENERAL IMPRESSION

Monroe appears to have deficits in textual oral reading and arithmetic computation, attention skills, and social-interpersonal behaviors. He is immature in his response to difficult tasks and his response to social rewards. He appears to be achieving considerably below his ability level, as indicated by his vocabulary and language skills. One of Monroe's primary problems appears to be motivation.

INITIAL TEACHING STRATEGY

1. Begin by using frequent food and toy reinforcers for task completion. Gradually shift to social praise. Try to enlist the aid of his father in praising Monroe for good school work and spending extra time with him as a reward for academic achievement.

2. Begin with simple tasks with which Monroe can be highly (at least 95%) successful. Gradually introduce more difficult tasks and reward him for making any attempt to complete them. Be firm in expecting that he will make some attempt to complete every task he is given.

3. Use tasks requiring oral responses as often as possible in the beginning. Gradually shift to tasks requiring written responses.

4. Initially, involve Monroe's peers in monitoring his oral responses (e.g., giving him an oral quiz) to facilitate social interaction. Also use instructional games whenever possible to increase appropriate peer contact.

5. In arithmetic, concentrate first on mastery of the basic addition and subtraction facts. One or more of the following activities may be helpful in addition to written exercises:

   a. Play hopscotch with addition and subtraction combinations chalked in the squares. The player must know the answer before he can hop on a square.

   b. Play arithmetic baseball, in which a basic number combination is called out by the "pitcher" and must be answered correctly within two seconds by the "batter" to advance a player.

   c. Have Monroe verbalize the problem and its answer as he writes the answers to the basic number combinations.

6. In reading, capitalize on Monroe's strengths in vocabulary, language, and phonics skills. Concentrate on word analysis and recognition in textual reading. It may be helpful to begin by:

   a. Using language-experience stories to see if Monroe will read textual material that he has dictated.

   b. Creating a story for him to read, using as many words as possible beginning with the same sound in order to force him to analyze entire words.

   c. Having Monroe read stories into a tape recorder and later listen to his performance.

   d. Teaching phonetic "word families" and using linguistic-based reading materials (e.g., Sullivan readers).

An initial teaching strategy suggests instructional goals. Instructional objectives must be stated explicitly so that teaching and learning can be evaluated.

II. State Instructional Goals as Performance of Specific Tasks

After using Type I information to initiate a remedial program, the teacher must give careful attention to instructional goals. Instructional objectives are of crucial importance because they result directly in the presentation and analysis of instructional tasks. Establishing adequate goals is the first step in the remedial teaching process itself.

A. *Objectify task performance*

Adequate instructional goals state clearly what the child will do, the conditions under which he will do it, and the criteria that will be used to judge his performance. If any one of these elements is missing, the goal is not stated adequately (Mager, 1962). Goals stated in performance terms indicate clearly what the teacher should teach and how effectively he is teaching. The following are examples of instructional goals which are inadequate because they are not stated in performance terms:

"To know the seven continents"
"To understand that an adjective describes a person, place, or thing"
"To tolerate other peoples' points of view"

The following goals are stated in performance terms:

"Given any map or globe, the student will be able to identify each of the seven continents by tracing its outline with his finger."
"Given any printed standard English sentence in which he can read all the words the student will be able to underline the adjectives with 100% accuracy."
"Given a situation in which he is conversing with someone who expresses an opinion or belief different from his own, the student will show tolerance for the other person's point of view by allowing him to speak without interruption and by refraining from physically attacking him."

B. *Determine immediate goals*

Every remedial teaching session should include immediate goals which can be accomplished during the session. It is important to have immediate goals so that time and effort are not wasted on irrelevant activities, so that the pupil can gain a sense of accomplishment, and so that the ultimate long-range goal is not lost.

C. *Formulate long-range goals*

Immediate goals should constitute successive approximations of long-range goals. Priorities for the child's learning must be established. Long-range goals must be formulated on the basis of the objectives' educational relevance for the child. When relevant long-range goals are established and immediate goals are successive approximations of them, remedial teaching and learning become an orderly progression of relevant tasks. An example of a long-range goal and several immediate goals which are approximations of it could be stated as follows:

Long-Range Goal

Given any clock or watch face, the child will be able to tell the time shown to the nearest minute.

Immediate Goals (Approximations)

1. Given a large clock face with arabic numerals, the child will be able to read correctly the o'clock and half past times for any hour or half hour.
2. Given such a clock face, the child will be able to count the minutes by fives proceeding clockwise from 1 (five) and continuing through 11 (fifty-five).
3. Given such a clock face, the child will be able to tell the time as ____ min. after ____ or ____ min. till ____ to the nearest five minutes for any position of the hands.

Instructional goals suggest remedial tasks. Performance goals provide a guide to the instructional tasks which will remediate the problem.

III. Analyze Tasks to Pinpoint Learning Problems

Instructional tasks are the essence of remedial teaching. By performing instructional tasks, the child moves closer to mastery of the skills in which he is deficient. Consequently, no aspect of remedial teaching competence deserves closer attention than the analysis of instructional tasks. *Task analysis may be viewed as a sequence of evaluative activities which pinpoints the child's learning problem and guides the teacher in planning an effective remedial sequence of instructional tasks.*[2]

A. *Specify the task*

A task is something to do. It is an observable, countable, repeatable behavior, as discussed in Chapter 2. It is described by what comes after the phrase "the child will be able to ..." in the statement of an instructional goal in performance terms. For example, the following are tasks:

"point to the red ball"
"write the lowercase alphabet in manuscript letters"
"copy a square"
"find the sum of three two-digit numbers"
"stay seated while taking the spelling test"

More important than defining *a* task is consideration of *the* task in question. *The teacher must specify what it is that he wants the child to do.* Otherwise, both the teacher and the child will become confused about what response is expected. Following oral directions demands a different response, and, consequently, is a different task than following written directions. Pointing to the correct object is a different task than naming it. Tasks must be defined precisely before their response requirements can be identified.

B. *Identify the task's response requirements.*

A task requires a response. Every response can be broken down into a set of sequential subskills or response requirements which are prerequisites for successful task performance. Identifying the response requirements for instructional tasks is of primary importance in task analysis. Only when the component responses of a task are known can the child's learning problem be pinpointed. The teacher must analyze the instructional task by asking, "What are the things a child must do to perform this task successfully?" For example, when given the oral direction, "Print your name at the top of the paper", the child must be able to:

1. Interpret (understand) the task directions
2. Find the top of the paper
3. Hold the pencil in writing position
4. Form each of the manuscript letters in his name
5. Print the letters in his name in sequence

Each of these five response requirements is a task in itself. As a task, it can be analyzed in terms of its own response requirements. Whether or not a response requirement must be further analyzed as a task depends on the child's performance.

C. *Note the child's errors*

Task analysis requires that the child be directed to perform the task. When the child's task performance breaks down, it is imperative that the teacher pinpoint his difficulty. This means that if a task is not performed successfully, the teacher must analyze the first response requirement on which the child makes an error. In the example, "Print your name at the top of the paper," the teacher must analyze response requirement #4 if the child has mastered response requirements 1-3 but does not form all of the letters in his name correctly. He must note which letters were not properly formed and identify the response requirements for the tasks of forming those letters. Then he must present the tasks of forming the letters (e.g., "Make the letter A") and note the child's errors on the specific response requirements for those tasks. This process of task presentation and error identification must continue until a task is given which the child can perform without error. His errors on more difficult tasks then clarify his performance difficulty.

D. *Describe the learning problem as a performance deficit*

Careful analysis of the child's errors will indicate what the child has not learned that is essential for successful task performance. His learning problem can then be described as a deficiency in performance which can be remediated. What the child should be taught follows logically. To return to the example of the task, "Print your name at the top of the paper," if a child named "Randy" consistently responds to the task by printing "Rnady" at the top of the paper, his performance deficit is that he reverses the order of the letters "a" and "n" in his name. Since it is known that he has mastered all of the other response requirements for completion of the task, it is obvious that what he must be taught is the correct *sequence* of letters. If, on the other hand, a child named "Sue" responds to the task by printing "2ƨ" at the top of the paper it is clear that the response requirement of forming the letters comprising her name must be analyzed as a set of separate tasks. If an analysis of the task of printing the letter "S" shows that Sue does not visually discriminate "S" from "2", although she reliably discriminates and copies some letter forms (e.g., "t" and "o"), her performance deficit (does not visually discriminate "S" from "2") indicates precisely what must be taught. Task analysis explicates what is required for performance, what the child can do, where the child's response breaks down, and what sequence of skills must be taught to remediate the problem.

IV. Present Tasks to Remediate the Problem

The teacher must design and present a sequence of remedial tasks which will enable the child to overcome his performance deficit. The nature of the tasks themselves and the manner in which they are presented will determine the child's progress in learning.

A. *Organize tasks for efficient presentation*

Tasks must be organized so that the child is not distracted or confused. The necessary instructional materials must be arranged so that tasks can be presented at a brisk pace and with a minimum of teacher effort. As soon as one task is completed the next task should be presented, unless the task is to be followed by a break for rest or reinforcement. If the teacher has to search for the needed material or cannot manipulate the material efficiently, the child's attention is more likely to stray from the task. Unneeded teaching materials and other objects which the child may want to manipulate or which may attract the child's attention should be removed from the teaching situation. The child's attention can then be focused more readily on the task to which the teacher wants him to respond. The teacher must be sure that he is in a position to direct the child's responses and manipulate the teaching materials easily and that the child is seated or positioned so that he can respond appropriately. In any remedial teaching situation the teacher must:[3]

1. Select the materials he is going to use to teach the task(s)
2. Be sure that he knows how to use the materials
3. Be sure that the materials are in proper order
4. Arrange the task environment for efficient presentation and response
   a. Remove unnecessary materials
   b. Have necessary materials within easy reach
   c. Be sure the child has an appropriate desk, table, chair, or other area in which to work
   d. Position himself within easy reach of the child and the materials

B. *Be directive*

The teacher must assume responsibility for directing the child's attention and responses to tasks. To do this effectively, he must establish a pleasant but controlling relationship with the child. He must be sure in his own mind what he wants the child to do. He must tell the child what to do and when to respond. Questions should be reserved for situations in which the child has a legitimate choice or the question is intended to elicit a correct answer to a task. For example, the teacher should avoid using questions in the following ways:

The teacher wants the child to put together a puzzle—
"Let's put this puzzle together, O.K.?"
The teacher wants the child to read the next paragraph
—"Do you want to read the next paragraph?"

If the teacher has determined that the child *should* do these tasks it would be better to direct the child as follows:

"Here's a puzzle to put together. See how well you can do it."
"Now read the next paragraph, please."

The child's task and the teacher's expectation must be made unambiguous. Teaching is most effective when the teacher pleasantly but firmly and clearly assumes the role of director of the learning activities.

Questions *are* appropriate when the teacher wants the child to choose one of two or more alternatives, any one of which is acceptable. For example, "Which do you want to do first, reading or arithmetic?" is an appropriate question when either choice is acceptable. "What is Barney doing in this picture?" is a question for which the teacher can expect a specific correct answer.

When a child does not respond correctly to oral directions the teacher must take action to help the child complete the task. He may do this by repeating and simplifying the directions or by using cues, prompts, and models.[4] (See also Chapter 10)

Repeat and Simplify Directions. The teacher must be absolutely certain that the child understands exactly what he is to do. Otherwise, the reason for the child's failure cannot be determined. If the child does not respond promptly and correctly to directions for performing a task, the directions should be repeated. Furthermore, the teacher must be sure that the child understands each part of the direction he gives. For example, if the task directions are stated as "Draw a straight line from the monkey to the house," the teacher must be sure that the child understands what it means to draw a straight line from one object to another and that he can identify the monkey and the house. Before assuming that the child cannot perform the task or prompting the child's response, the teacher should repeat the task directions and, if necessary, simplify the directions to make sure that they are understandable to the child. Directions can be simplified by using simpler vocabulary or by breaking them down into small, sequential steps.

Cue Responses. If the child does not respond to repeated or simplified directions the teacher must take further action. The child may respond appropriately when he is given a signal or cue. The teacher may cue a response by a word, a gesture, or any other auditory, visual, or tactile signal. For example, if a child tends to respond at an inappropriate time, the teacher may call the child's name, use a hand signal, touch the child, etc., to cue his response at the appropriate time. If the child is attending to the wrong stimuli (pictures, words, blocks, etc.), the teacher may use a pointing or tapping cue to direct the child's attention and response.

Use Prompts. If a child does not respond to the teacher's cue, his response may need to be prompted. When a response is prompted, the teacher physically assists the child in performing the task. For example, if the child cannot perform the task of drawing a square the teacher may take the child's hand and help the child draw the figure. Occasionally, only a partial prompt may be needed, as when the teacher helps the child to draw only three sides of the square. Prompts can be faded out as the child learns the task. A prompt should be faded by gradually dropping assistance *beginning at the point of completion.* For example, the prompt for drawing a square should be faded as follows:

1. Help the child draw all four sides
2. Help the child draw only the first three sides
3. Help the child draw only the first two sides
4. Help the child draw only the first side

Eventually the prompt may be dropped completely, the child completing the entire task independently.

Provide a model. A child can often learn a task more quickly if he has a model to follow. If a child does not make an appropriate response, the teacher may need to show him how to do the task. For example, if the child does not cut on the dotted line or clap his hands when told to do so, the teacher should demonstrate the correct response. The instructions "Watch me," "Do it like this," etc. should be given when the teacher models the response. In some cases it may be helpful to have another child provide the model.

C. *Present only essential tasks*

The child should be presented with tasks that are directly related to the concept the teacher is trying to teach.[5] Irrelevant tasks should be eliminated. Each task should be an essential step in reaching the next performance goal. As suggested in Chapter 3, the teacher must teach directly to the problem. If the objective of instruction is to teach the child to catch a ball, little is to be gained by providing tasks in picture naming. If the teacher wants the child to learn sight words, there is little benefit in asking the child to walk on a balance beam. Picture naming and balance beam walking are legitimate instructional tasks, but there is little reason to expect that competence on one task will generalize to a very different one. Generalization is much more likely to occur among very similar tasks. Therefore, the teacher should present tasks which are prerequisites for reaching the instructional goal.

D. *Present tasks sequentially*

The sequence in which tasks are presented affects the rate at which the child learns. Complex tasks are mastered by sequential learning of many simpler tasks (see discussion of shaping in Chapter 2). It is important for the teacher to be aware of the sequential development of academic, social, and perceptual-motor learning so that tasks can be ordered effectively. The teacher should familiarize himself with the sequential development of skills by consulting other sources.[6] To be effective in remediation the teacher must be well organized and directive. He must also present essential tasks in the proper sequence. However, tasks must be followed by feedback if they are to remediate the problem.

V. Provide Feedback on Task Performance

Competence in remedial teaching demands more than merely presenting appropriate tasks. To learn efficiently children must be informed frequently, immediately, and clearly of the adequacy of their performance. One of the advantages of programmed instruction and other highly structured teaching systems (e.g., Berieter & Engelmann, 1966) is that they provide such feedback. As discussed in Chapter 2, what happens immediately after a response determines whether or not that response is likely to occur again. Teachers who fail to give adequate feedback on task performance risk extinguishing the child's appropriate responses.

A. *Give clear feedback*

Ambiguous feedback on performance is worse than no feedback at all. Ambiguity will only heighten the child's anxiety and confusion. When the child makes a response to a task the teacher's feedback should leave no room for doubt in the child's mind about the correctness of his response. Feedback on correctness might include such statements as "That's perfect," "It's all right except for this part right here," "No, that's wrong," "Yes, it's a bicycle," etc. The teacher should also give explicit feedback regarding his affective reaction to the response. The teacher can communicate affective reactions clearly by smiles, hugs, pats, winks, and a variety of other physical and verbal responses.[7] It is necessary to give some children extrinsic rewards (e.g., candy, trinkets, stars, tokens, etc.) along with social rewards and knowledge of correctness in order to make the feedback completely clear.

B. *Give corrective feedback*

Positive feedback for appropriate performance is corrective in that it strengthens correct responses to remedial tasks. When the child gives an incorrect response to a task, the teacher's feedback should be corrective in that it tells the child how to improve his performance.[8] "Make this line a little straighter," "You have to put the second number right under the first one," etc., go beyond merely telling the child clearly that his response is wrong. Feedback can also be corrective in a third sense—that it helps the child to evaluate his own performance accurately. By giving corrective feedback, the teacher provides a model which can be incorporated into the child's own self-evaluation. When feedback is adequately corrective it reinforces correct responses, extinguishes incorrect responses, indicates how task performance can be improved, and provides a model of realistic evaluation.

C. *Give feedback immediately*

Feedback is usually most effective when it is given during or immediately after performance. When the teacher is continuously observing the child's performance, he should, if necessary, give encouragement and praise or correction *while* the child is performing the task as well as immediately after it is completed. When he is not able to observe the child continuously, he must establish a structure and routine which allow feedback to be given as soon after task completion as possible.

D. *Give feedback frequently*

Feedback is so vital to learning that very few, if any, responses should go without it in the beginning stages of remediation. Most teachers tend to overestimate the frequency with which they provide feedback and allow the child to make many responses to which they do not respond. This tendency should be corrected if teaching is to be maximally effective. A good rule is, "Give feedback at *every* opportunity." Feedback should be a consequence for task performance. As a consequence, feedback is an essential element of classroom structure.

VI. Structure the Learning Environment

In Chapter 3 it was suggested that remedial teaching must be highly organized. Such organization results in an environment which is structured for learning. A highly structured environment has been found helpful in teaching children with learning problems (Cruickshank, Bentzen, Ratzeburg, & Tannhauser, 1961; Haring & Phillips, 1962, 1972; Phillips, 1967). Structure includes classroom rules, routines, and consequences of behavior related to the rules. In a well-structured classroom environment, the rules and consequences of behavior are simple, primarily positive, and consistently applied. The structure creates an atmosphere which is conducive to learning and the development of a good teacher-pupil relationship.

A. *Keep the structure simple*

Rules for behavior need to be kept short and simple, as discussed in Chapter 2. This suggestion is appropriate for all classroom rules, including those that apply to academic responses and routines. The teacher should determine which rules and routines are essential for efficient classroom operation and concentrate on making them work. Routines for distributing and collecting materials, preparing to leave the room, and following a schedule of activities, as well as rules governing movement about the room, talking in turn, and completing assigned tasks, should not be complicated. When the structure of the classroom becomes elaborate, children are likely to become confused about what is expected, required, tolerated, and prohibited by the teacher.

B. *Build rewards into the structure*

Adults, including teachers, often tend to assume that appropriate performance is its own reward. For many children with learning problems, if not for most, this is not the case. A good classroom structure emphasizes explicit positive consequences for cooperative, productive behavior. The teacher must arrange rewards for good performance as an integral part of the structure. He can do this by scheduling positive consequences for appropriate responses (cf. Gallagher, 1970). The consequences need not be extrinsic rewards, such as candy or trinkets, although such rewards might be necessary for some children. Every child has a right to rewards which are meaningful to him no matter what his level of development. The teacher must develop competence in finding meaningful consequences and helping the child learn to work for rewards which are indicative of a higher level of maturity.

C. *Adhere firmly and consistently to the structure*

Rewards are effective only when they are kept in the proper relationship to performance. The teacher must be firm and consistent in providing rewards only *after* appropriate responses are made to the structure. The "reward now, perform later" plea of children must be resisted. Likewise, if the structure established by the teacher calls for leveling an aversive consequence for behavior, the teacher must not allow the child to dissuade him. The primary aspects of a structured classroom environment are clear directions, firm expectations, and consistent follow-through (Haring & Phillips, 1962). Consistency does not mean rigidity. There are circumstances under which routines should be varied and rules should be broken. But if the classroom rules and routines are varied at the whim of either the teacher or the children, learning will not be optimal.

D. *Develop a good teacher-pupil relationship*

A good teacher-pupil relationship is based on mutual respect and trust. Many children with learning problems neither respect nor trust teachers. It is the teacher's responsibility to respect and trust the child in spite of his lack of reciprocal regard. The child will learn respect if the teacher's behavior is fair, consistent, and task centered. It is misleading to assume that to be an effective teacher one must first become a confidant of the child. Lasting confidence grows out of a history of predictable interactions. The teacher can develop a sound and productive relationship with the child in the following ways:

1. Demonstrating concern for him as an individual by gearing teaching to his specific needs
2. Remediating his learning problems by offering skillful instruction

3. Making learning enjoyable by exciting his interest and providing rewards for appropriate performance
4. Remaining confident in the child's ability to learn
5. Being cheerful, pleasant, and fair but firm, consistent, and predictable in interactions with him

A well-structured classroom facilitates learning and development of a sound teacher-pupil relationship. It also simplifies documentation of the remedial process through careful record keeping.

VII. Keep Useful Records of Teaching and Learning

Good record keeping is an essential feature of effective teaching. Accurate, objective records serve the following purposes:

1. They provide feedback to the teacher regarding the adequacy of instruction.
2. They simplify communication with other teachers and parents.
3. They provide a guide to future instruction.

The teacher should keep two basic kinds of records: a log of teaching activities and charts of the child's performance. In addition, he should use *Type II* information to plan future teaching.

A. *Keep a log of teaching activities*

A teacher's log should provide a brief narrative account of what instructional tasks were presented, what materials were used, the child's responses to the tasks, and the teacher's evaluation of the outcome (see Chapter 3, Principle VII). It is important to date each entry so that the log is a chronology of instruction. Anecdotal records of the child's social-interpersonal behavior, as well as his responses to instruction, should be entered in the log so that the relationship between academic and social learning can be observed. The entries in the log, including the teacher's evaluation of instruction, must be kept accurate and objective if the log is to serve its purpose. If the teacher wishes to keep a record of his subjective impressions and feelings it should be kept as a separate set of notes. The log should summarize the teacher's instructional activities so that the child's educational experience can be documented for the child's parents (if they wish to have the information) and his future teachers. It is often helpful to append samples of the child's written work. In most cases the log will serve as the teacher's lesson plan. However, the teacher may need to write more detailed plans in some situations.

B. *Chart the child's progress in learning*

The child's progress in learning specific skills and behaviors may be plotted on a graph. The experience of graphing his progress can be exciting and motivating for both the child and the teacher. The visual feedback from a graph is more immediate and interpretable than the information obtained from written reports or summary tables. Whenever possible the child should be encouraged to maintain the graph himself, as graphing is often a reinforcing behavior for children. (See Chapter 2 for a discussion of graphing techniques.)

C. *Base future teaching on Type II information*

Type II information is obtained from the teaching process itself. It is the basis for day-to-day and moment-to-moment remedial teaching. It implies that the teacher will continuously monitor the child's responses to instruction and modulate his own behavior and the instructional tasks in order to increase his effectiveness. Type II information provides corrective feedback in a remedial teaching system. As a system, remedial teaching may be diagramed as shown in Figure 5-1.[9]

Before beginning remediation the teacher must use *Type I* information to formulate an initial teaching strategy. On the basis of his observation of the child, test results, and information obtained from other sources, he enters the remedial teaching system.

The teacher must first state a long-range instructional goal and an immediate goal which is an approximation of it. The instructional task which he presents will follow logically from the immediate goal. If the child performs the task without error, the cycle of stating an immediate goal and presenting the next task in sequence is continued until the long-range goal is achieved. When the long-range goal is achieved, the cycle includes the statement of a new long-range goal. If all of the teacher's long-range goals are reached, remediation is no longer necessary and can be terminated.

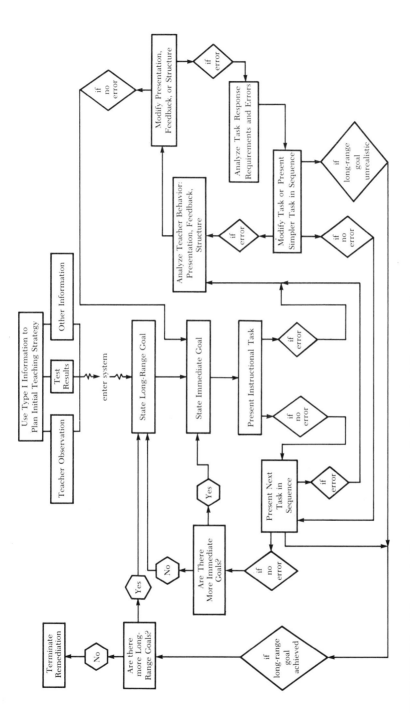

FIGURE 5-1   Schematic Representation of a Remedial Teaching System

117

If the child makes an error in task performance, the teacher must first analyze his own teaching behavior and modify the task presentation, feedback on task performance, and/or the structure of the learning environment. If the child is able to perform the task without error after the teacher corrects his own behavior, the cycle of restatement of the immediate goal and presentation of the next task in sequence is resumed.

When the child's task performance breaks down after the teacher has corrected his instructional behavior, the teacher must analyze the response requirements of the task and the child's errors. If modification of the task or presentation of a simpler task results in adequate performance, the next task in sequence is then presented. If the child continues to make performance errors, the teacher may either reanalyze instructional behavior or restate the long-range goal for the child to make it more realistic.

The use of *Type II* information to guide instruction requires both a high degree of technical competence and a high degree of self-awareness and sensitivity on the part of the teacher. Technical competence is demanded in sequencing and presenting remedial tasks. Sensitivity and self-awareness are necessary if the teacher is to analyze the role played by his own behavior in contributing to the child's learning problem.

Summary

Successful remedial teaching, whether accomplished by regular or special class teachers, requires specific competencies based on the principles of academic remediation and behavior management discussed in Part I. These competencies involve assessment, goal setting, task analysis, task presentation, feedback, structure, and record keeping. Mastery of these skills will enable the teacher to provide an environment in which the child can learn both academic skills and appropriate behavior.

NOTES

[1]We acknowledge the skillful assistance of Ms. Kay Rigling in obtaining the data for this report.

[2]For further discussion of task analysis see: Becker, Engelmann, & Thomas (1971), Engelmann (1969), Lerner (1971), and Stephens (1970).

[3]Additional suggestions for organizing tasks may be found in: Cruickshank, Bentzen, Ratzeburg, & Tannhauser (1961), Haring & Phillips (1962), and Phillips (1967).

[4]For a detailed analysis of presenting tasks see: Becker, Engelmann, & Thomas (1971) and Engelmann (1969).

[5]A model for teaching concepts is provided by Becker, Engelmann, & Thomas (1971).

[6]Chapters 6-11 include broad outlines of sequential development in specific skill areas. For more detailed discussion of sequential skill development, the reader is referred to the additional readings at the end of each chapter.

[7]For an extensive listing of approval and disapproval responses see Madsen & Madsen (1970).

[8]For discussion of correcting errors see Becker, Engelmann, & Thomas (1971).

[9]A more detailed model of teaching tasks is provided by Becker, Engelmann, & Thomas (1971).

ADDITIONAL
READINGS

Becker, W. C., Engelmann, S., & Thomas, D. R. *Teaching: a course in applied psychology.* Chicago: Science Research Associates, 1971.

Bereiter, C., & Engelmann, S. *Teaching disadvantaged children in the preschool.* Englewood Cliffs, N.J.: Prentice-Hall, 1966.

Berry, K. E. *Remedialdiagnosis.* San Rafael, Calif.: Dimensions, 1968.

Engelmann, S. *Preventing failure in the primary grades.* Chicago: Science Research Associates, 1969.

Haring, N. G., & Phillips, E. L. *Analysis and modification of classroom behavior.* Englewood Cliffs, N.J.: Prentice-Hall, 1972.

Hewett, F. M. *The emotionally disturbed child in the classroom.* Boston: Allyn & Bacon, 1968.

Otto, W., & McMenemy, R. A. *Corrective and remedial teaching.* Boston: Houghton Mifflin, 1966.

Peter, L. J. *Prescriptive teaching.* New York: McGraw-Hill, 1965.

Stephens, T. M. *Directive teaching of children with learning and behavioral handicaps.* Columbus, Ohio: Charles E. Merrill, 1970.

6

Behavior-
Management
Problems

Many children who have learning problems are not distinguished by their good work habits, productivity, cooperativeness, and social graces. Frequently, it is necessary to establish good work habits and eliminate interfering social behaviors before academic remediation can be accomplished. The objectives of behavior management should be to prepare the child for academic learning and increase the efficiency and effectiveness of instruction. As suggested in Chapters 2 and 5, the teacher must teach work habits and adaptive social behaviors directly. The teacher must concern himself with two basic problems:

1. What academic response patterns prevent the child from learning efficiently?
2. What social behaviors interfere with the child's learning?

Diagnosis

Teacher Observation

Diagnosis of behavior problems depends primarily on teacher observation and analysis of the child's behavior. The teacher must obtain baseline data and analyze the factors which control the child's behavior, as discussed in Chapter 2. Precise diagnostic methods have been described in detail by Lovitt (1967).

It is helpful to conceptualize the child's behavior in terms of excesses and deficits. When the teacher is diagnosing behavioral *excesses* he must find answers to the following questions:

1. What does the child do that is maladaptive?
2. How often does he do it under present conditions?
3. What environmental events serve to maintain his behavior?
4. How can I remove the events that support his undesirable behavior?

Essentially, diagnosis of behavioral *deficits* must answer the following questions for the teacher:

1. What do I want the child to do?
2. How often does he do it under present conditions?
3. What approximations of what I want the child to do can I identify?
4. What reinforcers for the child can I identify that are at my disposal?
5. How can I provide reinforcers for successive approximations of what I want the child to do?

These diagnostic questions are focused on positive expectations and positive consequences. The key to effective behavior management is finding ways to reward desirable actions of the child.

Informal Assessment

Screening instruments (several of which are described briefly in Chapter 4) and rating scales are available for identifying major problem areas. Hewett (1968) has developed an hierarchy of educational goals and a useful inventory of behaviors related to academic and social tasks. Walker (1969) has outlined a model for assessment of deviant behavior. However, effective management of specific problem behaviors depends on observational diagnostic methods which are more precise than rating scales and inventories.

Formal Tests

Few useful formal tests for diagnosing behavior-management problems are available. Although the disciplines of psychology, neurology, and psychiatry have developed a wide variety of personality measures and neurological tests, they provide little information which can be used in teaching. As Hewett (1968) has stated:

> It is not that the multi-disciplinary maps or viewpoints of psychiatry, clinical psychology, or neurology are inaccurate or irrelevant but that they seldom are truly useful in bridging the gap between description and diagnosis and practical classroom application . . . (p. 78).

Following are a number of suggestions for managing specific behavior problems. Each suggestion is based on classroom experience, but it must be remembered that its successful use with a given child depends on adaptation of the technique to meet the unique requirements of the individual.

**Interfering
Social Behaviors**

Social and emotional behaviors which interfere with learning must be brought under control before academic problems can be remediated. The child must learn to:

1. attend school willingly and regularly
2. accept the authority of the teacher and other school personnel
3. work cooperatively and constructively in the classroom
4. establish positive relationships with his peers
5. exhibit behavior indicative of a positive self-image
6. exhibit appropriate behavior outside the classroom

Diagnostic questions and teaching suggestions for remediating interfering social behaviors are listed below.

I. Does the Child Attempt to Escape or Avoid School?

    A. *Does the child resist coming to school?*

        1. Have a special treat or activity waiting for the child each day when he comes to school.

2. If the mother brings the child to school, arrange to have the father bring the child until he is able to walk or ride the bus by himself.
3. Award every child a star for each day's attendance at school. Have a party on Friday for all children who have had perfect attendance during the week.
4. Start a "club" in the area of greatest interest to the child (science, math, reading, music, etc.). Make participation in the weekly meetings depend on at least four days attendance since the last meeting.

B. *Does the child frequently run from the classroom?*

5. Increase your positive attention to the child when he is in the classroom. Keep your interaction with the child outside the classroom at a minimum (Haring, Hayden, & Allen, 1971).
6. Tell the child that if he does not leave the room without permission you will spend twenty minutes working with him on a favorite activity (e.g., sewing, model building, reading, etc.).

II. Does the Child Challenge Authority?

A. *Does the child disobey directions or requests?*

7. If the child refuses to recite in class, allow any child who does recite to bring a book or magazine of his choice to class for a specified period of private reading at the end of the class (Madsen & Madsen, 1970).
8. Provide the class with several specific examples of "good attitude." Include examples of obeying commands and complying with teacher requests. Later, praise the child by commending his "good attitude" when his behavior approximates obedience and compliance (Madsen & Madsen, 1970).
9. Arrange a "time-out" area in the room. If the child does not obey a direct command within fifteen seconds, place the child in the time-out area for five minutes. After five minutes allow the child to leave the time out area only if he is willing to follow your directions. Praise the child when he does obey commands.
10. Ignore the child when he disobeys a direction given to the class. Do not *allow* him to comply with your

next command to the class until he follows the first directive. Compliment the child for obedient behavior whenever he follows your directions.

B. *Does the child argue with the teacher?*

11. If you are certain that your judgment is correct, tell the child only once that his answer is unacceptable. Do not respond in any way to protestations or complaints that you are wrong (Hall, 1971a). Remember that you can make errors, and give the child the benefit of the doubt if an issue is unclear.

12. Whenever the child begins a dispute concerning an assignment or direction, stop all interaction with him by turning and walking away. If the child begins an assignment or follows a directive without arguing, praise him with a positive statement (Hall, Fox, Willard, Goldsmith, Emerson, Owen, Davis, & Porcia, 1971).

III. Is the Child Uncooperative or Disruptive in the Classroom?

A. *Is the child often out of his seat without permission?*

13. "Tie" the child to his desk by fastening a decorative ribbon across his lap with cellophane tape. Praise the child at frequent intervals if he remains at his desk. When he has permission to leave his desk, remove the ribbons. "Retie" him when he returns.

14. Make an explicit rule concerning movement about the classroom. Ignore children who do not follow the rule. Praise children who observe the rule (Madsen, Becker, & Thomas, 1968).

15. Allow any child who has remained in his seat during the work period to play musical chairs, eraser tag, seven-up or some other game involving movement.

16. Shuffle a deck of playing cards and let the child select a suit. For each academic task completed, allow the child to turn a card face up. If the card turned face up is a member of the chosen suit let the child get a drink of water from the fountain, visit the game corner for one minute, or make some other specific, quiet movement about the room. If the child gets out of his seat without permission, require him to forfeit

his next card-turn (Kauffman, Cullinan, Scranton, & Wallace, 1972).

17. Set a timer for varying brief intervals. If the child has remained in his seat during the interval, give him a small piece of candy and praise him for sitting.
18. Set a timer as in #17 above, but take care to hide it from the child's view. Have the child record whether he is in or out of his seat each time the timer rings.

B. *Does the child talk out or interrupt conversations?*

19. The suggestions provided in #14 under "out-of-seat" behavior can also be used effectively for talking out behavior (Madsen, Becker, & Thomas, 1968; Hall *et al.* 1971).
20. For each thirty-minute period during which the child does not talk out, allow him five minutes to play with a "magic slate" or some other educational toy (Hall, 1971a).
21. When the child talks out without raising his hand or interrupts a conversation, do not recognize him in any way. Turn your back or walk away if the child attempts to get your attention by tugging at your sleeve or standing in front of you. When the child does raise his hand and wait his turn to speak, recognize him immediately and compliment him.
22. If there are fewer than five talk-outs during a forty-minute study period allow the class a ten-minute break for casual conversations.
23. Move the child's desk away from children to whom he tends to talk, and near children with whom he is unlikely to converse.
24. Award the child a point for each five-minute period during which he works quietly without talking. When he has accumulated ten or more points allow him to exchange them for minutes during which he "interviews" other pupils and tape records the conversation for replay to the class.
25. Give the child a slip of paper on which he is to record his own talkouts during the study period. Have him return the slip to you at the end of class (Broden, Hall, & Mitts, 1971).

C. *Does the child ask inappropriate or unnecessary questions?*

   26. Handle this problem similarly to talking out or tattling; ignore the inappropriate or unnecessary questions and attend to the child when his questions are
appropriate and necessary.

D. *Does the child make distracting noises?*

   27. Ignore the child's noise making and praise children
who are being quiet. Give the noise-maker positive
attention and praise when he exhibits quiet behavior
(Hall, 1971a).

   28. If the child continues to make excessive noise with an
object after he has been warned, take the object from
him for a short, specified period of time.

   29. For each fifteen-minute interval during which the
child does not make the distracting noise, give the
child a point. Let him take roll the next day if he
accumulates ten or more points.

E. *Does the child have frequent crying spells or temper tantrums?*

   30. Tell the class that as long as the child is not crying
they must call him by his "big" name, e.g., Fred.
Whenever he cries, they may call him by his usual,
though nonpreferred name, Freddy (Kaufhold &
Kauffman, 1972).

   31. When the child begins a temper tantrum, immediately place him in an isolation or time-out area of the
classroom. Be firm but unemotional in dealing with
the child. After the child has been quiet for five
minutes, allow him to leave the time-out area.

   32. Give no attention to the child when he is crying or
tantruming. Attend to the child only when his behavior is appropriate.

   33. Observe the child's tantrums carefully. Notice the
first behavior the child exhibits when beginning a
tantrum (e.g., desk-hitting or foot-stomping). Tell the
child to repeat the behavior more forcefully for a
specific number of times (e.g., "That's it, stomp really
hard five times.") Tell the child to repeat the behavior
until he says he would like to stop.

   34. At the beginning of class give the child five colored
slips of paper with his name written on each. Each
time the child whines, cries, or complains during the

class period, take one name slip away from him. Warn him that this is what you are going to do (Hall, Axelrod, Foundopulos, Shellman, Campbell, & Cranston, 1971).

F. *Does the child destroy property of others?*

35. Desks and walls that are defaced by pen or pencil marks should, under close supervision, be washed by the child to the satisfaction of the teacher (Madsen & Madsen, 1970).
36. When wads of chewing gum are found under desks, establish gum-chewing privileges for Monday, Wednesday and Friday. If an individual is caught chewing gum on Tuesday or Thursday he loses one day of gum-chewing privileges and also has to remove five wads of gum from under a desk (Madsen & Madsen, 1970).
37. If a child destroys another child's property, require him to replace it with an equivalent item.
38. If the child steals or extorts tokens, invalidate all of the tokens he currently possesses and let him earn only distinctively marked tokens.

G. *Does the child swear in school?*

39. Give the student a list of ten alternative words to swearing. Tell the child that each time he has the urge to swear, he should use a word from the list.
40. Set a kitchen timer for successive thirty-minute periods. Praise the student for each thirty-minute period that he does not swear. (For some children the time periods may need to be as short as one minute.) After the student exhibits an ability to refrain from swearing for a given period of time, gradually increase the time periods.
41. Record the number of swears per hour, period, or day. Tell the child that swearing is inappropriate in the school and that it is his responsibility to eliminate this behavior. Have him record his swears on a graph. Praise him for a reduced number of swears per hour, period, or day.
42. Prepare a tape recorder so that it is ready to operate at a time when the child is likely to swear. Secretly record his swearing. In a private conference with the

student, play the tape and have him comment on the appropriateness of his language.

H. *Does the child use lewd gestures or write inappropriate messages?*

43. Establish a special ten-minute recess for the class. Place a set of cards numbered one through ten on the base of a desk calendar. Each time a lewd gesture is seen or reported, turn a card, which reduces the special recess by one minute (Sulzbacher & Houser, 1968).

44. Make a rule that if students are caught passing notes or secret messages, a special privilege will be withdrawn. Remind the students that notes and secret messages may be passed during a special three-minute communication period (Madsen & Madsen, 1970).

I. *Has the child failed to learn polite social behavior?*

45. When distributing materials, praise the children who say "thank you." Also praise those students who request material with the word "please."

46. Role play polite behaviors with the children. Praise those children who exhibit those behaviors at times other than role playing.

IV. Has the Child Established Negative or Inadequate Relationships with His Peers?

A. *Does the child hit or otherwise assault other children?*

47. Completely ignore the child who did the hitting—do not reprimand him, scowl at him, or attend to him in any way. Go immediately to the child that was hit and give him positive attention, care, or comfort.

48. Count the number of times the child commits an act of overt aggression against another person during a specified time interval, such as the recess period. Show the child the record of his behavior over a period of several days. Award points each day that the record indicates zero acts of aggression or fewer than the day before. Let the child exchange the points earned for special activities or treats.

49. Arrange a chair in a corner of the room which is away from any interesting objects or other children. Each

time the child hits, kicks, pinches, or otherwise hurts another child place him immediately and unemotionally in the chair and tell him he must sit there for five minutes. After five minutes let him rejoin the group. Be sure to tell the child what you are going to do before initiating the technique.

50. Observe the activity during which the most fighting takes place (e.g., music, recess, etc.). For each day that no fighting occurs during the chosen activity, allow the child to visit with the principal for five minutes. The principal must be willing to chat pleasantly with the child contingent on the child's good behavior (Madsen & Madsen, 1970).

51. Ignore aggressive behavior unless there is serious threat of bodily harm. Show approval and praise frequently for peaceful and cooperative behavior (Brown & Elliot, 1965).

B. *Does the child tease other children too frequently?*

52. Do not reprimand the teasing child. Arrange with the child who is being teased that he will earn the privilege of helping you for two minutes after school each time he is teased but makes no response.

53. When the teasing begins, go immediately to the child who is being teased, turn him physically away from the teaser, and engage him in a pleasant conversation *before* he reacts to the teasing. Ignore the child who is teasing.

54. Tell the child who teases that he may not tease his peers but he may tease you. Encourage him to tease you when he "feels the urge" and react dramatically to his teasing. Tease him appropriately in return. However, if he teases another child give him a brief but firm reprimand.

55. Have the teased child record the number of times he is taunted but makes no response to his tormentor. Check the reliability of his recording at frequent intervals. Give the child one Valentine candy for each occasion on which he makes no response to teasing. For each ten candies let the child earn an "I can take it" certificate, and after five certificates present him, with great ceremony, the "Medal of Bravery." The certificate and medal may be made from construction paper.

C. *Does the child interrupt other children who are working?*

    56. For each ten minute interval during which the child does not bother anyone else in the class, allow him, during a specified time, to spend one minute visiting socially with another child.

    57. Make a small isolation booth in a corner of the room by using a coatrack, bookcase, or other movable furniture. Each time the child interferes with the work of a classmate, send him to the "time-out" booth for ten minutes (Madsen & Madsen, 1970).

D. *Is the child reinforced by his peers for misbehavior?*

    58. Discuss the problem briefly with the class. Explain that for each work period during which the usual miscreant does not misbehave the entire class will have a ten-minute break.

    59. Each time the child misbehaves and is reinforced by his peers make a tally mark on the chalkboard. Reduce the usual free time or recess period by fifteen seconds for each mark given. Praise the child for working without distracting his peers.

E. *Does the child seldom talk to peers or the teacher?*

    60. Let the child record his own voice on a tape recorder and replay the tape immediately. Praise the child for recording his voice and gradually require more and more conversational speech from the child.

    61. Give the child a penny each time that you observe him talking with another child or he talks spontaneously to you. At first, give the penny even if only one word is spoken. When the child has begun making frequent one-word responses, gradually demand longer responses to earn the reward. Praise the child for talking when you give him the penny.

    62. Arrange to have the child's parents reward him for bringing home a daily "report card." Have the child keep a folded piece of colored construction paper with him at all times. Whenever you observe him talking appropriately to someone or he talks to you, draw a "happy face" on his report card. Review his card at the end of the day. Have him return it the following day with his parent's signature.

    63. Let the child work with an especially friendly child on a special project (e.g., building a model car) during a

fifteen minute period each day. Obtain the cooperation of the child's friend in asking him questions and responding positively to his comments. When conversation between the two children is established, add a third child to the group and let them begin a new project.

F. *Is the child rejected socially by his peers?*

64. When rewards (e.g., candy) or highly desired materials (e.g., art supplies) are distributed to the class, have the isolate child be the distributor (Kirby & Toler, 1970).

65. Keep the rejected child close to you. Let the other children observe you interacting pleasantly with him. Give special attention to children who imitate your model. Ignore children who overtly reject or avoid the child.

66. Choose some desirable behavior of the rejected child (e.g., looking at a book, writing neatly). Comment positively on his behavior within the hearing of the entire class and make it the occasion for a special "fun" activity (singing a song, taking a break, giving extra time at recess, etc.).

G. *Does the child cling to adults and avoid his peers?*

67. Ignore the child when he attempts to interact unnecessarily with you or another adult. Attend positively to the child when he is playing or working with other children (Allen, Hart, Buell, Harris, & Wolf, 1964).

68. Comment positively on the cooperative behavior of specific children at frequent intervals. Make certain that the isolate child hears your comments.

H. *Does the child spend long periods daydreaming?*

69. Make sure that the work is neither too easy nor too difficult for the child.

70. Make the task more interesting by giving novel directions or requiring an unusual mode of response (e.g., let the child "print" the answers to arithmetic problems involving two-digit sums by using a library date stamp).

71. Set a timer to ring at brief random intervals. Explain that when the bell goes off the child will be allowed

to pull an item from a "fun box" if he is working hard. To make the fun box, write directions on slips of paper and fasten them to strings. Put them in a box with only the ends of the strings showing. On the slips, write a wide variety of directions such as, "Give one M&M candy to every person who is working and take one for yourself," "Go back to your work until you can earn another try," "Take this note to the principal and he will give you five cents," "Choose six other people to play one game of seven-up right now," etc.

I. *Does the child "tattle" on others?*

72. Ignore the tattling or simply say, "I don't care to hear about it."
73. When a child tattles, change the topic of conversation abruptly and continue as if the tattling had not occurred.

V. Does the Child Exhibit Behavior Indicative of Immaturity or a Negative Self-Image?

A. *Does the child maintain a sloppy or dirty appearance?*

74. Make a life size cutout of a boy and girl with hair combed, hands clean, fingernails clean, teeth brushed, shirt tucked in, and shoes shined. Have a morning grooming check and post the name of each child that approximates the appearance of the cutout.
75. If you are using a token system in your classroom, the store should contain a number of self-care items (e.g., soap, comb, toothbrush, aftershave lotion, perfume). Don't overprice these items. Have frequent sales.
76. Model appropriate grooming skills for the children. Let the children observe you wash your hands, comb your hair, use a fingernail brush to clean your nails. Compliment children who imitate your model of good grooming.
77. Set up a style show for girls to model clothes made in their sewing class. Make participation in the style show a reward for good grooming.

B. *Does the child suck his thumb or fingers?*

78. Ignore the child when he is sucking his thumb and give attention and praise for behaviors other than thumbsucking (Skiba, Pettigrew, & Alden, 1971).

79. During story time, stop reading to the child immediately when he puts his thumb in his mouth, and do not resume reading until he removes it. (Note: This procedure may also be suggested to parents. See Kauffman & Scranton, 1972.)

C. *Does the child exhibit repetitive or self-injurious behavior?*

80. Obtain the assistance of several responsible pupils. Have the pupils sit next to the child who is grimacing or performing a tic and praise him when his behavior is appropriate. For example, "Good, Ogden, you're not gnashing your teeth now" (Gallagher, 1971).
81. When the child begins a self-injurious behavior, shout **"STOP IT"** as loudly as possible. Make your shouting as aversive as possible for the child. Do not sooth the child or comfort him while caring for his wound if he purposely hurts himself. Give the child a great deal of positive attention when he is not engaged in self-injurious behavior. (Note: *See comments on the use of punishment in Chapter 2.*)

VI. Does the Child Exhibit Inappropriate Behavior Outside the Classroom?

A. *Does the child refuse many foods at lunch?*

82. Plan a unit of instruction on foods of another culture. For example, have a series of lessons on food of the Orient and let the children wear coolie hats that they have made on the days when chop suey is served (Cooper, Payne, & Edwards, 1971).
83. Let the children who have eaten all of their food add a part, such as a leaf on a tree or a cotton ball on Santa's beard, to a special bulletin board (Cooper, Payne, & Edwards, 1971).
84. Let the child observe you eating and enjoying foods which he does not eat.

B. *Is the child too active or noisy at the lunch table?*

85. Arrange with the parents that you will send home a daily report of the child's lunchroom behavior. The report will simply state whether or not he has earned the privilege of staying up for an extra thirty minutes before bedtime. Give good reports contingent on improved behavior.

86. Seat the children in boy-girl-boy-girl order at the lunch table. Reward children who are talking quietly and using good manners with attention and praise.

C. *Is the child disruptive on the bus?*

87. Record several sing-along songs on a cassette tape recorder. Have a responsible student operate the recorder enroute to and from school. The use of recorded songs stimulates children to sing rather than fight while they ride (Payne, Feingold, & Cooper, 1971).
88. Have the child carefully observe what is happening on the bus. Have him write what he sees on a special piece of paper given to him by the bus driver. Reward him for the number of words that he uses to describe the activities on the bus.
89. If a token system is operating in the classroom, the bus driver can be given tokens to dispense for good behavior on the bus.

Academic
Response Problems

To be a successful learner in any area of the curriculum, the child must make appropriate academic responses as directed by the teacher. Specifically, the child must:

1. Accept the tasks provided by the teacher
2. Complete the tasks within a reasonable amount of time
3. Work neatly and accurately
4. Participate in group activities

Following is an outline of diagnostic questions and teaching suggestions to remediate commonly observed academic response problems.

VII. Does the Child Actively Resist Academic Tasks?

A. *Does the child refuse academic tasks?*

90. Present the child with two or three alternative tasks which involve similar skills (e.g., $4\overline{)12}$, $12 \div 4$, $12/4$, divide 12 by 4). Let him choose the one he prefers.

91. Ignore comments such as, "I don't want to" or "I ain't going to do this stuff." If the child destroys his work, be prepared to give him another identical task. Do not allow the child to participate in another activity until he has begun the task. As soon as the child has begun the task, comment positively on the fact that he is doing it.

92. Require only a small amount of academic work, after which the child is immediately allowed to make his next move in a checker game which you are playing with him. Gradually require more work for each move.

93. Record the number of times the child verbally refuses work each day and plot the data on a graph. At the end of a week show the child the graph of his refusals. Then have him begin to record daily his own refusals. If he has fewer refusals than the day before, present him with a smiling face.

B. *Does the child destroy his own work?*

94. Give the child a decorative sticker or decorative seal for each paper completed and turned in (not destroyed). Let the child keep the stickers or seals in a special notebook (Gallagher, 1971).

95. For each paper completed but not mutilated or defaced, allow the child to work on an art activity for ten minutes (drawing, painting, cutting, etc.).

C. *Does the child fail to follow directions?*

96. Present the directions in the form of a "code" or secret message (e.g., "NO EGAP 12 FO RUOY HTAM KOOBKROW OD YLNO EHT TSRIF EERHT SWOR. DOOG KCUL, XAM. TNEGA 99."). Challenge the child to demonstrate that he has "cracked the code."

97. Simplify the directions. Give each step in the directions separately and praise the child for following each step.

98. Record the directions on the tape recorder. Let the child listen to the directions at the listening station.

D. *Does the child fail to return promptly to task after a break?*

99. Shuffle a deck of playing cards and show them to the child. Have him pick a suit, e.g., clubs. Explain that if

he returns to his work within two minutes after the end of his break (recess, free time, etc.) he will be allowed to cut the deck. If he turns up a club, he may have an additional five minutes of free time immediately (Kauffman, Cullinan, Scranton, & Wallace, 1972).

100. Five minutes before the break is over, give the child a warning signal. As each minute passes, inform the child of how many minutes are left before the break will be over.

101. Arrange to have the child's favorite seatwork activities (e.g., cutting, coloring, crosswords, reading, math puzzle) following the break. Give the seatwork in two parts, one of which the child may do immediately after the break and one of which he may do only after he has completed the usual task which he tries to avoid.

102. Allow the children who quickly return to their work to listen to their favorite popular music at the listening station.

103. Establish the time at which children must return to the room after recess. Post a chart on the bulletin board and record daily the name of each child who returns to the room on time (Hall, Cristler, Cranston, & Tucker, 1970).

VIII. Does the Child Fail to Complete Academic Tasks?

A. *Is the child slow getting started on work?*

104. Record how many minutes pass after the task is assigned before the child actually begins the work. If the child begins sooner than the day before, award a point. When five points are accumulated allow the child to engage in a favorite activity or have a special treat.

105. When the task is assigned, set a kitchen timer for one minute. If everyone in the class has begun the task when the bell rings, allow the class an additional five minutes of recess time.

106. Ignore the child until he completes some small portion of the task. As soon as he begins, praise him for having begun his work and reduce the assignment by

50 percent or more. Gradually lower the reduction in work as the child learns to begin immediately.

107. Have the child begin his work at a desk where there are fewer distractions. When he has completed the first part of the task let him return to his own desk.

108. Play "working chairs." Set a timer for variable intervals ranging from thirty seconds to three minutes. Make the rule that any child who is working when the timer goes off *may* move to the next chair if he wishes. Children should rotate around the classroom. Those who are not working must remain in their chairs or go to a "time-out" chair.

109. Make cross-word puzzles shaped like several worms. "Early birds" (children who begin their work immediately) get the worms. Other special activities, such as pictures to color or forms to cut and paste, may be substituted.

110. Give the child a simpler or shorter task than usual and note whether he begins more quickly. If he does, continue giving the easier task until the child establishes a pattern of beginning immediately. Then very gradually increase the difficulty or length of the task.

B. *Does the child begin but not complete tasks?*

111. Break the task down into smaller units (e.g., assign one row of math problems or an individual problem rather than a page). As the child completes each part of the task, praise his accomplishment and assign another small unit. Gradually lengthen the assignment.

112. If you are certain that the task is one which the child is capable of doing, do not allow him to engage in any other activity until the task is completed. As soon as the task is completed, praise the child and allow him to engage in a favorite activity. Avoid nagging the child to finish the task. State the arrangement positively (e.g., "You may go to recess when you have finished your reading").

113. Allow the child to check his own work as soon as he finishes it.

114. Give five points for each completed task. When fifteen points have been earned, allow the child to skip the next similar assigned task.

115. Make up a daily "report card" on which you report number of tasks assigned and number of tasks com-

pleted. At the end of each day send the child to the office with his report card. Arrange to have the principal talk with the child for a few minutes if the report card is better than the day before. If the report card shows a decrease, the principal is to say "I'm sorry, but I can't see you today," and send the child back to the room.

C. *Does the child work too slowly after he gets started?*

116. Record the child's rate of work (problems completed correctly per minute or words read per minute, etc.). Have him plot his rate on a graph each day.

117. Have the child choose a partner with whom he would like to compete. Make "speedometer" charts by drawing a speedometer dial on a sheet of paper. Do not include the indicator. Let the children draw the indicator on the speedometer to show their rate of work for the day. The child with the highest speed wins.

118. Find the speed of various animals (e.g., turtle, goose, cheetah, horse, dog, etc.). Post cutouts of each animal and its speed on the bulletin board. Compute the child's rate of work for the day and allow him to wear the cutout that most closely approximates his rate. (Note: The child's rate of response per minute should be considered the animal's speed in miles per hour in most cases.)

119. If the child completes his assignment by the end of the work period allow him to be "Mercury" for the day and take messages to the office or other teachers.

120. Children in the intermediate grades often are fascinated by measures of rate. Compute the child's rate of working each day. Provide one point for reaching a minimum rate and additional points for working at progressively higher rates. For example, give the child one point for doing his math assignment at the rate of three problems per minute, three points for a rate of five problems per minute, ten points for eight problems per minute, etc. Let the child exchange his points for special activities, treats, or privileges (Lovitt & Esveldt, 1970).

D. *Does the child resist working independently?*

121. Break the task into very small work units (e.g., one math problem or operation, one comprehension

question, etc.). Require the child to complete the first small unit on his own. When he has done that, work with him while he does the next unit. Alternate short, independently completed tasks with tasks on which you give assistance. Gradually require more independent work before giving help. (Note: Make certain that the child has the prerequisite skills to do the work independently.)

122. Talk with the child about the need to work independently. Measure the child's height in inches. For each ten minute period of time that he works independently, let him color in one inch toward his total height. When he reaches the goal of his total height, let him have a special privilege.

E. *Does the child resist new tasks?*

123. Assign some very small portion of the new task (e.g., one simple subtraction problem) which must be completed before the child goes on to an old, familiar task (e.g., several addition problems). Gradually increase the ratio of new tasks to familiar tasks.

124. Discuss with the child his unwillingness to attempt new tasks. Make an "adventurer" badge and explain that he may wear it for a specified period of time if he attempts a new task without hesitation. When five badges have been earned give the child his choice of an explorer's helmet or showing an "adventure" film strip.

125. Make a "Look What I Tried" scrapbook in which is written each new task the child has tried. Let the child illustrate each new task and take the scrapbook home.

IX. Does the Child's Work Lack Accuracy and Neatness?

A. *Is the child's work inaccurate?*

126. If the child's work reaches a predetermined level of accuracy, allow him to be a "foreman" and help other children with their work.

127. Have the child verbalize each math problem before writing the answer (Lovitt & Curtiss, 1968).

128. Allow children to go to their play area only when their writing reaches a reasonable standard of accuracy (Salzberg, Wheeler, Devar, & Hopkins, 1971).

129. For each day's assignment, compute percent correct. Have the child plot his percent correct on a graph each day.

130. Divide the class into two "teams." Compute the average percent on the assigned work for each team. Designate the team with the greatest accuracy the "Eagles" and let each member of the team wear an Eagle badge for the day. Allow the Eagles to choose the game to be played during a special ten minute recess.

B. *Is the child's work done sloppily?*

131. State specific criteria for neatness (e.g., all letters formed on the line, heading in the proper place on the paper, no numerals touching each other, etc.). Post papers which approximate the criteria under a heading on the bulletin board. Gradually increase the standard for posting work and add additional criteria.

132. Establish a level of neatness and accuracy for completed work. Praise the child for meeting the criterion and allow him to engage in a favorite activity immediately. If the criterion is not met, do not allow the child to engage in the activity. Set the criterion slightly above the child's usual level of performance and gradually require better work (Hopkins, Schutte, & Garton, 1971).

133. If a child improves the neatness of his work, allow him to be a "secretary" and write "messages" which you dictate to him. These may be complimentary comments on the work of other pupils, notes to the principal or other teachers, letters ordering materials, or a complimentary note to his parents.

134. Do not allow the child to use a pen for any work until he meets a reasonable standard of neatness. Then allow him to use a pen (or a special pen which you provide) unless the neatness of his work deteriorates.

X. Does the Child Avoid Group Participation?

A. *Does the child respond infrequently in class?*

135. Ask several class members to give positive feedback (smile, make a complimentary comment) to the child whenever he makes a response in class. It is important

that the class members be taken into your confidence and that they are liked by the child who seldom responds.

136. If a child responds well in the presence of one other pupil, plan activities in which he has ample opportunity to do so. Then add a second peer to the group, later a third, and so on, until the group approximates the entire class.

137. Begin by asking simple questions that require only a yes or no answer (e.g., "Are you ready to go to recess?"). Don't allow the child to engage in the activity until he answers the question. When a one-word response is firmly established, gradually require two words, then three, then a phrase, and eventually a complete sentence.

138. Have the child record the number of times he volunteers an answer in class and plot the results on a graph. Check the reliability of his record by occasionally counting his behavior over a given period of time (Gallagher, 1971).

139. Frequently send the child on errands which require that he talk to someone (e.g., deliver messages, request materials, make announcements, etc.).

140. See also the suggestions in Chapter 10, Oral Language.

B. *Does the child resist cooperation with peers in group work?*

141. Make the child a group leader and assist him, if necessary, in obtaining the cooperation of his peers. Praise him for approximations of good leadership. Gradually introduce situations in which he must cooperate with another group member who is a temporary leader.

142. Teach the child specific group skills (e.g., listening to others, contributing suggestions, offering help) in a role-playing situation. Record his cooperative behaviors in actual group situations and let him plot them on a chart. If necessary, begin by planning situations in which he must work cooperatively with only one other child and gradually increase the size of the group.

143. Ignore the child when he is not cooperating with his group (except to stop destructive behavior) and give

him positive physical contact and praise for successive approximations of cooperation. Cue his peers to respond to him in the same way. Reward the entire group with praise when the child is cooperating.

Potential
Reinforcers

Listed on the following pages are some activities that may serve as reinforcers for children. It must be remembered that for any given child, a specific activity may or may not be a reinforcer. Additional lists of potential reinforcers may be found in Madsen and Madsen (1970) and Gallagher (1971).

1. Helping in the cafeteria
2. Assisting the custodian
3. Cleaning the erasers
4. Erasing the chalkboard
5. Using colored chalk
6. Watering the plants
7. Leading the Pledge of Allegiance
8. Decorating the bulletin board
9. Leading the line to recess or the lunchroom
10. Using a typewriter
11. Running the ditto machine
12. Stapling papers together
13. Feeding the fish or animals
14. Giving a message over the intercom
15. Writing and directing a play
16. Picking up litter on the school grounds
17. Cleaning the teacher's desk
18. Taking the class roll
19. Carrying messages to other teachers
20. Holding the door during a fire drill
21. Serving as secretary for class meetings
22. Raising or lowering the flag
23. Emptying the wastebasket
24. Carrying the wastebasket while other children clean out their desks
25. Distributing and collecting materials
26. Using an overhead projector
27. Operating a slide, filmstrip, or movie projector
28. Recording his own behavior on a graph

29. Writing with a pen or colored pencils
30. Correcting papers
31. Teaching another child
32. Playing checkers, chess, Sorry, tiddlywinks or other table games
33. Choosing a game to play
34. Being captain of a team
35. Working with clay
36. Doing "special," "the hardest," or "impossible" teacher-made arithmetic problems
37. Reading the newspaper
38. Reading or drawing a road map
39. Listening to the radio with an earplug
40. Arm wrestling
41. Reading or writing poetry
42. Learning a "magic" trick
43. Lighting or blowing out a candle
44. Being allowed to move desks
45. Sitting beside a friend
46. Going to the library
47. Helping the librarian
48. Writing to the author of a favorite book
49. Looking at a globe
50. Making or flying a kite
51. Popping corn
52. Making a puppet
53. Carrying the ball or bat to recess
54. Visiting with the principal
55. Making a book
56. Recording time taken to do a task
57. Having a spelling bee
58. Doing a science experiment
59. Telling the teacher when it is time to go to lunch
60. Sharpening the teacher's pencils
61. Opening the teacher's mail
62. Sitting next to the teacher at lunch
63. Doing crossword puzzles or math puzzles
64. Sweeping the floor of the classroom
65. Weighing or measuring various objects in the classroom
66. Reading a wall map
67. Giving a spelling test
68. Adjusting the window shades
69. Sewing
70. Having an arithmetic contest at the chalkboard

ADDITIONAL
READINGS

Books

Ackerman, J. M. *Operant conditioning techniques for the classroom teacher.* Glenview, Ill.: Scott, Foresman, 1972.

Becker, W. C., ed. *An empirical basis for change in education.* Chicago: Science Research Associates, 1971.

Becker, W. C., Engelmann, S., & Thomas, D. R. *Teaching: a course in applied psychology.* Chicago: Science Research Associates, 1971.

Blackman, G. J., & Silberman, A. *Modification of child behavior.* Belmont, Calif.: Wadsworth, 1971.

Bradfield, R. H., ed. *Behavior modification: The human effort.* San Rafael, Calif.: Dimensions, 1970.

Buckley, N. K., & Walker, H. M. *Modifying classroom behavior.* Champaign, Ill.: Research Press, 1970.

Carter, R. D. *Help! These kids are driving me crazy.* Champaign, Ill.: Research Press, 1971.

Clarizio, H. F. *Toward positive classroom discipline.* New York: John Wiley, 1972.

Fargo, G. A., Behrns, C., & Nolen, P. eds. *Behavior modification in the classroom.* Belmont, Calif.: Wadsworth, 1970.

Gallagher, P. A. *Positive classroom performance: Techniques for changing behavior.* Denver, Colo.: Love Publishing Co., 1971.

Gnagey, W. J. *The psychology of discipline in the classroom.* New York: Macmillan, 1968.

Hall, R. V. *Managing behavior.* Lawrence, Kan.: H & H Enterprises, 1971.

Haring, N. G. *Attending and responding.* San Rafael, Calif.: Dimensions, 1968.

Harris, M. B., ed. *Classroom uses of behavior modification.* Columbus, Ohio: Charles E. Merrill, 1972.

Homme, L. *How to use contingency contracting in the classroom.* Champaign, Ill.: Research Press, 1969.

Madsen, C. H., & Madsen, C. K. *Teaching/Discipline.* Boston: Allyn & Bacon, 1970.

Meacham, M. L., & Wiesen, A. E. *Changing classroom behavior: A manual for precision teaching.* Scranton, Pa.: International Textbook Company, 1969.

Mikulas, W. L. *Behavior modification: An overview.* New York: Harper & Row, 1972.

Neisworth, J. T., Deno, S. L., & Jenkins, J. R. *Student motivation and classroom management: A behavioristic approach.* Lemont, Pa.: Behavior Technics, 1969.

Patterson, G. R., & Gullion, M. E. *Living with children: New methods for parents and teachers.* Champaign, Ill.: Research Press, 1968.

Phillips, E. L. "Problems in educating emotionally disturbed children." In N. G. Haring & R. L. Schiefelbush, eds. *Methods in special education.* New York: McGraw-Hill, 1967.

Stainback, W. C., Payne, J. S., Stainback, S. B., & Payne, R. A. *Establishing a token economy in the classroom.* Columbus, Ohio: Charles E. Merrill, 1973.

Stephens, T. M. *Directive teaching of children with learning and behavioral disorders.* Columbus, Ohio: Charles E. Merrill, 1970.

Sulzer, B., & Mager, G. R. *Behavior-modification procedures for school personnel.* Hinsdale, Ill.: Dryden Press, 1972.

Tharp, R. G., & Wetzel, R. J. *Behavior modification in the natural environment.* New York: Academic Press, 1969.

Zifferblatt, S. M. *You can help your child improve study and homework behaviors.* Champaign, Ill.: Research Press, 1970.

Journals

Exceptional Children 37, no. 2 (October 1970).

Teaching Exceptional Children 3, no. 3 (Spring 1971).

Educational Technology 11, no. 4 (April 1971).

Journal of Applied Behavior Analysis (all issues).

7

Visual-Motor Problems

The concept of learning readiness is a complex and controversial topic (Smith, 1969b). During the last few years, increased attention has been given to the role of motor development and readiness for learning. Theories and models proposed by Barsch (1965, 1967, 1968), Delacato (1966), Getman (1965), and Kephart (1963, 1967, 1971) have had wide impact and appeal to individuals in many disciplines concerned with children experiencing learning problems.

Our attention, in this chapter, is focused upon visual-motor skills. As one aspect of total perceptual-motor development, visual-motor processes are considered crucial to future academic learning. The teacher must be particularly concerned with two basic questions:

1. What motor skill deficiences prevent the child from succeeding academically?
2. What visual-perceptual problems interfere with the child's learning?

Diagnosis

Teacher Observation

The alert classroom teacher will be able to expertly use observational methods as an important source of diagnostic information. Chaney and Kephart (1968) advise the teacher to "look for a pattern of difficulties and try to relate that which is observed to the overall problem" (p.42). More specifically, Smith (1969b) suggests the following as important considerations:

(1) how the child holds his pencil and the manner in which he draws and writes;
(2) how well he can copy and trace;
(3) the technique which he uses to form numerals and letters;
(4) whether a consistent pattern of reversals is evidenced;
(5) how well he organizes materials for play and work;
(6) how well he can move about the room without bumping into or tipping over objects;
(7) how well he can identify and separate foreground objects from the background;
(8) the degree to which discrimination among sizes, shapes, and colors is a problem;
(9) how well the child can accomplish a task that requires a certain sequence of activities; and
(10) whether objects in space appear confusing to him (p.62).

Detailed observational checklists for use in the regular classroom have also been developed by Chaney and Kephart (1968).

Informal Assessment

Many of the teaching suggestions that are subsequently listed under specific headings can be used as informal procedures to evaluate particular visual-motor skills. The child's performance serves as a measure of skill development within a certain area. Careful and precise utilization of informal tests provides the teacher with exacting information that can be used in planning an instructional program.

Formal Tests

A number of formal evaluative devices are also available for the assessment of visual-motor skills. The following are among the more widely used formal tests in this area: *Purdue Perceptual Motor Survey* (Roach & Kephart, 1966), *Southern California Test Battery for Assessment of Dysfunction* (Ayres, 1969), *Marianne Frostig Developmental Test of Visual Perception* (Frostig, Lefever, & Whittlesey, 1964), *Lincoln - Oseretsky Tests of Motor Proficiency* (1965), and the *Bender Visual-Motor Gestalt Test* (Bender, 1938; Koppitz, 1964). Most of these tests require specialized training for proper administration. However, classroom teachers should be encouraged to become familiar with these tests since the results, in most cases, are directly applicable to classroom instruction.

The teaching suggestions which follow are not organized to represent the tenets of any particular theory or model. The activities are organized to provide the teacher with a sampling of suggestions for developing visual-motor skills.

<h3 style="text-align:center">General
Movement Patterns</h3>

The child with deficient motor skills may appear clumsy and awkward in basic movement patterns. Overcoming motor problems involves developing:

1. Adequate gross motor skills
2. The ability to maintain balance and move rhythmically
3. Body image and body awareness
4. Lateral consistency in body orientation
5. Directional orientation
6. Adequate fine motor skills

Diagnostic questions and teaching suggestions for remediating general movement difficulties are listed below.

I. Has the Child Mastered Skills Necessary for Adequate Movement Patterns?

A. *Does the child have difficulty with gross motor movements?*

1. Have children practice various walking movements including walking freely forward, backward, sideward, zigzag, on tiptoes, on heels, with legs stiff, on a straight line, etc.
2. Have the child practice various running movements including running in place, around and between objects, in slow motion, and following another child.

Also, have the child run and stop on signal or change directions on signal.

3. Have the child practice jumping, hopping, and leaping across lines, forward, for height, for distance, with partners, over hurdles, and as quietly as possible.

4. Teach the child to skip as high off the ground as possible, in narrow areas, backwards, in a square or circle, and while clapping hands.[1]

5. Have the child work on throwing and catching a ball by throwing the ball back and forth with a partner using a push pass. Later, add the over-the-head toss and the underhand toss. Have the child bounce the ball before he throws it or try to throw the ball into a basket.

6. Provide the child with a number of tires to jump in and out of, to leap over, to run around, to walk on the rim, or to be used in an obstacle course.

7. Many of the balance beam suggestions discussed in activity #21 may be used to develop gross motor skills.

8. Have the child practice motor movements on the trampoline or skateboard. Activities involving these devices should be closely supervised and kept simple until the child becomes more skillful in gross motor movements.

9. Use "training" steps so the child can practice going up and down steps. Hackett and Jensen (1966) suggest making steps one foot deep and ten feet wide. They also provide additional suggestions for constructing training steps.

10. Use "Simon Says" and "Jumping Jacks" games so the child can practice various movement skills such as running, hopping, jumping, walking, throwing, etc.

11. The AAHPER Youth Fitness Test (President's Council on Physical Fitness, 1967) can be used as a guide to developing overall gross motor movements. The test includes the following seven skills:
    a. *Pull-up:* for judging arm and shoulder girdle strength.
    b. *Sit-up:* for judging efficiency of abdominal and hip flexor muscles.
    c. *Shuttle run:* for judging speed and change of direction.

    d. *Standing broad jump:* for judging explosive muscle power of leg extensors.

    e. *Fifty-yard dash:* for judging speed.

    f. *Softball throw for distance:* for judging skill and coordination.

    g. *Six hundred-yard run-walk:* for judging cardiovascular efficiency.

B. *Does the child have difficulty with balance and rhythm?*

12. Use rhythm records[2] to teach children to walk, run, hop, and skip to the beat of the music. Also, use rhythm band instruments to teach different beats.

13. Use the trampoline to develop balance. Have the child learn to sit and bounce on his seat before bouncing on his feet. Gradually, have the child bounce straight by bending his knees and thrusting against the bed with his feet. Be sure to have adequate protection on all four sides of the trampoline. Allow only one child on the trampoline at a time.

14. Have the child learn to jump rope in rhythm while listening to a record or according to a particular beat or chant sung by the children. Use different types of rope turning (e.g. *cradle,* in which the rope is swung back and forth as a pendulum; *back turns,* in which the rope is moved away from the jumper at the bottom of the turn).

15. Teach the child some of the following stunts.[3]
Raggedy Ann. Walk like a rag doll with very relaxed head, body, and arms.
Elevator. Stoop slowly to a three-quarter squat position. Keep body and head erect throughout with the arms remaining at the sides.
Bear Walk. Assume all-fours position. Walk forward slowly, rolling from side to side, moving right arm and leg, then left arm and leg.
Leg Roll. Lie flat on back, arms extended over head, legs straight, feet together. Slowly roll over and over on mat without using arms or elbows to propel body.
Heel-toe-Walk. Walk forward, touching heel to toe on each step. Gradually build up speed with practice.

16. Teach the child to bounce a ball to a rhythmic beat. Bouncing is taught first with two hands and then with one. Walking while bouncing should also be practiced, along with bouncing the ball to a partner.

17. Use hopping on one foot, hopping on two feet, and skipping in a variety of patterns. Alternate hops forward, backward, and sideward. Hop twice on the right foot, twice on the left, etc.; hop twice on the right foot, once on the left, etc.; and skip twice, hop once, etc.

18. Valett (1967) suggests setting the metronome at a slow speed or using bongo drums, alternating simple beats, to teach children to walk rhythmically.

19. Have relays where each child lines up in a row and at the signal raises the ball over his head and passes it to the player behind him. Each player repeats the action until the last person in line receives the ball. He runs with the ball to the front of the line and begins the overhead passing. This continues until the first player heads the line again.

20. Teach the child to use rhythm in hitting ping-pong or tennis balls. Gradually encourage the children to use the skills in actually playing these games.

21. Have the child walk on a balance beam. Chaney & Kephart (1968) list sixty-nine variations for balance-beam walking, including walking forward with hands on hips, walking the beam sideward with eyes closed, and walking backward with an eraser balanced on top of the head. They suggest a standard beam size of 2" X 4" X 10' with supports which prevent the board from tipping over. As children improve in balancing skills, the width of the beam should be narrower.

22. Prepare an obstacle course composed of chairs, tables, tires, balance beams, and hoops. Have the child move through the course in many different positions including crawling, walking, running, hopping, and jumping.

C. *Does the child have difficulty with body image and awareness?*

23. Assume different poses involving the entire body and have the child imitate the position. Slowly change positions and gradually speed up the tempo. Children can also take turns in assuming different poses.

24. Touch different parts of the body and have the children imitate you. Have the children call out the names of body parts as they touch a given part. In-

clude identification of the head, shoulders, ankles, hips, elbows, back, wrists, etc.

25. Have children lie on the floor with their eyes closed. Ask the child to slowly raise different parts of the body off the floor.

26. Chaney & Kephart (1968) suggest sticking small pieces of gummed paper on various body parts and having the child locate and remove them or hiding parts of the body with a towel or sand and having the child uncover them.

27. Play "Hoky Poky" with the children. Have them stand in a circle and give the following directions:

    "Put your left arm in."
    "Take your left arm out."
    "Put your left arm in and shake it all about."
    "Put your right foot in."
    "Take your right foot out."
    "Put your right foot in and shake it all about."

28. Lerner (1971) suggests having children pantomime actions of bus drivers driving a bus, policemen directing traffic, etc., or having the child look at pictures of people and tell whether the person is happy, sad, etc.

29. Have children draw around parts of themselves (e.g., fingers, foot, etc.) or trace an outline around another child. Ask the child to draw in body and facial parts.

30. Provide the child with puzzles of people or animals to put together. Initially have the child replace just certain body parts and eventually permit the child to work on the entire puzzle.

31. Have the child step, walk, or run in empty space. Gradually have the child control his movement by jumping or stepping into hoops on the ground (Hackett & Jensen, 1966).

32. Play "Simon Says" with the children. Have the child follow different commands such as "Simon says, touch your knee," or "Simon says, close your eyes and touch your ears." Allow a child to be the leader of this game.

33. Have the child lie flat on his back on the floor with his arms at his sides and his feet together. Ask the child to play *Angels-in-the-Snow* by moving his feet apart as far as possible with knees stiff. Have the child bring his feet together by clicking his heels. Arms are simi-

larly moved. Kephart (1971) further explains a number of variations of this activity.

34. Provide children with clay to model human figures. Clay modeling can be done initially as a group exercise.

35. Prepare pictures of humans with different body parts missing. Ask the child to tell what is missing or have him draw in the missing part.

D. *Does the child have difficulty with laterality (complete motor awareness of the two sides of the body)?*

36. Have the child use the balance beam as suggested by Chaney and Kephart (1968). Use a variety of activities in working with the balance beam including forward, backward, and sideward.

37. Provide the child with climbing apparatus on which he can coordinate the use of both hands and legs in climbing. Climb ladders, jungle gyms, hand bars, etc.

38. Have the child practice throwing, catching, and kicking through various games involving the use of large balls. Kickball and soccer are particularly good games for developing these skills.

39. Play darts, archery, and target shooting to develop eye dominance. Encourage the child to sight the target with his dominant eye (Valett, 1967).

40. The trampoline teaching suggestions described in activity #13 help to develop total body control and balance.

41. Have the child engage in a variety of head, shoulder, trunk, arm, and leg differentiation exercises. Benyon (1969) lists a number of suggestions for each of these areas.

42. Have the child practice creeping by extending the arm and leg in various combinations. Creep on the floor, up and down stairs, around and over objects, and through tunnels.

43. Abernethy, Cowley, Gillard, and Whiteside (1970) present a wide range of suitable activities for laterality difficulties. They include individual, partner, and group activities to be used with or without equipment.

44. Draw footprints on the floor and have the child place his feet on the prints and follow the direction of the

footprints. Gradually reduce the space left between footprints.

E. *Does the child have difficulty with directionality (right-left, up-down, forward-backward, etc.)?*

45. Prepare a series of maze puzzles. Ask the child to verbalize the directions that he takes with his pencil.
46. Call out or have the child call out commands to the class. For example:

> "Bob, stand *by* the door."
> "Ben, crawl *through* the hoop."
> "Mary, walk *to the right side* of Jeff's desk."

47. Put a mark (e.g., removable paint, masking tape, etc.) on the hand or foot of the side to be taught. Give directions or play "Simon Says" directing the child to raise certain body parts involving right and left, up and down, front and back, etc.
48. Prepare a worksheet of sample pictures with instructions to follow. For example:

> "Put a line *under* the house."
> "Put an X *on* the apple."
> "Put a circle *around* the boy."

49. Have the children sort and identify right and left boots, shoes, gloves, hand outlines, etc. (Valett, 1967).
50. Have two children face each other with one calling out directions such as "Clap left hands," or "Touch fingers." The other child follows the directions (Wedemeyer & Cejka, 1970).
51. Provide on the child himself a cue for right-left such as a ring on the left hand or a watch on the right arm (Johnson & Myklebust, 1967). Freckles or other marks on the hands also serve as right-left reminders.
52. Construct on paper a large map of a town. Have the child guide toy cars on the roads verbalizing turns and directions. Give the child some specific directions to follow on the map. Have him guide the car to the final destination using the directions given to him.
53. Provide the child with a pegboard and a number of different pegs. Direct the child in placing the pegs in the pegboard by providing specific directions. For example:

"Put the green peg *over* the blue peg."
"Put the red peg to the *left* of the brown peg."
"Put the orange peg *under* the yellow peg."

54. Play games in which the child closes or covers his eyes. Make various sounds in different parts of the room and ask the child to identify the direction of the sound.

55. Valett (1967) suggests teaching map directions by marking the sides of the room North, South, East and West. Play games where children place themselves according to map directions such as "Rose, go to the north of John" or "Gertrude, stand to the west of Vin."

56. Prepare a scrapbook of pictures that illustrate position words such as *in, out, above, below, under, on, up, down,* etc. Ask the children to find pictures in magazines that illustrate these words.

57. Use red and green margin markers to emphasize left-right progression or use masking tape to provide a tactile clue for letter placement in writing exercises.

58. The obstacle course described in activity #22 can be used to develop understanding of position words such as *under, over, in, out,* etc.

F. *Does the child have difficulty with fine motor movements?*

59. Have the child weave boot laces or yarn through picture lacing boards. Lerner (1971) suggests making the lacing boards from a cardboard punched with holes or a pegboard with a design or picture made on the board.

60. Ask the child to sort beads according to color, size, or shape. Provide the child with a pattern to duplicate with beads or ask the child to create his own pattern.

61. Provide the child with model clay to manipulate. Ask the child to mould particular objects (e.g. balls, fruits, etc.) or have the child create his own figures.

62. Have the child fold a paper following a step-by-step procedure after observing the teacher. Start with simple patterns and repeat the folding procedure several times. Children can eventually be asked to fold patterns from memory.

63. Provide children with zippers to zip, buckles to buckle, locks to open with keys, snaps to fasten, shoes

to lace, boots to tie and untie, and buttoning activities.

64. Manipulation of tools or kitchen utensils provides excellent fine motor practice. Screw drivers, hammers, and wrenches along with egg beaters, spoons, and cutlery can be used in a variety of situations.

65. Play various card games with the child where the child must manipulate a number of cards at one time, deal cards, and shuffle the deck.

66. Ask the child to duplicate a design or picture by providing the child with some specific pasting material (e.g., paper, felt, macaroni, toothpicks, etc.).

67. Wedemeyer & Cejka (1970) suggest fastening a large button at the center of a cardboard square and stapling loops of narrow elastic around the edge of the board. Direct the child to stretch and fasten each loop around the button.

68. Provide the child with a small wooden ladder and ask the child to "climb up" and "climb down" the ladder with one finger. The child can also "walk" the ladder while it is in a horizontal position, "stepping" from one rung to the next (Murphy, 1971).

69. Have the child throw, catch, bounce, and roll various objects such as balls, balloons, etc. Provide targets for the child, such as boxes and cans.

70. Have the child play games such as "Pick up sticks" or "Jacks," both of which require finger dexterity.

71. Encourage the child to make letters in the air during the beginning stages of writing. Movements in letter formation should be gross and gradually become finer.

72. Have the child practice various strokes at the chalkboard. Make lines, triangles, squares, etc. In making circles have the child practice with one hand and two hands, both clockwise and counterclockwise (Kephart, 1971).

Visual-Perceptual
Skills

Many children with visual-perceptual problems are unable to master various academic skills such as reading and writing. Competency in visual perception is dependent upon the ability to:

1. Discriminate the constancy of form
2. Perceive objects in foreground and background and to meaningfully separate them
3. Perceive different parts of an object in relation to the observer
4. Coordinate vision with movements of the body

Diagnostic questions and teaching suggestions for remediating visual-perceptual difficulties are listed below.

II. Has the Child Mastered Skills Necessary for Adequate Visual Perception?

A. *Does the child have difficulty discriminating the constancy of form?*

73. Have the child sort objects according to *shape*. Beads, blocks, paper shapes, etc., can be used for sorting activities.
74. Use templates at the chalkboard for tracing. Eventually have the child trace smaller templates at his desk. Use circle, square, triangle, rectangle and diamond templates. Gradually lead the child to trace the form from memory.
75. Have children match manipulable shapes (made of wood, plastic, tag board, etc.) to similar shapes on a paper. Use blocks which directly match block designs on paper.
76. Provide the child with a bag full of different-sized wooden shapes. Have the child *feel* and *describe* one shape in the bag.
77. Arrange four checker patterns, three identical and one slightly different. Have the child pick out the different pattern and explain the difference. This activity may also be used with dominoes, blocks, sticks, pegs, etc., (Valett, 1967).
78. Play the game "Twenty Questions" using shapes within the room. Have one child choose an object in the room and let other children ask questions about the shape.
79. Have children toss bean bags to particular shapes. Before each toss, instruct the child to "toss the bean bag to the square holes" or "toss the bean bag to the round holes."

80. Present the child a series of identical designs, numbers, or letters with one smaller or larger than the others. Have the child choose the one that is different (Vallet, 1967).

81. Older children can match letters presented in manuscript, cursive, and typed forms. Also, ask children to identify letters or numbers presented in a variety of positions.

82. Have children match lower- and uppercase letters. This activity can be varied by having children find and cut out as many A's, M's, etc., as they can find in magazines.

83. Behrmann (1970) suggests providing children with a worksheet similar to the example below and having them circle the word that is the same as the word at the top of the column.

clock	floor	lead
cling	flute	leaf
click	flour	lead
clock	flood	leak
clear	float	lean
clean	floor	leap

84. The Frostig (1964) program provides sequentially structured activities for developing form-constancy perception.

B. *Does the child have difficulty in perceiving objects in foreground and background and in separating them?*

85. Keep the child's desk and work area as free as possible of visual stimuli. Portable study carrels often provide an effective noncluttered environment for some children.

86. Have the child sort different objects according to size, color, texture, or shape. Gradually build up the number of objects to be sorted.

87. Play games such as *Hide the Thimble* and *Huckle Buckle Beanstalk.* These group activities help a child to focus attention on a single object.

88. Place a series of red and white X's on the floor. Play

a record and have the children march around, stepping only on the red X's (Compton, 1965).

89. Have children play games to discriminate objects in a room. Ask the child to find the square objects, the wooden objects, the objects larger than a chair, etc.
90. Prepare pictures with "hidden" figures. Ask the child to find all the shoes, pencils, or cups in the picture.
91. Provide the child with a picture and ask him to point to various objects. For example:

> "Point to the *smallest* child."
> "Point to the *upstairs* window in the house."
> "Point to the girl's *earrings*."

92. Behrmann (1970) suggests having a child stand in front of the room and letting the other children study him for a short period of time. Have the child leave the room and change something (e.g., removing a belt, changing bracelets to another hand, etc.). On his return to the room, let the other children try to determine what is different.
93. Draw overlapping figures and designs for the child to visually differentiate (Valett, 1967). Acetate overlays can be placed over pictures, and the child can locate specific objects with a grease pencil or his finger.
94. Older children can be asked to find a certain sequence of letters in a word, a sequence of sentences in a paragraph, or a name in a telephone directory.
95. Underline sentences to be copied from the board with colored chalk and place a crayon line of corresponding color on the paper (Compton, 1965).
96. The Frostig (1964) program includes a variety of exercises that can be used in developing figure-ground perception.

C. *Does the child have difficulty with spatial perception?*

97. Draw lines on the floor to represent a road. Ask the child to walk *across* it, *along* it, *beside* it, down the *middle,* etc.
98. Have the child stand, sit, or lie *on, in, under,* in *front* of, *behind,* and *beside* various objects. Have the child verbalize these positions as he performs the action.
99. Use toy garages, houses, farms, etc., to have the child

manipulate objects upon command. For example, ask the child to:

"Put the car *in* the garage."
"Put the doll *into* the bed."
"Place the truck at the *back* of the house."

100. Provide the child with a block design with blocks in specific patterns. Have the child duplicate the design exactly.

101. Instruct the child in building simple projects using Lincoln Logs, tinker-toys, and erector sets. Have the child build various models using model building kits.

102. Present the child with various geometric forms (e.g., cones, cubes, cylinders, pyramids, etc.). Have the child feel and build spontaneous structures using the forms (Valett, 1967).

103. Present the child with a design made of checkers on one half of a checkerboard. Have the child duplicate the design on the other half of the board.

104. Give the child dot-to-dot puzzles to complete. The puzzles should become increasingly more difficult. Have the children develop their own dot-to-dot puzzles for other children to complete.

105. Provide the child with scrambled sets of words and sentences to unscramble. Also, give the child a list of words all spelled correctly except one. Ask the child to circle the misspelled word.

106. Have the child build words by using link or anagram letters, or cut flash strip sentences into separate words and have the child rebuild the sentence (Compton, 1965). Children may also print words by using a rubber stamp.

107. Have children locate specific positions on maps and globes. Give each child a road map and ask them to draw a line from one city to another using the shortest route possible.

108. The *Fairbanks-Robinson Program of Perceptual-Motor Development*[4] offers a comprehensive list of activities emphasizing a developmental approach to spatial relationships.

D. *Does the child appropriately coordinate eye movements with hand movements?*

109. Have the child participate in physical activities such

as bean bag games, ball throwing, and rolling a hoop.

110. Give the child simple dot-to-dot puzzles to complete. Initially dots may be connected at the chalkboard. Later dot-to-dot worksheets may be assigned as seatwork.

111. Have the child copy various designs from the chalkboard. Gradually increase the complexity of the design. This activity may be varied by having the child copy a design from a card at his desk.

112. Practice writing vertical, horizontal, diagonal, and curved lines at the chalkboard, at the painting easel, on writing paper, and in the air. These strokes can also be practiced in sand, finger paint, or clay.

113. Give the child pictures, stencils, and templates to trace. Ask the child to color and cut the traced copy.

114. Ask the child to clip clothespins onto a line or box. Keep a graph showing the child's progress over a period of time.

115. Provide activities that involve cutting with scissors. Simple straight lines should be cut first, followed by slanted and curved lines. The double-handed scissors[5] may be needed for the child with severe difficulties in this area.

116. Provide the child with a hammer to pound pegs into holes, nails into boards, or nails into various designs.

117. Give the child a needle to thread or have the child sew with yarn to complete various designs. Small weaving looms can be used to make pot holders, etc.

118. Have the child play dominoes, darts, marbles, or checkers to develop eye-hand coordination.

119. Direct the child to use tongs or tweezers to pick up a series of objects (beads, pencils, etc.) and place them in a small-necked bottle or a box with a small hole at the top (Wedemeyer & Cejka, 1970).

120. Have the child play the game of jacks. Start with a larger ball and work initially with only one jack. Gradually, increase the number of jacks and reduce the size of the ball.

121. Many of the teaching suggestions for fine motor skills (see activities #59 through #72) can be used for developing eye-hand coordination because of the close association between these two skills.

122. Suspend a ball from the ceiling with elastic. Have the

child swing the ball to a specified target within the room.

NOTES

[1]See Abernethy, Cowley, Gillard, & Whiteside (1970); Chaney & Kephart (1968); Hackett & Jensen (1966); and Lerner (1971) for additional locomotor movement teaching suggestions.

[2]A variety of LP rhythm records may be obtained from Educational Activities, Inc., Box 392, Freeport, Long Island, New York 11520.

[3]Further stunts and games are discussed in Neilson (1956).

[4]The Fairbanks-Robinson program may be obtained from Teaching Resources, 100 Boylston Street, Boston, Massachusetts 02116.

[5]Double-handed scissors may be obtained from Developmental Learning Materials, 7440 North Natchez Avenue, Niles, Illinois 60648.

ADDITIONAL
READINGS

Abernethy, K., Cowley, J., Gillard, H. & Whiteside, J. *Jumping up and down.* San Rafael, Calif.: Academic Therapy Publications, 1970.

Arena, J. I., ed. *Teaching through sensory-motor experiences.* San Rafael, Calif.: Academic Therapy Publications, 1969.

Barsch, R. H. *A movigenic curriculum.* Madison, Wisc.: Department of Public Instruction, Bureau for the Handicapped, 1965.

Barsch, R. H. *Achieving perceptual-motor efficiency,* Vol. 1. Seattle: Special Child Publications, 1967.

Barsch, R. H. *Enriching perception and cognition,* Vol. 2. Seattle: Special Child Publications, 1968.

Behrmann, P. *Activities for developing visual-perception.* San Rafael, Calif.: Academic Therapy Publications, 1970.

Buktenica, N. A. *Visual learning.* San Rafael, Calif.: Dimensions, 1968.

Bush, W. J., & Giles, M. T. *Aids to psycholinguistic teaching.* Columbus, Ohio: Charles E. Merrill, 1969.

Chaney, C. M., & Kephart, N. C. *Motoric aids to perceptual training.* Columbus, Ohio: Charles E. Merrill, 1968.

Cratty, B. J. *Developmental sequences of perceptual-motor tasks.* Freeport, Long Island, N. Y.: Educational Activities, Inc., 1967.

Cratty, B. J. *Learning and playing.* Freeport, Long Island, N. Y.: Educational Activities, Inc.

Delacato, C. H. *The treatment and prevention of reading problems.* Springfield, Ill.: Charles C. Thomas, 1959.

Delacato, C. H. *Neurological organization and reading.* Springfield, Ill.: Charles C. Thomas, 1966.

Frostig, M., & Horne, D. *The Frostig program for the development of visual perception: Teacher's guide.* Chicago: Follett, 1968.

Getman, G. N. The visuomotor complex in the acquisition of learning skills. In J. Hellmuth, ed., *Learning disorders,* Vol. 1. Seattle: Special Child Publications, 1965, pp. 49–76.

Getman, G. N., Kane, E. R., & McKee, G. W. *Developing learning readiness programs.* Manchester, Mo.: McGraw-Hill, 1968.

Hackett, L. C., & Jenson, R. C. *A guide to movement exploration.* Palo Alto, Calif.: Peek Publications, 1967.

Kephart, N. C. *The brain-injured child in the classroom.* Chicago: National Society for Crippled Children and Adults, 1963.

Kephart, N. C. Perceptual-motor aspects of learning disabilities. In E. Frierson & W. Barbe, eds. *Educating children with learning disabilities.* New York: Appleton-Century-Crofts, 1967, pp. 405–13.

Kephart, N. C. *Learning disability: An educational adventure.* West Lafayette, Ind.: Kappa Delta Pi Press, 1968.

Kephart, N. C. *The slow learner in the classroom.* 2nd ed. Columbus, Ohio: Charles E. Merrill, 1971.

Kirshner, A. J. *Training that makes sense.* San Rafael, Calif.: Academic Therapy Publications, 1972.

Lerner, J. W. *Children with learning disabilities.* Boston: Houghton Mifflin, 1971.

Magdol, M. S. *Perceptual training in the kindergarten.* San Rafael, Calif.: Academic Therapy Publications, 1971.

Murphy, P. *A special way for the special child in the regular classroom.* San Rafael, Calif.: Academic Therapy Publications, 1971.

Neilson, N. P. *Physical education for elementary schools.* New York: Ronald Press, 1956.

Piaget, J. *The origins of intelligence in children.* New York: International Universities Press, 1952.

Schurr, E. *Movement experiences for children.* New York: Appleton-Century-Crofts, 1967.

Valett, R. E. *The remediation of learning disabilities.* Palo Alto, Calif.: Fearon Publishers, 1967.

Van Witsen, B. *Perceptual training activities handbook.* New York: Columbia University Press, 1967.

Wedemeyer, A., & Cejka, J. *Creative ideas for teaching exceptional children.* Denver: Love Publishing Co., 1970.

8

Specific Reading Problems

Difficulties in learning to read have been recognized as the most important single cause of school failure (Strang, 1969). Many children who encounter reading difficulties experience academic problems in other areas of the curriculum. Smith (1968) regards reading as "the most significant common denominator for adequate achievement" in areas such as arithmetic, communication, and social and personal adjustment (p.129).

The skills involved in learning to read adequately are many and complex. For some children they are a confusing puzzle. Teachers of children with reading problems must be aware of the specific skills with which particular children are experiencing difficulties. They must also be aware of methods and materials to alleviate the reading problem. The responsibility for knowing the needs and strengths of each child in the class rests with the classroom teacher.

Among the general reading problems with which the teacher must be concerned, the following are most basic:

1. What visual skills in reading prevent the child from reading adequately?
2. What auditory skills in reading prevent the child from reading adequately?
3. Does the child comprehend the material that he reads?

Diagnosis

A substantial amount of diagnostic data can and should be obtained by the classroom teacher. As suggested in Chapter 3, diagnostic evaluation involves teacher observation, informal assessment, and formal tests. Appropriate instruction stems from the information obtained during each level of diagnosis.

Teacher Observation

Daily observations and contacts with individual children can provide valuable diagnostic information. Little is required in the way of diagnostic materials. Moreover, the *normal* classroom setting provides the teacher with the opportunity to clearly observe the characteristic behavior of individual children in many different instructional situations. Oral reading, silent reading, group discussion of reading material, seatwork activity, and selection of library books are but a few of the situations in which teachers can informally obtain diagnostic data.

Essentially, the teacher must seek answers to the following questions:

1. How does the child approach reading tasks?
2. How does the child attack unfamiliar and difficult words?
3. How does the child respond to instructional help?
4. How does the child feel about reading?
5. What are the child's specific difficulties?
6. What progress is the child making?
7. What are the child's reading interests?
8. What is the child's reading potential?
9. What conditions are causing the child's reading difficulty?
10. Which of these conditions can be modified?[1]

Informal Assessment

Numerous informal tests may be used to assess specific skill development. Informal tests are usually teacher made and, therefore, are inexpensive, flexible, rapidly administered, and relatively easy to construct. Many informal tests may be used as a supplement to standardized tests. Informal tests combine the diagnostic values of observation with content that is closely geared to instruction. In addition to the examples provided in Chapter 3, further informal tests may be found in Englemann (1969), Lerner (1971), and Wallen (1972).

Formal Tests

Many standardized reading tests are available for use with those children for whom additional information is required. An important consideration in selecting a standardized test is the direct applicability of the information to instruction. As discussed in Chapter 3, *teachable tests* provide the classroom teacher with usable instructional data.

Della-Piana (1968) has indicated that the four major individually administered reading diagnostic batteries currently available are the Durrell (1955), Gates-McKillop (1962), Monroe (1932), and Spache (1963) tests. All of these tests provide instructional data which may be used in helping a child overcome a reading problem. However, teachers must be flexible and judicious in their use of formal tests.[2] There are indications, as stated in Chapters 3 and 5, that teachers' observations of children's day-to-day performance in reading provides the best possible basis for diagnostic teaching (Strang, 1969).

The teaching suggestions that follow are grouped according to specific skill deficiences. A number of the activities may be easily adapted for use in several skill areas.

**Visual Skills
in Reading**

Many children who have normal visual acuity experience difficulties in differentiating, interpreting, or remembering different shapes, letters, or words. Basically, children with visual skill deficiencies must learn to:

1. Discriminate sizes and shapes
2. Discriminate specific letters
3. Discriminate the directionality of specific letters
4. Remember letter names and words
5. Remember particular words learned mainly by sight
6. Recognize structural parts of words

Diagnostic questions and teaching suggestions for remediating visually oriented reading problems are listed below.

I. Has the Child learned the Visual Skills Necessary for Reading?

A. *Has the child mastered the skills prerequisite for visual discrimination of letters?*

1. Place a number of objects (cup, pencil, ruler, block, eraser, nail, etc.) in front of the child. Display a duplicate object, such as a pencil or block, and ask the child to pick up the similar object. Initially, only three or four objects should be included. As time progresses, and the child improves in this skill, increase the number of objects.

2. Display a number of buttons of different sizes (or nails, blocks, pieces of the same color paper, etc.) in front of the child. Instruct him to match the buttons according to sizes or shapes.

3. Match pictures of objects with the actual objects. Variations of this activity could include allowing the child to cut pictures from magazines to match with actual objects or matching pictures to pictures.

4. Give children various shapes of macaroni to sort. Initially, the child may group the various macaroni according to shape and place them in small boxes. Later, the macaroni may be colored and sorted according to shape and color.

5. Show the child a picture with missing parts. Direct the child to draw in the part that is omitted. Some examples include:

   a. A tree without a trunk
   b. A cup with a handle missing
   c. Faces with various parts missing (nose, ear, etc.)
   d. A child without a shoe
   e. A house without a door

   Begin by requiring the child to draw in parts to match the sample drawing. Gradually make the missing parts less obvious.

6. Display three triangles and one square. Ask the child to identify the shape that is unlike the other. Various geometric shapes may be included. As you proceed with this activity, increase the number of shapes to be discriminated. Shapes of different colors may be used after the child learns shape discriminations.

7. Encourage the child to become aware of sizes and shapes. Cut out different sizes of squares, circles, triangles, etc. Explain to the child that a square is still a square even though it might be smaller than others. This activity might be extended by having the child find all of the square shapes in a room or all of the circle shapes in a magazine.

8. Describe an object that is very familiar to the child. Ask the child to find that object among four pictures (or objects) that are presented to him. For example, "I am thinking of something that is round, that bounces up and down, and that you need to play baseball."

9. Have children complete dot-to-dot pictures of familiar objects, animals, etc. Gradually increase the detail of the pictures and ask the child to describe them.

10. Present the child with different arrangements of blocks, geometric shapes, familiar objects, etc. Ask the child to choose the one arrangement that is different from the others and to explain why. For example,

B. *Can the child discriminate among letters?*

11. Have the child match capital and lowercase letters: Aa, Mm, Pp, Bb, etc.

12. Play letter bingo with small groups of children. In this activity, cards with different letters printed on them are passed to each child. The teacher or another child covers the appropriate letter. The first child to fill a card is the winner.

13. Have children trace various letter templates and stencils.

14. Let the child use the typewriter to find specific letters. Children can be instructed to find certain letters in a given amount of time.

15. Present rows of four- or five-letter cutouts to the child. Ask the child to circle the same two letters in each row. Gradually work to finer discriminations, such as b and d, m and n, p and q, etc. This activity may be duplicated for seatwork.

16. Present letters of varying size to the child and ask him to match the same letters. A large M can be presented with a very small M, along with a medium-size, lowercase m.

17. Pictures that closely correspond to the shapes of individual letters can be presented with the letter as a memory device for children. For example, a wiggly snake can be presented with the letter S, a telephone pole with the letter T, a wheel with the letter O, etc.

18. Present children with partially completed letters and ask them to identify and/or complete them. For example, etc.

19. Show the child the alphabet with specific letters omitted. Ask the child to fill in the missing letters. For example, a b ___ d ___ f g h ___ ___ k ___ m, etc. The number of missing letters is increased as the child progresses.

20. Tape an individual alphabet to each child's desk to provide children with a quick reference and guide.

21. Dot-to-dot pictures may be used with letters. The teacher can direct this exercise by instructing the child to: "Draw a line to the letter p, now a straight line over to the letter s, down to the letter b, etc." This activity can also be planned so that the lines are drawn in the exact sequence of the alphabet.

C. *Does the child reverse letters?*

22. Have the child make an association for letters that are reversed. For example, children with a freckle on the left hand can remember that a *d* points in that direction. Likewise, children who wear a ring on one of the fingers on the right hand can associate the ring with the direction of the letter *b*.

23. Print frequently reversed letters on oak tag strips. These letters should also be outlined on tracing paper. Let the child match the tracing paper letter with the oak tag strip by placing the tracing paper over the letter.

24. Instruct the child to trace specific letters on sandpa-

per, salt trays, etc. Be sure that the child says the
name of the letter as he traces it.

25. Describe a letter and have the child find that letter
among three or four placed in front of him. For example, "I am thinking of a letter that is a straight line up
and down and another line straight across."

26. Give children words with missing letters accompanied by matching pictures. This exercise may emphasize frequently reversed letters. For example,

27. Place words that are frequently reversed on flash
cards and use them for periodic drills. Arrow cues may
be added for help. For example,

28. Place words on flash cards and present them to the
child by covering up all but the first letter. Slowly
uncover additional letters until the child correctly
pronounces the word. The activity emphasizes left-to-
right orientation. An overhead projector may be
used.

29. Present children with a stimulus word and four
choices from which to choose the matching word. For
example,

pot	otp	top	tip	pot
lap	pal	pil	lap	alp
war	row	war	raw	awr

D. *Does the child remember visual stimuli, including letters
and words?*

30. Place several articles, such as eraser, block, pencil,
chalk, etc., in front of the child. Allow the child a short
time to view them. After you have removed the
items, ask the child to recall as many of them as he
can. This activity can be varied by removing one or

two articles at a time and asking the child to tell what is missing.

31. Present the child with an uncluttered picture of an object known to him. Allow the child a short time to study the picture. After you have removed the picture, ask the child to describe what he saw.
32. Flash a picture or geometric design on a screen through an opaque or overhead projector or tachisto-scope. Instruct the child to match the flashed form with a similar form on a worksheet.
33. Present pictures with missing parts to the child and ask him to either draw in the missing part or tell which part is missing.
34. Allow children to view pegboard, marble board, or bead designs for a short period of time and then ask them to duplicate the design. Children working in pairs may also construct their own designs.
35. Encourage children to use a toy telephone to learn the telephone numbers of their friends.
36. Print letters or words on removable gummed labels on the squares of a checkerboard. Let the children play checkers but require them to name a letter or word before they make a move.
37. Paint the alphabet on a piece of oil cloth. Place the cloth on the floor and have a child walk at random from one letter to another. Ask children to reproduce the sequence. This activity may be varied by walking through letters that spell specific words. Ask children to reproduce the letter and say the word.
38. Letters or parts of words may be color cued for memory. For example in the word raining the *ing* may be color coded red.
39. Printing words with a rubber stamp set provides an interesting activity for some children. This activity calls attention to the sequence of letters.
40. Children can also work with three-dimensional letters. Encourage the child to discuss the differences among letters.
41. Cut apart cartoon strips and paste them on oak-tag. Ask children to reassemble the cartoon in the correct order.
42. Trace words and letters in any of the following media: finger painting, salt, sandpaper, felt, instant pudding, clay, or wet sand.

43. Provide children with words in a mixed-up order and ask them to arrange the letters correctly. For example, present *cat* as atc, *bag* as agb, etc.
44. Write a number of letters on the chalkboard. While the children's eyes are closed, erase one letter. When the children open their eyes, ask them to identify the missing letter. Words can also be used for this activity.
45. Give the child dotted forms to trace. Gradually reduce the number of dots so that there are only a few remaining. See if the child can remember how to make the letters or words. For example,

E. *Does the child recognize sight words?*

46. Write five sight words on the chalkboard. Read each one aloud and ask the children to close their eyes. Erase a word and ask, "What is missing?" Continue until all the words are erased. Following this, ask the children to remember the five original words and write them again on the board. See who can read the entire list.
47. Use the Language Master to teach new words or review those previously taught. Use the blank cards to program the most persistently miscalled words.
48. Prepare a tape recording of the most common sight words. Have the child listen to the tape through earphones and follow a worksheet. The teacher's voice says, "Number 1 is *guess*, Number 2 is *could*," etc. To test a child, give him a word list without numbers and let him mark the worksheet as follows: "Put number 1 in front of *guess*; Put number 2 in front of *could*"; etc. Check by using a key.
49. Duplicate a sheet with groups of words that are similar in configuration. Direct the child to circle the word you read. For example,

    1. *at* is it in
    2. see saw *sea* sip

    You may record the stimulus words in order to make use of a tape recorder with this activity.

50. Picture dictionaries can be helpful in learning words and associating meaning. Encourage children to make their own dictionaries with either magazine pictures or their own illustrations.
51. In a group of assorted words written on tag board, write all difficult sight words in red to alert the child that he must recall the word by memory.
52. With sight words on cards, a child can occasionally review words previously learned by placing the words he knows in a "Friends" pile and the troublesome words in an "Enemies" pile. Students may work in pairs.
53. Draw a baseball diamond on the chalkboard. Place sight words printed on flash cards on the chalk ledge. Label the words single, double, homerun, etc. Groups of children can play baseball by reading the words. This activity can also be adapted to football, fishing, mountain climbing, etc.
54. Tracing may be beneficial for children with poor visual memories. The child says the word as he traces it. Trace in the air, on the chalkboard, in salt trays, on large pieces of paper, etc.
55. Words can be presented to children in pairs to facilitate memory. For example, salt and pepper, bread and butter, black and white, hot and cold, etc.
56. Have the child match a stimulus word from a list of visually similar words, such as those illustrated in the following chart.

bed	bid	bad	bud	dab	bed
hop	hip	hop	bop	hup	dip
run	run	rat	run	sun	nun

This activity might be varied by calling out the stimulus word.
57. Word Bingo, similar to Letter Bingo (see #12 p. 168) may be played with small groups of children.
58. Label objects around the room and periodically review these labels with the children. Mix the labels and have a child put them in the proper place.

59. Some basic sight words are listed below (Dolch, 1953):

a	did	had	made	said	under
about	do	has	make	saw	up
after	does	have	many	say	upon
again	done	he	may	seven	us
all	don't	help	me	see	use
always	down	her	much	shall	
am	draw	here	my	she	very
an	drink	him	myself	show	
and		his		sing	walk
are		hold	never	sit	want
around	eat	hot	new	six	warm
as	eight	how	no	sleep	was
ask	every	hurt	not	small	wash
at			now	so	we
ate	fall			some	well
away	far	I		soon	where
	fast	if	of	start	which
	find	in	old	stop	white
be	first	into	on	sent	who
because	five	is	once		why
been	fly	it	one		will
before	for	its	only	take	wish
best	found		open	tell	with
better	four	jump	or	ten	work
big	from	just	our	thank	would
black	full		out	that	write
blue	funny	keep	over	the	yellow
both		kind	own	their	yes
bring	gave	know		them	you
brown	get		pick	then	your
but	give	laugh	play	there	
buy	go	let	please	these	
by	goes	light	pretty	they	
	going	like	pull	think	
call	good	little	put	this	
came	got	live		those	
can	green	long	ran	three	
carry	grow	look	read	to	
clean			red	today	
cold			ride	together	
come			right	too	
could			round	try	
cut			run	two	

F. *Does the child recognize prefixes, suffixes, and compound words?*

60. Provide the child with a list of words and direct him to circle the root (graphemic base) in each word. For

example, *sing*ing, *jumps*, *end*ed, etc. This activity may be separated for prefixes and suffixes.

61. Provide the child with a list of root words on oak-tag strips and an envelope of endings that may be added to these root words. Ask the child to list as many words as he can.

62. Give the child a series of sentences to which prefixes or suffixes must be added to complete certain words. Have the child complete each sentence. For example:

    1. Mary walk____ to the store each morning.
    2. She is ____ sure of the correct street.
    3. They are play____ in the yard.
    4. He did not ____ connect the refrigerator.

63. For older children, give a root word and a meaning of a new word. Ask them to write the new word. For example, read—to read something again (*reread*). The concentric circles described on page 180 can be made for root words and suffixes. Have the child rotate the circle and say the root words that are made.

65. Under two columns, list words that can be made into compound words. Leave a third column blank so that the child can complete the compound word.

Column A	Column B	Column C
base	ball	_____
cow	boy	_____
light	house	_____

66. The above activity may be varied by leaving blank either column A or column B, in addition to column C. Another variation could include placing a drawing in either of the first two columns.

Column A	Column B	Column C
base		_____
	boy	_____
light		_____
_____	man	mailman

67. The words utilized in the above exercises can be varied in random order. Ask the child to put together as many compound words as he can. For example,
    ball, house, flash, boy, base, light, cow, boat, etc.

68. Prepare a paragraph with missing parts of compound words. Ask the child to complete the missing parts. For example,
    John and Tom play base (ball) or (basket)ball every after (noon) on the (play) ground. (Some) times they also play (horse) shoes or play in the sand (box). In the winter, they build (snow) men and make snow (balls).

69. Children can make their own compound words. Have them provide a definition for each word they make.

Auditory Skills
in Reading

Children with auditory skill deficiencies may have normal hearing acuity. However, they experience difficulties in differentiating, synthesizing, and remembering the sounds of different letters and words. The child must learn to:

1. Discriminate among sounds
2. Discriminate initial and final letter sounds
3. Synthesize letter sounds into words
4. Remember the sounds of letters and words

Diagnostic questions and teaching suggestions for remediating auditory-based reading problems are listed below.

II. Has the Child Learned the Auditory Skills Necessary for Reading?

A. *Has the child mastered the skills prerequisite for auditory discrimination of letter sounds?*

70. Select two different sounds, such as a bell and a drum. Stand behind the child and ring the bell. Ask the child to point to the object used to make the sound. Gradually increase the number of sounds that can be discriminated. Discriminations should also become finer as the child progresses.

71. With the aid of a tape recorder, ask the child to iden- tify common sounds such as an airplane, a car, various animals and household appliances, etc. These sounds can be gradually moved to voices of familiar individu- als.

72. In working with the sounds of letters, work initially with grossly different sounds, such as /m/ and /p/, /s/ and /b/, or /a/ and /v/. Gradually work into the finer discriminations such as /v/ and /f/ or /m/ and /n/.

73. Associate a sound with a picture or with a real object. The following pictures or items are often helpful to most children (Russell and Karp, 1938):

a — apple	n — nest
b — boat	o — orange
c — cat	p — pail
d — duck	q — queen
e — egg	r — rooster
f — fox	s — sack
g — goat	t — tail
h — house	u — umbrella
i — ice cream	v — vest
j — jacks	w — wagon
k — kite	x — xylophone
l — lamp	y — yard
m — mouse	z — zebra

74. Read a word, such as "fat." Ask the child to repeat the word. Then read a list of words, and have the child clap when he hears a word that rhymes with the stimulus word.

75. The rhyming activity described above can also be used for nonrhyming words. The rules change so that the child claps when a nonrhyming word is called. For example, the teacher may use "fat" as the stimulus word, and then "mat, cat, pot, sat, dog." Gradually, the discriminations should become finer.

76. Write sounds on large pieces of paper and place them on the floor. As you say a word beginning (or ending) with a specific sound, the child must walk to the sound he has heard.

77. Read a sentence to the child with a word omitted. For example, "We play baseball with a ball and a *(bat)*." Instruct the child to change the omitted word to one that rhymes with it. Acceptable responses for this example include, "cat, mat, fat, sat, etc."

78. Give the child a box containing a number of different toy objects, such as boats, cars, plastic dishes, chalk, pencils, erasers, etc. Ask the child to select all the objects that begin with the /p/ sound. You may have five or six boxes which emphasize different sounds.

79. Give children a list of words and ask them to circle all the words which rhyme with a given stimulus word. This activity may be varied by giving the child a list of words and instructing him to list a word which rhymes with the given word.

80. Listen to commercial records which teach auditory awareness of sounds.[3]

81. Provide the child with a number of different pictures. Direct the child to match those pictures whose names rhyme. This activity may be varied by duplicating pictures for seatwork.

82. Give the child a list of rhyming words and direct him to circle the parts of the words that are alike. This activity provides a check to see if the child is aware that rhyming words have parts that are spelled similarly.

B. *Can the child discriminate initial and final sounds?*

83. Say a word, such as "sad," and require the child to provide a word which rhymes with it but has a different initial consonant.

84. Ask the children to say all the words they know that begin with a specific sound.

85. Make up nonsense sentences with the child using the same letter at the beginning of each word. Examples could include, "Bad Billy bit blueberries," or "Holy Harry has hot hands."

86. Provide children with a number of individual oak-tag cards with one sound on each card. Instruct the child to listen carefully and hold up the letter he hears at the beginning (or end) of each word.

87. Give the children two cards numbered one and two. As you say a word instruct them to listen for a specific sound and indicate whether they heard it at the be-

ginning or ending of the word by holding up card #1 or card #2.

88. Instruct children to classify a number of pictures according to initial or final sounds. Appropriately labeled boxes are helpful for this activity. Have the children place pictures with the beginning /s/ sound in one box, the beginning /f/ sound in another box, etc.

89. Give each child the same number of oak-tag cards with words written on them. Ask for all the cards that begin with a certain sound, rhyme with a word, etc. For example, ask for all the cards that "end with the same sound as *bag*." Continue to ask questions until each child's pile of cards is depleted.

90. Call out words which have the same blend in either the initial or final position in all the words. Let the child tell where he hears the blend. For example, chip, chum, charge, search, patch, march, etc.

91. Give the child the name of someone in the room. Let the child make up two descriptive words which have the same initial consonant sound. For example, prim, pretty, Paula or skinny, silly, Sam.

92. Ask children to blend different consonants to a specific word family. For example, blend initial consonants to the *"in"* family (e.g., pin, fin, tin, etc.).

C. *Can the child blend letter sounds into words?*

93. After children know specific sounds, give them three-to five-letter nonsense syllables. Ask them to blend the sounds. The syllables can become progressively longer as the child improves in this ability.

94. Ask the child to blend specific sounds to a given list of phonograms. For example, blending the /p/ sound to "at," "in," "it," "an," etc. This activity may be duplicated for seatwork or done at the chalkboard.

95. Provide the child with a picture of a specific object, such as a block. Below the picture, appears:

_____ _____ o c k

Have the child supply the missing consonant blend, either by writing in the missing part or saying it.

96. Prepare a series of three stimulus words. Pronounce one of the words in each series. Have the children listen and underline the word you pronounce (Heilman, 1968). For example:

blue	black	drum	plain	dress
blow	plank	dear	plant	dire
brake	blank	drink	party	drive

97. Have children draw a word from a box containing words with blends. The child must pronounce the word he chooses and give another word which begins with the same blend.

98. Print words with blends on oak tag and cut the word after the blend. Mix up a number of word parts and have the child sort them correctly. Gradually increase the number of words as the child succeeds with this task.

99. Make two concentric circles, one with blends and the other with phonograms. Have children rotate the circle and read the words. Circles for initial consonants can also be made.

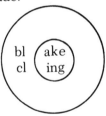

100. Give each child a large piece of paper with a blend written on it. Write a phonogram on the chalkboard and ask children to make a word with their blend and the phonogram on the chalkboard.

D. *Does the child remember sounds, including the sounds of letters and words?*

101. Tap or clap out rhythm patterns and have the child repeat the pattern.

102. Ask a child to repeat a sentence or phrase that you have said to him.

103. Present a series of verbal commands to the child. Instruct the child to follow the sequence of the commands. For example, "John, throw this paper in the wastepaper basket, then pass out these books to the boys, and then erase the chalkboard."

104. Present a series of movements to a small group of children and have them follow the sequence. For example, "Jump, hop, clap, and skip."

105. Ask a child to describe another child in the room. Using only the pertinent characteristics, draw a picture of the child. After a number of these have been completed, ask individual children to identify and describe certain pictures.

106. Play a record of a story or tell a story to a small group of children. Upon completion of the story, have the children divide a paper into equal sections and draw the events of the story in sequence.

107. Instruct the child to close his eyes. While his eyes are closed, tap some object in the room or make another sound. When the child opens his eyes, ask him to identify the sound from among three that are presented. Include sounds such as crushing paper, knocking on the door, tapping on glass, whistling, animal sounds, writing on the chalkboard, etc.

108. Prepare treasure maps for each child. Give several instructions at one time (e.g., go up the green path by the white house and follow the circular drive). Children may compete to reach the treasure.

109. Ask children to trace and write letters or manipulate three-dimensional letters as they hear the name of a letter. Feeling and noting the way the speech organs perform in making different sounds is also helpful.

110. Give children a blank piece of paper. Direct the children to perform a variety of tasks. For example, "Make a circle in the upper-right-hand corner, draw a straight line in the middle of the paper, write your name on the line, etc. This activity may be made more structured by preparing worksheets with various geometric designs and directing the children to perform specific tasks. For example, "Write the first letter of the alphabet inside the square, color in the triangle with your red crayon," etc. (The verbal directions for these activities may be placed on a tape recorder.)

111. Help children play successive addition games. For example, "I went to the zoo and saw a lion." The next child adds another animal. "I went to the zoo and saw

a lion and a tiger." Continue adding animals with
each successive child.

112. Take a walk with the children around the playground
listening, watching, and observing. Once you are
back in the classroom, have the children list by categories (e.g., animals, transportation) what they heard.
This activity can also be used on field trips, walking to
and from school, etc.

Reading
Comprehension

Johnson and Myklebust (1967) indicate that the major problem of the
child with reading difficulties is not in *understanding* what he reads,
but in *processing* printed material. Consequently, once specific visual and auditory skill deficiencies have been corrected, teachers will
often find corresponding improvement in reading comprehension.
Teaching suggestions for remediating comprehension difficulties
which persist when visual and auditory skills are adequate are listed
below.[4] Basic comprehension skills include:

1. Reading to get the main idea
2. Remembering specific details

III. Does the Child Comprehend What He Reads?

A. *Does the child get the main ideas?*

113. A basic consideration in reading comprehension is to
be sure the material is worth the effort the child will
make to read it. In addition, the reading material
should not be at a level that is too difficult for the
child.

114. Give the children a series of written true-false statements to answer. For example:

a. Cats have three legs.
b. A square has four sides.
c. Triangles have five sides.

115. Give the children a series of absurd short stories to
read. Ask them to find the absurdity. For example:

"The children put on their bathing suits. They
collected their shovels, pails, and snowballs to take
to the ocean to swim."

116. Have students read newspaper articles from which the headlines have been deleted. Students select the correct headline from a group arranged on the teacher's desk.

117. Have children read untitled stories. Upon completion of each story, request that they write an appropriate title.

118. After the children have read a story, print a list of phrases on the chalkboard. Some of the phrases should be related and others unrelated to the story. Ask the children to choose those that pertain to the reading selection.

119. Point out devices used by authors to emphasize certain passages. Emphasize chapter titles, headings, subheadings, italics, indentions, etc.

120. After reading a story, discuss it with the children, listing the main ideas in the story. Select children to illustrate specific story events with drawings. The story can be retold by rolling the drawings on a "TV" screen or overhead projector in sequence.

B. *Does the child remember specific details?*

121. After reading a story, ask the children to compose a telegram repeating the events of the story or of a certain part of the story. Limit the telegram to a specific number of words.

122. After students have read a story, distribute three or four sentences which indicate a sequence of events pertaining to the story. Have the students arrange them in proper order.

123. Ask children to read a stimulus sentence and four multiple-choice responses. Have the children select the correct multiple-choice responses. To insure exacting reading, more than one response may be correct. For example,

> Mary and John are eight-year-old twins in the third grade at Smith School.
> a. John is one year older than Mary.
> b. John and Mary go to the same school.
> c. John and Mary were probably born in the same year.
> d. Mary and John do not have any other brothers and sisters.

124. Encourage students to indicate exactly where in a particular story they first knew it was sad, funny, etc.
125. Let one child take the role of a character in a story that the class has read. The rest of the class should try to guess the identity of the characters by considering clues given to them by the impersonator.
126. Have children read a story on "how-to-do" some activity. Upon completion, ask them to perform the activity in sequence, e.g., building a kite, making soap, baking a cake, etc.
127. Distribute specific instructions on paper slips. Request children to carry out the instructions. For example, "Put all of the books in the library corner in order." or "Pass out a yellow piece of paper to each girl in the room."

NOTES

[1]These and similar questions are further discussed in Strang (1969).

[2]Further discussion of standardized tests may be found in Della-Piana (1968), Kaluger & Kolson (1969), Strang (1969), and Wilson (1967).

[3]Commercial LP records may be obtained from: Ginn and Company, 72 Fifth Ave., New York, N. Y. 10011; Mafex Associates, Inc., Box 519, Johnstown, Pa. 15707; and Scott, Foresman, & Co., 433 E. Erie St., Chicago, Ill. 60611.

[4]More detailed analysis of reading comprehension is discussed in Heilman (1972), Russell & Karp (1938), Spache & Spache (1969), and Wilson (1967).

ADDITIONAL READINGS

Arena, J. I. *Teaching educationally handicapped children.* San Rafael, Calif.: Academic Therapy Publications, 1967.

Bateman, B., ed. *Learning disorders,* Vol. 4. Seattle: Special Child Publications, 1971.

Bush, W. J., & Giles, M. T. *Aids to psycholinguistic teaching.* Columbus, Ohio: Charles E. Merrill, 1969.

Carrillo, L. W. *Informal reading-readiness experiences.* New York: Noble and Noble, 1964.

Cohen, S. A. *Teach them all to read.* New York: Random House, 1969.

Della-Piana, G. M. *Reading diagnosis and prescription: An introduction.* New York: Holt, Rinehart and Winston, 1968.

Engelmann, S. *Preventing failure in the primary grades.* Chicago: Science Research Associates, 1969.

Gillingham, A., & Stillman, B. W. *Remedial training for children with specific disability in reading, spelling, and penmanship.* Cambridge, Mass.: Educators Publishing Service, 1960.

Hall, N. A. *A handbook of remedial reading techniques for the classroom teacher.* Stevensville, Mich.: Educational Service, 1969.

Hegge, T. G., Kirk, S. A., & Kirk, W. D. *Remedial reading drills.* Ann Arbor, Mich.: George Wahr Publishing Company, 1940.

Heilman, A. W. *Principles and practices of teaching reading.* Columbus, Ohio: Charles E. Merrill, 1972.

Johnson, D. J., & Myklebust, H. R. *Learning disabilities: Educational principles and practices.* New York: Grune and Stratton, 1967.

Kaluger, G., & Kolson, C. J. *Reading and learning disabilities.* Columbus, Ohio: Charles E. Merrill, 1967.

Karnes, M. B. *Helping young children develop language skills.* Arlington, Va.: The Council for Exceptional Children, 1968.

Lowell, E. L., & Stoner, M. *Play it by ear.* Los Angeles: John Tracy Clinic, 1960.

Medlin, V. L., & Warnock, H. H. *Word making methods book.* Salt Lake City, Utah: Word Making Productions, 1958.

Orton, J. L. *A guide for teaching phonics.* Winston-Salem, N.C.: The Orton Reading Center, 1964.

Platts, M. E., Marguerite, S. R., & Shumaker, E. *Suggested activities to motivate the teaching of the language arts.* Stevensville, Mich.: Educational Service, Inc., 1960.

Russell, D. H., & Karp, E. E. *Reading aids through the grades.* New York: Teachers College Press, 1938.

Schubert, D. G., & Torgerson, T. L. *Improving reading through individualized correction.* Dubuque, Iowa: William C. Brown, 1968.

Spache, G. D. *The teaching of reading.* Bloomington, Indiana: Phi Delta Kappa, 1972.

Spache, G. D., & Spache, E. B. *Reading in the elementary school.* Boston: Allyn & Bacon, 1969.

Strang, R. *Diagnostic teaching of reading.* New York: McGraw-Hill, 1969.

Valett, R. E. *The remediation of learning disabilities.* Palo Alto, Calif.: Fearon Publishers, 1967.

Wallen, C. J. *Competency in teaching reading.* Chicago: Science Research Associates, 1972.

Wilson, R. M. *Diagnostic and remedial reading for classroom and clinic.* Columbus, Ohio: Charles E. Merrill, 1967.

9

Written Language Problems

Written language is one of the highest forms of language and essentially the last area of language to be learned (Johnson & Myklebust, 1967). It is usually preceded by the development of skills in listening, speaking, and reading.

Children with written language difficulties come to dislike the idea of written communication and either devise elaborate mental schemes to compensate for deficits in written language or simply avoid all written activities (Compton, 1965). To help a child overcome these difficulties the teacher must be concerned with three specific questions:

1. What particular difficulties prevent the child from correctly manipulating the writing utensil to form letters?
2. What skill deficiencies interfere with producing the correct graphic form for each word?
3. What interferes with the child's ability to translate ideas into words and syntactic patterns?

Diagnosis

Teacher Observation

Direct observation of written language skills will provide the teacher with exacting data in knowing *precisely* what a child can and cannot do in this area. The teacher who closely observes the child during instructional periods will know the specific types of errors that are being made and, thereby, have a basis for initiating remediation. Copying exercises done at the chalkboard or at the pupil's desk, various types of dictation, and creative writing exercises provide ideal situations for direct observation of handwriting, spelling, and written expression skills. The teacher should be particularly observant of the following:

1. Consistent difficulty in copying or revisualizing specific letters
2. Patterns of linguistic errors in the spelling of specific words
3. Misapplication of various spelling rules
4. Pencil grasp and body posture problems
5. Consistent syntactical or grammatical errors in the written expression of ideas
6. Difficulties with the writing form (manuscript or cursive) being used

Informal Assessment

Many skill deficiencies can be individually assessed through various informal, teacher-made tests. The analysis of errors on informal measures provides the teacher with pertinent diagnostic information that may be directly utilized in an instructional program. Otto and McMenemy (1966) and Smith (1969b) provide examples of screening instruments and informal tests for written language.

Formal Tests

The formal appraisal of written language skills has long been neglected in standardized tests. Very few formal tests are available in this area. Spelling and written expression subtests, which have been a part of larger achievement batteries, have inadequately served the diagnostic needs of this area because of the emphasis on grade- and age-level scores. The Slingerland (1962) screening test does provide valuable instructional information in handwriting and spelling. The Myklebust (1965) writing test is also instructionally helpful, and it provides norms for ages seven through seventeen. Smith (1969b) briefly reviews a number of other standardized tests in this area.

Following are a number of teaching suggestions for remediating written language problems. The activities are grouped according to particular skills. However, many suggestions may be used in several skill areas.

Handwriting
Skills

Children who experience handwriting problems basically have difficulties executing the motor patterns that are required for writing letters, words, or numbers. Basic handwriting skills include the following abilities:

1. Holding a writing utensil properly and performing various motor readiness activities (e.g., drawing lines, circles, etc.)
2. Properly using manuscript writing
3. Properly using cursive writing
4. For left-handed children, properly positioning the paper, hand, and posture.

I. Does the Child Write Without Difficulty?

    A. *Has the child mastered the skills prerequisite for writing?*

        1. Have the child perform body movements, such as up and down, left and right, forward and back, out and in, etc., with gross body exercises. These activities should be done first without pencils, chalk, etc. For example, direct the child to:

> "Raise your right hand *up* in the air."
> "Make large circles with your writing hand in *front* of your body."
> "Bring your arms *in* toward your body."
> "Make long straight lines with your writing hand going from *top* to *bottom.*"

2. Use the chalkboard for some of the exercises listed above. For example, direct the child to:

"Make a long line from *left* to *right.*"
"Draw a circle *in toward* your body."
"Make a line going from *bottom* to *top.*"

3. Some children must be taught how to hold the writing utensil. Practicing with a paint brush while painting may be helpful. McKenna (1970) also suggests the following finger exercises: finger-tapping on a desk, firmly and rhythmically; lifting and lowering designated fingers on command; sorting cards; and "playing the piano" on a desk, with hands arched properly and fingers pressing down firmly.

4. Some children may have difficulty in remembering how to hold a pencil. Johnson and Myklebust (1967) suggest placing a piece of adhesive on the pencil, cutting a small notch in the wood, or painting the specific area where the fingers should be held.

5. Use geometric-figure templates for tracing with fingers, on the chalkboard, on paper, etc. Gradually encourage the child to make the figures freehand, using the template as an example. Templates may be made from oak tag, wood, plastic, foam rubber, etc.[1]

6. Use dot-to-dot figures on the chalkboard or on duplicating paper to teach a sequence of lines. Initially, circles and squares can be used. Gradually the figures can include actual letters.

7. Children can trace figures and letters by placing tracing paper over the figure to be duplicated. During the beginning stages of this activity, the tracing paper might need to be taped or tacked to the desk.

8. It is helpful for some children to reproduce figures with their fingers in wet sand, salt trays, pudding mixes, or finger paint.

9. Ask children to identify wooden figures or letter forms while their eyes are closed. If wooden forms are unavailable, letters can be drawn with the finger on the back of the child's hand or on his back. Children can work in pairs and tally points. Particularly difficult figures and letters can be stressed.

10. Children can draw the beginning strokes for most letters through various games. For example:

Vertical Lines

a. "Finish building the house."

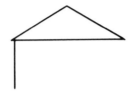

Sharp Peaks

b. "Put a crown on the king's head."

Wavy Lines

c. "Make some wiggly snakes."

Circles

d. "Finish the man's face and eyes."

Half-circles

e. "Put the handles on the other cups."

11. Gradually, children should be able to reproduce different shapes upon verbal direction of the teacher.

12. A number of children must be taught the correct body posture and paper angle for good handwriting. A detailed description for teaching these skills is provided by Croutch (1970).

B. *Does the child have difficulty with manuscript writing?*

13. Beginning letters can be taught through the aid of boxes for correct formulation. All of the basic vertical and horizontal letters may be taught by utilizing boxes, as shown below:

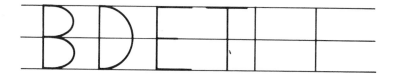

As the child progresses, the boxes should be gradually faded out.

14. Masking tape may be used in providing a tactile clue for margins and different letter placements. A section of masking tape along the left side of the paper provides the child with a clue for directionality. Smaller pieces of tape can be used for specific letter directions.

15. Arrow clues for specific letters can also be helpful. For example,

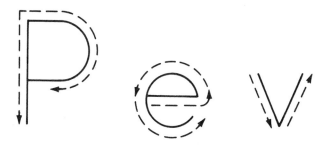

16. Some children are also aided by placing a little green dot at the starting position for the letter stroke, and a small red dot at the termination point for the letter:

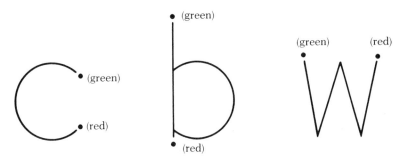

17. The basic strokes comprising most letters can be taught sequentially. For example, the letter t can be taught as two separate strokes $|$ and $-$. Likewise, h , is comprised of $|$ and $\mathsf{\cap}$. Eventually the basic strokes can be joined together.

18. Letters with easier strokes should be taught first. The following are considered the *least* difficult for children to learn: *c, i, l, o, t, v.*

19. A helpful device for some children is an individual alphabet taped to their desks. Dittoing the alphabet or parts of the alphabet at the top of a child's seatwork may also be helpful.

20. Clean, lined paper is necessary for children with aligning and spacing difficulties. Use color-coded paper or different-colored ditto masters.

21. Capital letters should be introduced by means of familiar words, such as the child's name, his city, the state in which he lives, etc. The techniques used for teaching lowercase letters (boxes, color cues, masking tape, etc.) can be employed in teaching capital letter formation.

22. Teach children to "talk-out" strokes in making specific letters. For example:

n — short line down, back up, around and down

W — slant down, slant up, slant down, slant up

i — short line, dot

t — tall line down, cross near top.

23. For children with spacing difficulties, use plastic, wooden, felt, or oak-tag letters. Instruct children to match the spacing in given words. Likewise provide words with improper spacing and instruct children to space the letters properly.

C. *Does the child have difficulty with cursive writing?*

24. Cursive writing should not be taught to children who are still experiencing difficulties with manuscript writing. In all likelihood, children who experience extreme difficulties with manuscript will also experience failure with cursive writing.

25. Children who know the formation of manuscript letters can be shown the similarity to cursive writing by writing heavy cursive letters over the corresponding manuscript letter. For example,

etc. This technique may be varied by using a different-color pencil or a felt-tipped pen for the cursive letter.

26. Many of the cursive strokes can be practiced through games similar to those listed under #10, p. 190.

For example:

stringing the beads

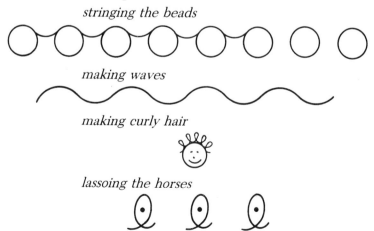

making waves

making curly hair

lassoing the horses

27. Make any of the above strokes on ditto paper and have a child trace over them with his finger, pencil, crayon, etc. The commercially available *Trac-a-Bit*[2]

allows children to trace letters using an erasable grease pencil or crayon.

28. Letters with similar movement patterns should be taught sequentially. The following four groups contain similar strokes:

a	c	d	g	o		
b	h	f	k	l	e	
i	j	p	r	s	t	u	w
m	n	v	x	y	z		

29. In the beginning stages of cursive writing, above-the-line "stops" and below-the-line "stops" may be provided as a cue for letter formation. The "stops" can consist of colored dots or short lines, masking tape, etc. For example,

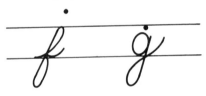

30. Dot-to-dot or dash-to-dash letters can be used for completion exercises. The dots or dashes should be gradually faded out, allowing the child to make the complete letter.

31. For a child who has difficulty in keeping his wrist on the desk in the proper position, a heavy (possibly weighted) bracelet or wristband will help to keep the wrist in place.

32. Cursive letters can also be broken into steps in order for strokes to be analyzed and taught sequentially (see activity #17 p. 192). For example, the letter *f* can be taught by slowly joining the following parts:

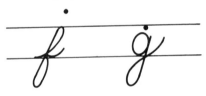

33. Spacing difficulties in cursive writing can be helped by working with cursive letters cut from oak tag or wood. Children can match spacing in a number of given words, join letters to spell words given verbally by the teacher, etc.

34. Verbal cues may be utilized in cursive writing. If letters of similar strokes are learned in sequence, the verbal cues can easily be "seen" by the child. The *a* strokes, for example, could be used in teaching the *g* strokes. "First come around like the a, then go up, etc."

D. *Does the left-handed child position his paper, head and body correctly?*

35. Paper and arm positioning are important ingredients for good left-handed writing. Left-handers need to be taught the "bear left"[3] position for the arm and the paper. Taping the paper to the desk in the correct position serves as a reminder in the beginning stages of handwriting.

36. The commercially available writing frame (a wire guide attached to the pencil)[4] is an excellent device for teaching left-handers the correct hand position while writing. The frame can also be used for right-handers.

37. The incorrect hooked-wrist position observed in many left-handers may be helped by practice with paint brushes, chalk, crayons, magic markers, etc. Constant reinforcement of holding writing utensils properly will help many left-handed children to also hold pencils in the correct manner.

38. The left-hander's writing should be slightly sloped to the left, although the slope appears to be somewhat "backhand." Left-handed children should be given appropriate sloping examples to follow. Teachers can make use of left-handed teachers in the same school, older left-handed students, and left-handed children in the same classroom to help provide exemplary work and patterns. This suggestion is appropriate only if the other left handers provide good models.

39. Special equipment, such as left-handed scissors and left-handed desk-chairs, should be provided whenever possible.[5]

40. Trembly (1970) reported that a Southpaw Club was organized for left-handers in one school. Children in the group were able to pool their ideas and experiences. The boys in the club even organized a baseball team and challenged a group of right-handers.

41. The *Plunkett* writing exercises serve as a commercial aid for left-handers. These materials offer a sequentially developed program of writing exercises.[6]

Spelling
Skills

Spelling is believed to be a more difficult task than reading because, as Lerner (1971) points out, the opportunity in spelling to draw upon peripheral clues is greatly reduced. In reading, the child may use contextual, structural, or configuration clues. However, in spelling, the child must:

1. Remember the form of letters
2. Remember the letter sequences and rules for particular words

II. Does the Child Spell Accurately?

A. *Does the child remember letter forms?*

42. Many of the activities suggested for the development of visual memory are also applicable here.

43. Analyze the type of spelling errors that a child is encountering in order to distinguish the specific letter(s) that seem to be consistently troublesome. In addition, ask the child to write specific letters of the alphabet from dictation. Pronounce different letter sounds and ask the child to write the symbol which denotes that sound. This information may be used in formulating a remedial program.

44. Provide children with a sheet of letters with similar configurations. Say a letter and direct the child to circle the correct one. As the child progresses, ask him to write the letter from dictation. Still later, ask the child to "write the letter that comes after *b* in the alphabet."

45. Following the above activities, ask children to "write the letter that the word *b*all begins with" or "write the letter that cu*p* ends with", etc.

46. Ask children to complete missing words by filling in the omitted letter(s). For example, "They like to (*s*)ing song(*s*). Mary (*s*)at on the (*s*)ixth chair. The dog(*s*) were very (*s*)ick." This activity may be varied by concentrating on specific letters in the initial, medial, or final positions.

47. Provide the child with a word, such as *tablecloth*. Ask the student to write as many words as possible beginning with *t* or *l* (or any other letter) using only the letters in tablecoth. Children may compete to write the most words. Variations of this activity include letters in other positions, writing just three-letter words, etc.

48. The revisualization of specific letters may be strengthened by tracing the letter in various media, such as clay, salt, sand, etc. Providing tactile exercises such as sandpaper, felt or wooden letters is also helpful.

49. Ask the child to spell certain words, with the emphasis on specific letters, by providing him with letter cutouts and permitting him to arrange the correct sequence of letters.

50. Print difficult words on flash cards for periodic review by the child. Especially troublesome letters can be printed in red to denote caution. A child's attention is then concentrated on the difficult letter(s).

51. Show a letter to the child for a short period of time, and have the child circle the correct choice of four letters written on a worksheet. As the child improves with this activity, the exposure time may be shortened, multiple letters may be exposed, words may be gradually added, or the child may be asked to write the letter(s) that were exposed. A tachistoscope is very useful for this procedure, but the letters or words may be presented on flash cards.

52. Children can be asked to write letters that are verbally described by the teacher. For example, "Write the letter that looks like a wiggly snake(s)," or "write the letter that looks like a small circle (o)." Eventually, words can be spelled in this manner, and other children can be asked to describe letters verbally.

53. Give the child partially completed letters to complete. Omit additional parts of the letters progres-

sively. For example, ask the child to complete the following:

54. Particularly troublesome letters can be assigned memory clues. If this technique is used it is important to assign clues to a minimum number of letters or the clues may be as difficult to remember as the letters. Associations provided by the child himself are much more effective than teacher-assigned clues. One child we know remembered the "i" by an upward-pointing arrow and the "a" by a circular arrow .

55. Tracing letters on the back of the child's hand or his back, as described earlier, can be utilized with words. Children must keep the visual image of each letter in their memory until the word is completed. Then they write the word on the chalkboard or on paper. Two- or three-letter words should be used for this activity at first.

56. Cover up an entire word and gradually expose each succeeding letter until a child can guess the correct word. Letter clues such as "The next letter comes after 'm' in the alphabet" can be supplied.

B. *Does the child remember the letter sequences in words?*

57. Provide children with sets of four words and ask them to circle the correctly spelled version of the word. For example:

mega	gmae	game	gaem
talbe	table	taebl	tabel
bread	braed	brdae	bader

58. Make crossword puzzles of particularly difficult words. The puzzles may be made by other children.

59. Present configurations of specific words to the child and ask him to match a given set of words with the configurations. For example:

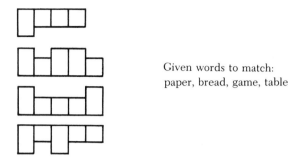

Given words to match:
paper, bread, game, table

60. As a child progresses with the above activity, ask him to identify similar configurations in words without being provided the visual forms. Present groups of four words and ask the child to circle the two words with similar configuration. For example:

      come   ball   park   talk

61. Use the Language Master as a visual/auditory/kinesthetic reinforcement for the child. Whole words can be used, spelling the word letter-by-letter. The child can trace the word once it has been placed through the recorder.

62. Assign children in the room different letters, blends, endings, etc. Call on a child to spell a word. The child must choose the easiest way to spell the word by selecting children who have the correct letters or groups of letters. For example, the word *jumping* can be more easily spelled by choosing a child with *ing,* rather than three separate children, one with *i,* one with *n,* and another with *g.* Children should be encouraged to look for the easiest way to spell a word (Arena, 1968).

63. Individual alphabet charts on each child's desk can be a helpful revisualization device.

64. Introduce a word family, such as <u>at</u>. Ask a child to list words in that family. This activity may be made more specific by directing children to add certain letters, blends, or endings and then pronouncing the word.

65. Write difficult words on the chalkboard. Ask children to study the word for a few seconds. Then erase the word and ask the children to write the word from memory. Underline or circle difficult parts of the word as a memory device.

66. Present children with a sentence composed of words with missing letters, words with mixed-up letters, and words portrayed by pictures. Ask them to complete the sentence. For example,

a. The [figure] wen(t) swimm(i n g) itwh her (M)oth(e r) at the ceona. (ocean) (with)

b. The [figure] is fly(i n g) gihh in the (s)k(y). (high)

67. Make a spelling file box of difficult words. Have the child copy the words correctly on flash cards and periodically review them. Encourage the child to study his own flash cards and write them from memory on the back of the card or on a piece of paper. Words may be deleted and others added as time progresses.

68. Ask children to circle all the little words contained within a list of larger words. This activity often serves as a letter recall device for individual spellings of words. Some examples include:

    friend, follow, report, oral, hand, easy

69. Encourage associative relationships for word spellings. Some associations may be peculiar, but they serve as meaningful memory devices for individual children. Individual associations can often be the most effective method for revisualizing certain words.

70. A self-discovery technique described by Wahl (1970) helps a child become aware of what he is doing wrong in spelling by pronouncing his misspelling the way he has written it and then respelling the word correctly. Wahl cautions the teacher to select reasonably phonetic words to be used with this technique.

Written
Expression

Children with written expression difficulties experience problems in properly transposing thoughts into written communication. Adequate written expression is based upon:

1. Abundant oral expressive experiences
2. Understanding and usage of correct syntactical and grammatical patterns

3. Ability to organize ideas into the appropriate communication form

III. Does the Child Have Difficulty in Expressing Ideas in Writing?

A. *Does the child have an adequate vocabulary?*

71. Give children a word, such as *run,* and ask them to list as many words as they can that are similar in meaning to *run.* For example, *rush, scat, flashed, hurry, dash,* etc. These words may be kept in a notebook to be used as a reference when children are writing stories.

72. Play word tennis with teams of children. In this activity, two teams are chosen and the first person in one team says a word, such as *happy.* Synonyms are provided by successive team members, switching back and forth until one member can no longer think of a synonym. Variations in scoring can include total points for each side for all synonyms, points against the team for running out of synonyms, etc.

73. Give the child a word with multiple meanings and ask him to write sentences using the different meanings. Upon completion, discuss the different meanings with the child. Examples of some appropriate words include: hit, run, show, bat, fan, fly, watch, file.

74. Give children a list of meanings and a second list of words which must be matched with the meanings. To make the activity more challenging, choose unusual meanings of words. For example:

Word Meanings	*Words to choose from*
a wispy puff of color in the sky	juice
mostly liquid, and sometimes good to drink	humid
sticky and moist	cloud

75. Provide the child with a list of general categories and a large number of words which must be classified according to category. For example, categories such as *transportation, food,* and *music* may be used. Words to be classified include: tugboat, drum, soup, rocket, feet, orchestra, sandwich, singer, etc. The

child should be able to make finer discriminations as he progresses with this activity. Eventually, the child is supplied only the categories and must provide the words under each category.

76. Provide children with a list of questions which they answer by either selecting the correct word that fits the sentence or answering the question affirmatively or negatively. For example:

"Does the spendthrift or the thrifty man save his money?"

"Are the jagged rocks harder to climb than the slick, rounded rocks?"

"Is the senior citizen an oldster?"

77. Have children "invent" new words by joining together two familiar words. Definitions should be provided for the new words. For example, *squabbit* (cross between a squirrel and a rabbit) or *glup* (combination of a glass and a cup).

78. Have the children find specific words in a story that answer questions asked by the teacher. For example, "Find the word in the third paragraph which describes the size of the town in which Tom lived," or "Find the expression on page thirty-six which tells you that Jane was very sad."

79. Unusual or colorful words which children have read or heard (e.g., "argy-bargy"—a Scotch expression meaning argument or controversy) may be kept in a special notebook or placed on the bulletin board. Encourage the children to use these words in their written assignments.

80. Provide children with input experiences such as field trips, reading stories, discussion periods, and oral-language activities. Many children will need a variety of experiences to stimulate ideas for written expression.

B. *Does the child use correct syntax and grammar?*

81. Provide the child with sentences having grammar and/or syntax errors which he must correct. Initially, the exercises should be concentrated on one type of grammatical or syntactical error. Gradually, the sentences should progress to multiple errors. Sentence errors can be underlined during the beginning stages of this activity.

> Mary *have* two apples.
> John *in the morning* has breakfast.
> She *were* running down the path.
> Girls *plays* with dolls.

82. The above exercise can be varied by working on a specific skill, such as plurals, and leaving the emphasis word blank for the child to complete. Children may also be given a choice between two words for the correct answer. For example,

> Susan and Jane (play, plays) together each day.
> He (run, runs) to school.
> They (like, likes) to ride bikes.
> The children played many (game, games).

83. Provide the child with a scrambled set of flash cards that matches a sentence that you verbalize. The child must place the words in the correct order to match your sentence. A tape recorder may be used for this activity.

84. Provide children with a list of words for which they must furnish the past tense. For example:

> come   (came)
> go   (gone)
> run   (ran)
> see   (saw)

85. The above exercise can be expanded into sentences where children are asked to provide the correct tense.

> He *play* with me yesterday.
> After he *jump,* John hurt his finger.
> Yesterday, Sally *ride* her horse.

C. *Does the child have difficulty in formulating ideas in writing?*

86. Children experiencing difficulty in expressing their thoughts in writing will initially need very specific instructions, activities, and exercises. These children will respond to structured assignments that tell them exactly what to do. As the child progresses, the structure and specificity can be gradually decreased.

87. Give each child an uncluttered picture of a specific object (or the actual object) and ask him to write its name. Gradually add descriptors until a sentence de-

velops (e.g., *This is a small, red apple.*). Some children may need experience in naming pictures before they progress to describing them.

88. Give each child an action picture, such as a stock-car race. Instruct each child to write a one-sentence description of what is happening in the picture.

89. Read an exciting story to the class, omitting the ending. Request children to finish the story by writing an ending to it.

90. Have the child dictate a story on a specific topic using the tape recorder. Type the story on paper, leaving key words blank. Ask the child to read the story, completing the missing words. He can verify his choices by replaying the original tape.

91. Provide the child with a number of different sentences. Ask the child to rewrite each sentence, saying the same thing in a different way without changing the meaning of the sentence. Examples include:

    The circus is an exciting place to visit.
    It rained very hard last night.
    She looked pretty in her new pink dress.

92. Provide the child with a list of words and a paragraph with missing words. Ask the child to complete the paragraph using the list of words. For example:

    Today it (rained) all day. We had to stay in the (house) to (play). The television was (broken), so we listened to the (radio) for awhile. We also played some (games) and painted some (pictures). The best part was when (mother) read us some (stories).

    stories   play   rained   pictures
    radio   broken   house   games   mother

93. Give the child a list of words and ask him to write a short story using the words given. The story can be structured by providing the child with a title for the story.

94. A daily diary may be kept by the class. Initially, let the class write the daily entry as a group. Eventually, permit individual children to write daily entries. Ultimately, each child in the class can keep his own diary.

95. Ask children to write a sentence summarizing a story that was read to them, a film that they viewed, a record that was played to them, or a story that they

read. Gradually, increase the length of the summary
or abstract.

NOTES

[1]Commercially prepared templates may be purchased from Developmental Learning Materials, 7440 North Natchez Avenue, Niles, Illinois 60648.
[2]Available from Zaner-Bloser Company, 612 North Park Street, Columbus, Ohio 43215.
[3]The paper is positioned the reverse of the correct right-handed position with the arm kept parallel with the edge.
[4]The writing frame may be purchased from Zaner-Bloser Company, 612 North Park Street, Columbus, Ohio 43215.
[5]Left-handed equipment may be obtained from Anything Left-handed, Inc., Box 4669, San Jose, California 95126.
[6]*Plunkett* materials are published by Educators Publishing Service, Cambridge, Massachusetts 02138.

ADDITIONAL
READINGS

Arena, J. I., ed. *Building spelling skills in dyslexic children.* San Rafael, Calif.: Academic Therapy Publications, 1968.

Arena, J. I., ed. *Building handwriting skills in dyslexic children.* San Rafael, Calif.: Academic Therapy Publications, 1970.

Barbe, W. B. *Creative writing activities.* Columbus, Ohio: Highlights for Children, Inc., 1965.

Clark, M. M. *Left-handedness.* London: University of London Press, 1957.

DeHirsch, K., Jansky, J. & Langford, W. S. *Predicting language failure.* New York: Harper & Row, 1966.

Dolch, E. W. *Better spelling.* Champaign, Ill.: Garrard, 1960.

Fernald, G. M. *Remedial techniques in basic school subjects.* New York: McGraw-Hill, 1943.

Gillingham, A., & Stillman, B. *Remedial training for reading, spelling, and penmanship.* Cambridge, Mass.: Educators Publishing Service, 1965.

Glaus, M. *From thought to words.* Champaign, Ill.: National Council of Teachers of English, 1965.

Johnson, D. J., & Myklebust, H. R. *Learning disabilities: Educational principles and practices.* New York: Grune & Stratton, 1967.

Lerner, J. *Children with learning disabilities.* Boston: Houghton Mifflin, 1971.

Otto, W. & McMenemy, R. A. *Corrective and remedial teaching: Principles and practices.* Boston: Houghton Mifflin, 1966.

Platts, M. E. *Anchor: A handbook of vocabulary discovery techniques for the classroom teacher.* Stevensville, Mich.: Educational Service, Inc., 1970.

Spalding, R. B., & Spalding, W. T. *The writing road to reading.* New York: Morrow, 1957.

Strauss, A. & Lehtinen, L. *Psychopathology and education of the brain-injured child.* Vol. 1. New York: Grune & Stratton, 1947.

Valett, R. E. *The remediation of learning disabilities.* Palo Alto, Calif.: Fearon, 1967.

IO

Oral
Language
Problems

The oral aspects of language are unique to man and are recognized as one of man's greatest achievements (Lerner, 1971). The close relationship between language and learning has been recognized by many as extremely important (Freud, 1953; Piaget, 1952; Skinner, 1957). Children with oral language problems are handicapped in understanding and using the spoken word. Consequently, difficulties in acquiring basic academic skills are also observed in many individual cases.

Deficits in oral language can be very complex in nature. Many children require specialized remediation by highly trained language therapists. A speech clinician should be consulted for guidance and assistance in helping children with significant language deficits. The development of oral language skills must, nevertheless, be recognized as an important goal for the classroom teacher. The teacher must be aware of the three basic aspects of language acquisition and the difficulties usually associated with each of them.

1. What *inner* language disorders prevent the child from acquiring basic language skills?
2. What *receptive* language problems interfere with the child's ability to comprehend the spoken word?
3. What *expressive* language difficulties preclude the development of adequate spoken language?

Diagnosis

Teacher Observation

Observations of children during both formal and informal school activities will provide the teacher with important instructional data. Spradlin (1967) feels that *observations* of oral language skills often provide information which can be obtained in no other way. Long-term daily interaction with a child gives the teacher ample opportunity to observe all facets of a child's oral language development. A number of behavioral symptoms with which the teacher should be familiar have been provided by Myklebust (1954). Detailed grade-level competencies in oral language are listed by Otto and McMenemy (1966).

Informal Assessment

Specific skill development can be informally measured by the classroom teacher through teacher-made tests. Based upon his observations, the teacher may more closely evaluate a child by having the child answer particular questions, complete skill worksheets, or participate in evaluative games and exercises. The classroom teacher may also use informal oral language scales, based upon chronological age levels, which have been developed by Mecham (1959) and Zimmerman, Steiner and Evatt (1969). Additional informal tests are described by Myers and Hammill (1969) and Myklebust (1954).

Formal Tests

Many standardized language tests are currently available. However, a large number of these tests require specialized training for proper administration. The more widely used language tests include the *Illinois Test of Psycholinguistic Abilities* (Kirk, McCarthy, & Kirk, 1968); the *Peabody Picture Vocabulary Test* (Dunn, 1959); and the *Receptive-Expressive Emergent Language Scale* (Bzoch & League,

1971). These tests provide data which is useful in planning individual   structional programs. Nonetheless, Spradlin (1967) cautions
"standard testing procedures have the disadvantages of restricting
the settings in which language is sampled and in the type of language
sampled" (p. 124).

Many of the following teaching suggestions may be easily adapted
for the use in several skill areas due to the interrelatedness of inner,
receptive, and expressive language and the obvious dependence of
one upon the other.[1]

<h3 style="text-align:center">Inner Language
Difficulties</h3>

Inner language disorders have been described as the most complex
of all language difficulties (Johnson & Myklebust, 1967; Lerner,
1971). Inner language can be defined as the language which one uses
to communicate with oneself (Goldstein, 1948) or the language with
which one thinks (Johnson & Myklebust, 1967). Inner language development is dependent upon the child's ability to:

1. Establish verbal imagery for sounds, words, concepts, etc.
2. Use the complex maze of skills needed in a logical thinking
   process

Diagnostic questions and teaching suggestions for developing inner
language skills are listed below.

**I. Has the Child Mastered the Skills Prerequisite for Adequate Inner
   Language?**

A. *Does the child have difficulty with verbal imagery?*

1. As words such as book, nail, water, etc., are introduced, provide the child with the object to hold, feel,
   smell, taste, etc. Have the child perform the action for
   more abstract words such as hop, run, kick, etc.
2. Point to and name objects during a walk around the
   school grounds (e.g., door, flagpole, table, etc.). Eventually, point to particular objects and have the child
   provide the name.
3. Provide the child with pictures of objects or animals
   that produce particular sounds (dogs, cats, telephone,
   fire truck, etc.). Record the sounds on a tape recorder.
   Play particular sounds simultaneously as the child is

looking at the matching picture. Gradually, have the child match sounds with the picture or vice versa.

4. Provide the child with a wide variety of experiences such as going on field trips, constructing models, playing with manipulative toys, etc. Name and discuss items which are unfamiliar to the child.

5. Select one child in the class and provide the other children a one-sentence description of this child (e.g., "It wears glasses."). "It" (the child) repeats one word from that sentence (e.g., "wears") and the other children try to guess the identity of "it" (Wagner, Hosier, & Blackman, 1970).

6. Present pairs of objects (e.g., a guitar and a violin; a ruler and a tape measure; etc.) and point out the similarities and differences. Provide experiences where the child can use the objects.

7. Read a short sentence to the child (e.g., "The sun was very bright"). Have the child draw a picture illustrating the dictated sentence.

8. Play "charades" where the child is asked to act out a role, such as a swimmer diving into the water or a carpenter hammering a nail (Bush & Giles, 1969) or have the child guess the role being acted out.

9. Use finger plays[2] or "Simon Says" to give the child the opportunity to involve parts of the body while listening to directions.

B. *Does the child experience difficulty in thinking skills?*

10. Provide the child with a series of pictures having one part missing from each picture. Ask the child to find the missing part.

11. Provide the child with a collection of items which have something in common but which are somewhat different in appearance (e.g., a watch and a clock; a shoe and a boot; a glass and a cup; etc.). Ask the child to find two items used for drinking or give the child one item and ask him to look for the related item (Karnes, 1968).

12. Read a series of analogies to the child and have him complete each sentence. For example:

"A banana is to an apple as squash is to _____ _____."

> "A boy is to a girl as a _____ is to a woman."
>
> "A ring is to a _____ as a bracelet is to a wrist."

13. Read a series of three words to a child and have him choose the two words that are related. For example:

    > "dog, cat, apple"
    > "chair, table, knife"
    > "milk, stone, water"

14. Bush and Giles (1969) suggest asking questions similar to the following to develop logical relationships:

    > "Does a bird have wings?"
    > "Do you read with your ears?"
    > "Would you go the a grocery store to see a movie?"
    > "Do you lick an ice cream cone with your knees?"

15. Read a story to the child and stop before finishing it. Ask the child to think of an ending for the story.

16. After reading a story, ask the child specific questions which require interpretation and imagination. For example, ask the child to imagine he was the hero. Would he have acted differently? Or what would happen if the story took place in a different country, season, or century?

17. Use simple riddles to describe familiar people, places, animals, etc. Ask the child to guess the identity based upon the description. Have the child think of riddles to be asked of other children.

18. Karnes (1968) suggests asking two children to stand before the class. Have one child think of ways in which he and the other child are alike (e.g., "We both wear glasses," "We both are boys," etc.).

19. Ask the child to list all the things that he can think of that have wheels, that are smaller than an ant, or that have hair (Smith, 1968).

20. Myers (1965) suggests asking some of the following questions:

    > "How could a blind person know when food on the stove is burning?"
    > "How are a turtle and a fish alike? How are they different?"
    > "Why may it be easier to make a dress shorter than to make it longer?"

Receptive
Language Difficulties

Receptive language is the ability to understand the spoken language of others. The child with difficulties in this area *hears* what is said but he is unable to *comprehend* what is said. Adequate receptive language involves the ability to:

1. Auditorally perceive speech sounds
2. Comprehend concrete and abstract words
3. Understand the linguistic structure of sentences
4. Follow directions
5. Listen critically and make judgments

Diagnostic questions and teaching suggestions for developing receptive language skills are listed below. Teaching suggestions for auditory memory, an important skill for developing receptive language, are listed in Chapter 8.

II. Has the Child Mastered the Skills Prerequisite for Adequate Receptive Language?

A. *Does the child have difficulty in understanding various speech sounds?*

21. Present various isolated speech sounds to the child. Ask the child to listen for a specific sound, such as /m/. Present a sequence of sounds to the child, such as /m/, /p/, /t/, /s/, /m/, /v/, /k/, /m/, /n/, /s/, /m/, and ask the child to raise his hand each time the /m/ sound is heard.

22. Gradually, introduce pairs of sounds (e.g., /m/ and /b/) and ask the child to tell if the sounds are the same or different. The child may respond by shaking his head, raising his hand, etc.

23. Have the child listen for a particular sound at the beginning of words read aloud. Present words that are phonetically very different at first, and eventually present words with beginning sounds that are more alike. Final and medial sounds can be introduced in a similar fashion.

24. Introduce blends, digraphs, and vowel sounds using somewhat the same procedure suggested in # 23. The sequence should progress from isolated speech sounds to listening for the sounds in words.

25. Provide picture clues and objects for those children who need additional help in associating speech sounds with letters and words.

26. Give the child a picture which contains many objects, such as an advertisement. Ask the child to point to an object that begins with the same sounds as a stimulus and that you provide (Heilman, 1968). This procedure can also be used for final sounds, rhyming, blends, etc.

27. Play bingo with children who recognize some letter sounds, using initial consonants or other speech sounds for the bingo squares. Call out different words and have the children cover appropriate squares.

28. Lerner (1971) suggests having the child identify objects, pronouncing the name of the object by separating the individual phonemes. For example: "Pick up the p – ĕ – n."

29. Provide children with experiences in listening for rhyming words. Prepare a worksheet with pictures of different objects. Present a rhyme to the children and ask them to circle the picture that rhymes with the sentence, e.g., "The man was holding a _____." The worksheet drawing cards include pictures of a dog, fan, book, and a baby.

30. Pronounce various words and ask the child to determine the number of syllables in each word by holding up the appropriate number of fingers, clapping or tapping out the number of syllables, etc.

B. *Does the child have difficulty in comprehending various words?*

31. Johnson and Myklebust (1967) advise that only meaningful words should be taught and that words are meaningful only "when the individual has the experience with which they are to be associated" (p. 87).

32. Begin training by working with real objects or pictures. Give the child a chance to feel and play with the object. Say the name of the object a number of times while the child has the object or picture before him.

33. Have the child match an object, such as a banana, with a picture of a banana or have the child match similar objects or pictures.

34. Gradually place three or four objects before the child and ask him to point to the one that you pronounce.

If the child is able to correctly point to an object, encourage him to say its name.

35. Have the child match an object to another object which is basically different in form and physical features but belongs to a similar category. For example, ask the child what you do with a *lock.* Provide him with a *nail, key,* and *cork* to select from (Eisenson, 1972). As the child progresses, have him match pictures instead of objects.

36. Have the child classify words into categories such as people, food, and animals by sorting pictures and words into groups.

37. Teach more abstract words, such as verbs, by having the child perform the activity. Jumping, walking, etc., can be repeated until the child understands the meaning of the word.

38. Smith (1967) suggests having the child clap for various reasons when he is being read to. For example:

    "Clap for every word that describes something."
    "Clap for every person's name."
    "Clap for every word that rhymes with _____."

39. Have the child follow simple directions. For example:

    "Give me the book."
    "Stand next to the door."
    "Show me the paper."
    "Jump up and down."

40. Have the child match objects that produce particular noises with the actual noise. Eisenson (1972) suggests using telephone rings, the vacuum cleaner whir, drum beats, bell clangs, or toy animals that approximate the sounds of the live animal.

41. Teach descriptive words by providing the child with a variety of pictures and having the child pick out the *happy* boy, the *sad* clown, the *dirty* towel, etc.

42. Provide the child with contrasting sets of experiences to teach the attributes of objects such as *hot* and *cold* water, *rough* and *smooth* stones, *little* and *big* animals, etc., (Lerner, 1971).

C. *Does the child have difficulty in comprehending sentences?*

43. Gradually add verbs to nouns (e.g., *"throw* ball," *"eat* candy," etc.) and adjectives to nouns (e.g., "a *small*

truck," "a *sad* girl," etc.) by having the child choose
the correct picture or perform the action (Eisenson,
1972).[3]

44. Have the child respond *yes* or *no* to the following
    questions (Bush & Giles, 1969):

    "Do flowers grow?"
    "Do dogs bark?"
    "Do rabbits hop?"
    "Do you have four ears?"

45. Read a short sentence to the child and ask him a series
    of questions about the sentence. Children may re-
    spond by shaking their heads or merely saying *yes* or
    no. For example: "Jean and Jeff go to the ocean and
    mountains during the summer."

    "Do Jean and Jeff go to the mountains during the
    winter?"
    "Do Jean and Jeff go to the ocean during the sum-
    mer?"

46. As the child progresses, longer and more detailed sen-
    tences and paragraphs can be read to the child. Ques-
    tions may be provided before the story is read to
    enable the child to listen for specific answers.

47. Read a list of sentences to the child and have the child
    sit with his thumbs up. As soon as the child hears a
    sentence that answers the question, "How," he puts
    his thumbs down. Sentences that answer "When,"
    "Where," and "Who" could also be used (Wagner,
    Hosier, & Blackman, 1970). Sentences that answer
    "How" include:

    "The boys run fast."
    "Virgil eats slowly."
    "Joyce looks pretty."

48. Zigmond and Cicci (1968) recommend having the
    child select the word in a sentence that does not make
    sense. For example:

    "It snows during the summer."
    "We drink milk out of a book."
    "We use a ball to write."

49. Read a poem or story to a child with obvious missing
    words. Have the child supply the missing part. For
    example:

"Chuck built a snowman with _____.
He used a carrot for the _____ and coal for the snowman's _____. When the sun came out, the snowman _____."

50. Lerner (1971) suggests having the child listen to a sentence and supply the correct word. For example:

    "I am thinking of a word that tells us what you eat soup with."

51. Prepare a worksheet with various drawings. Ask the child to perform specific directions. For example:

    "Draw a circle around the truck."
    "Put an X on the little girl."
    "Draw a line under the house."

52. Ask children questions which require them to make a comparison. For example:

    "Who wears dresses, boys or girls?"
    "Who shaves every morning, mother or father?"
    "Who barks, a rabbit or a dog?"
    "Who puts out fires, a policeman or a fireman?"

53. Johnson and Myklebust (1967) suggest preparing a worksheet with a series of pictures and reading sentences of varying difficulty according to individual needs. Ask the child to follow a specific direction after hearing the sentence. For example:

    "Mother bought some apples at the store."
    Circle what mother bought at the store.

54. Pass out various objects to each child in the class. Ask children to stand if they have the object that is described. For example:

    "Stand if you have the animal that meows."
    "Stand if you have the object that cuts meat."
    "Stand if you have the toy truck that delivers milk."

55. Provide a signal that can be used to attract a child's attention in order for him to listen for directions that will be given. For example, flick the lights, play a few notes on the piano, hold up an arm over the head, say "Listen," etc. Use one particular signal consistently for a group of children.

D. *Does the child have difficulty in following directions?*

56. Play "Simon Says" and have the child perform simple motor tasks which gradually become more complex as the child progresses. Permit individual children to take turns as the leader.

57. Give the child step-by-step directions for folding a piece of paper to make a certain number of squares or rectangles or provide the child with precut geometric shapes and direct him to assemble step-by-step an ice cream cone or a balloon (Karnes, 1968).

58. Direct the child to a specified place in the school building by providing him with a series of directions to get there. For example:

> "Go out the door and turn left. Walk straight down the hall and take your first right. At the gymnasium, turn left. Go through the first door on your right."

59. Call children to reading groups or dismiss children for recess or lunch by using row numbers, clothing colors, first-name initials, or other specific directions.

60. Ask particular children to repeat directions that were given to the class or a reading group. This procedure provides an immediate check before the child proceeds with an assignment.

61. Have two children play *Master and Robot* by appointing one child the "Master" who gives directions (e.g., go to the blackboard, draw a circle, turn around, sit in your chair, etc.) to the child appointed the "Robot." Have the children change places after a period of time (Wagner, Hosier, & Blackman, 1970).

62. Provide each child with a paper. Call out various directions for the child to complete on the paper. For example:

> "Draw a circle in the upper right-hand corner of the paper."
> "Make a triangle in the lower left-hand corner of the paper."
> "Write the number "7" in the circle."
> "Make a square in the middle of the paper."

The directions can be placed on a tape recorder for the child to complete with earphones.

63. Read directions for making a kite, baking cookies, or building a model. Have the children perform the activity by following the step-by-step directions.

64. Prepare a series of direction cards for children who can read. Allow the child to continue choosing cards from a pile as long as he is able to follow the commands. The cards might include:

    Go to the library table and find a brown book.
    Hop over to the door, turn around, and skip to the window.
    Pass out a pencil and the math workbooks to all the children in the first three rows.

E. *Does the child have difficulty in listening critically and making judgments?*

65. Prepare a worksheet with a list of words. Describe a word and direct the child to place a number before that word. For example:

    "Write the number 1 before the word that tells us it is the cold time of the year."
    (winter)
    "Write the number 2 before the word that describes a fruit that is long and yellow."
    (banana)

66. Read a list of statements and ask the child to tell whether the statements are *true* or *false*. For example:

    "Elephants can fly in the air."
    "We swim during the summertime."
    "We run with our hands."

67. Have one child stand in front of the room while the children sitting at their seats describe another child in the room. The child in front must guess the identity from the description provided by members of the class (Wagner, Hosier, & Blackman, 1970). The clues might include:

    "He has freckles."
    "He rides a bike to school."
    "He is wearing a blue shirt."

68. Smith (1967) suggests reading a short paragraph containing several words that have similar meanings. Ask the child to pick out the words that mean the same.

"Soon the *little* man came to a *small* dining room. He peered through the *tiny* door and saw a lovely, *petite* room all set up with *miniature* furniture. There were even *minute* dishes on the dining room table" (p. 88).

69. Read a list of nouns that fit in a particular category (furniture, fruit, animals, etc.). Direct the child to clap his hands when a noun is read that does *not* belong to a specified category. For example:

    "chair, desk, *man,* couch, table, *apple,* etc."

70. Use the flannel board while telling a story and plan for obvious errors between what is placed on the board and what is said. Ask the child to find the mistake (Lerner, 1971).

71. Have children arrange scrambled oral sentences in the correct order without using pencil or paper.

72. Wagner, Hosier, and Blackman (1970) recommend reading several statements to the child and asking him to decide if a statement is *fact* or *opinion.* For example:

    "George Washington was our first president."
    "Thomas Jefferson was our greatest president."
    "There were eight dogs in Tom's boat."

73. Read a short story to the child and stop periodically, asking the child to predict what will happen next.

Expressive Language Difficulties

Expressive language can be viewed as the spoken language the child uses in communicating with others. Adequate expressive language is dependent upon acquiring meaningful units of experience and establishing comprehension (Johnson & Myklebust, 1967). In addition, the child must be able to:

1. Produce various speech sounds
2. Formulate words and sentences
3. Use correct grammatical and syntactical language patterns
4. Exhibit an adequate spoken vocabulary

Diagnostic questions and teaching suggestions for remediating expressive language problems are listed below.

III. Has the Child Mastered the Skills Prerequisite for Adequate Expressive Language?

A. *Does the child have difficulty in producing various speech sounds?*

74. Johnson and Myklebust (1967) recommend taking an inventory of movements and phonemes that the child can produce. They suggest utilizing these sounds to make the child aware of movements and sounds.

75. Encourage the use of *any* vocal utterances which have some meaning to the child in order to provide a process of communication for the child and to provide motivation for learning more symbolic language. Gradually require vocal productions which more closely approximate the sounds of words or parts of words.

76. Begin training by facing a mirror with the child and slowly articulating a sound in isolation. Have the child imitate the movements. The first isolated sounds to be established, according to Eisenson (1972), should include $/m/$, $/p/$, $/b/$, $/k/$, $/g/$, $/n/$, $/t/$, $/d/$, $/l/$, and $/r/$.

77. Place the child's hand on your throat or face as sounds are being made in order for him to feel the movements. Have the child place his hand on his own throat.

78. Manually guide the child's tongue or lips to produce certain sounds if the child is unable to imitate a sound by observing. A tongue depressor may be used for appropriate tongue movements.

79. Provide children with verbal cues if they are needed. For example, Johnson and Myklebust (1967) suggest "close your lips and hum" for m or "bite your lip and blow but do not use your voice" for f (p. 128).[4]

80. Have the child practice various tongue and mouth movements such as opening the mouth wide, placing the tongue behind the teeth, moving the lips to a whistling position, etc.

81. Provide the child with pictures of various tongue and mouth positions that are used for particular sounds. Hold the picture up to a mirror and have the child imitate the position.

82. Have the child close his eyes while he is making certain sounds, so that visual memory may be used as a

basis for recalling the movements that are made for particular sounds (Eisenson, 1972).

83. Gradually blend known sounds together, as the child progresses in learning isolated sounds. Provide consonant-vowel and consonant-vowel-consonant combinations for the child. Use many of the same procedures suggested in the above activities.

B. *Does the child have difficulty in formulating words and sentences?*

84. Provide the child with familiar objects to name. Use fruit, clothes, toys, etc. Say the words and have the child repeat them. As the child progresses, use the word in a short sentence.

85. Proceed to naming pictures of animals, furniture, food, etc. Work on the classification of pictures into categories.

86. Facilitate word recall by teaching word association through pairs of words (e.g., hard-soft, salt-pepper, hot-cold, etc.). Pictures may be used to supplement the words (Johnson & Myklebust, 1967).

87. Build known words into sentences through the use of repeated phrases. For example:

   "This is a dog."
   "This is a chair."
   "This is a boy."
   "This is a book."

88. Bereiter and Engelmann (1966) expand upon repeated phrases by asking questions (e.g., "Is this a book?") and by adding second-order statements (e.g., "This book is red."). They also introduce "not" statements (e.g., "This is *not* a book.").[5]

89. Prepare a series of sentences with key words missing. Read a sentence to the child and ask him to supply the key word. For example:

   "A dog makes noise by _____."
   "Bicycles have _____ wheels."
   "We have _____ fingers."

90. Expand upon the "Show and Tell" period by asking the child specific questions about an object that he brings from home.

91. Prepare a grab bag of familiar objects. Have the child

choose one object and describe the object in as much detail as possible. Permit other children to guess the object being described.

92. Show a picture to a child and ask him to describe what is happening in the picture. More direct questions, specific to a particular picture, can also be asked. Smith (1968) also recommends having the child tell what went on before the picture was taken, and what happened afterward.

93. Have the children paint pictures at easels. Ask particular children to describe their pictures to the rest of the class.

94. Provide children with a set of sequence pictures or a comic strip cut into frames. Ask a child to "tell the story" by describing the sequence of events.

95. Have children repeat familiar nursery rhymes while following a record. Eventually have the child recite the rhyme without the record.

96. Use play telephones, tape recorders, or walkie-talkies to have the child focus upon using words and sentences as a means of communication.

97. Provide puppets for the child to use during free-play and more structured periods. Cheyney (1967) provides instructions for making puppets out of various materials.

98. Smith (1968) suggests having the child respond to questions emphasizing verbal fluency where nearly any response a child gives is acceptable. For example:

    "What would happen if we didn't have electricity?"

99. Give the child practice in using articles and prepositions by providing him with certain key words (e.g., house, boy, door) and having the child build a sentence around these words.

100. Karnes (1968) recommends asking the child *"Tell me how," "Why do we,"* or *"Tell me where"* questions. For example:

    "Tell me how . . .

       you tie your shoes.
       you play kickball.
       your father washes the car."

101. Gather a number of kitchen utensils or tools. Have a child describe the use of one utensil or tool without using gestures.

C. *Does the child have difficulty in using correct grammatical and syntactical forms?*

102. Correct grammar and syntax errors by providing the child with the correct usage. Osborn (1968) recommends telling the child to "Say it the way I do," or "This is the way you say it in school."

103. Encourage the child to respond in sentences. Incorporate a child's one-word responses into a sentence and have the child repeat the entire sentence. Groups of children can also repeat particular sentences together.

104. Use choral speaking to emphasize correct language usage. Bryan (1971) lists over one-hundred original verses that can be used in the primary grades.

105. Display a picture before the child and describe the picture in a sentence. For example, "This boy is running." Have the child repeat the sentence. Eventually, omit certain words for the child to insert as he repeats the sentence.

106. Provide pictures which illustrate past, present, and future tense of verbs. Sequences of an individual about to do something, doing something, and completing the same act can be described and discussed (Johnson & Myklebust, 1967).

107. Have the child describe an activity as he is jumping, skipping, etc. For example, "I *am jumping.*" Upon completion have the child say, "I *jumped* very high," or "I *jumped* over the box."

108. Provide the child with two different-sized tin cans, a red poker chip, and a white poker chip. Place the red chip in the large can. Ask the child "Is the red chip in the large can?" Gradually, have the child verbalize different situations. Vary the manipulation and questions, or verbalize incorrect statements and let the child catch your error (Karnes, 1968).

109. Have the child repeat words and sentences emphasizing plurals, verb tense, etc., using the Language Master. As the child progresses, provide use of the tape recorder for making statements about pictures, objects, etc.

110. Give the child an eraser and instruct him to place it in various places. Have the child describe each situation. For example:

    "The eraser is *on* my head."
    "The eraser is *in* the desk."
    "The eraser is *under* the chair."

111. Use the flannel board to demonstrate situations to which the child is required to respond. Stress plurals, prepositions, etc. Permit the child to create flannel board situations which he might verbally describe.

112. Write a sentence on the chalkboard with the words in an incorrect order and have the child arrange the words in the correct order. Flash cards containing single words can also be arranged into sentences.

113. Prepare a series of sentences with missing words. Read these to the child and have him supply the omitted word. Plurals, adjectives, prepositions, etc., can be emphasized with this activity. For example:

    "We went _____ the store."
    "The boat is _____ the water."
    "The plane is _____ the sky."

114. Provide the child with various pictures showing single and multiple units of different objects. Ask the child to point to the *girl* in one picture or the *girls* in another picture. Eventually, have the child make a statement about the pictures, such as "The *girls are* playing ball" (Karnes, 1968).

115. Wedemeyer and Cejka (1970) recommend preparing small cards with nouns, verbs, and adjectives written on them. Group the noun cards on one ring, the verbs on a second, and the adjectives on a third. Attach the cards to a folded cardboard stand in order for them to be flipped over easily. Have the child form appropriate sentences (e.g., "Rabbits are soft.").

116. Provide children with phrases (e.g., the big dog, to the mountains, under the house, etc.). Have the child build a sentence using the phrases in the standard syntactical form.

117. Bush and Giles (1969) suggest reading a number of sentences to the child, leaving out a word, and having the child fill in the correct ending. For example:

"I have many dresses but I have only one blue
_____."

"Yesterday we played ball, and today we will
_____ ball."

"I like to jump rope, but after I have been ____
_____ for a while I get tired."

D. *Does the child have an inadequate oral vocabulary?*

118. Provide children with experiences to stimulate vocabulary development and word usage. Field trips, reading stories, oral discussions, etc., can be used to develop vocabulary.

119. Collect colorful and exciting pictures, cartoons, paintings, etc. Have the child describe the action by listing descriptive words. Discuss the words with the entire class.

120. Have the child build a list of words from one common root, such as *ball* or *man.* Assign a point for each word. The child with the most points wins the game.

121. Have the child list the possible synonyms for particular words such as *cars, babies, days,* etc. (Smith, 1967).

122. Play "hangman" where children fill in the blends of a word by guessing letters. For each letter guessed incorrectly additional parts of the body are added until the individual is "hung."

123. Write any ten letters on the board and have children compose a ten-word telegram using the letters on the board as the initial letters for the ten words. Vary the activity by specifying the nature of the telegram (Platts, 1970).

124. Ask the child to name all the objects in a room or a picture during a specified time limit. Keep a graph to note improvement (Lerner, 1971).

125. Stop periodically while reading a story and have the child supply a word that fits with the context of the story.

126. Provide the child with a sentence (e.g., "It rained very hard last night."). Ask the child to say the same thing in as many different ways as possible. Encourage the use of unusual words.

127. Read a story to the child and have him retell the story to another child. Encourage the child to retell the story in his own words.

128. Introduce a "word of the day" and encourage children to use the word throughout the day. Permit particular children to present words on certain days (Platts, 1970).
129. Provide children with a word that has multiple meanings, such as "run." Have each child in turn use the word in a sentence employing a different meaning each time.

NOTES

[1]For detailed language development programs for various age levels, see: *Peabody Language Development Kits,* American Guidance Service, Inc., Circle Rines, Minn. 55014; *Distar Language,* Science Research Associates, 259 E. Erie St., Chicago, Ill. 60611.

[2]See Steiner and Pond (1970) for a listing and description of numerous finger plays.

[3]Eisenson (1972) offers additional suggestions for basic language constructions, such as adding nouns to verbs, nouns to predicate adjectives, etc.

[4]Gray and Wise (1959) and Van Riper (1963) list additional tongue and lip positions for various sounds.

[5]See Bereiter and Engelmann (1966) for a more detailed description of this program.

ADDITIONAL READINGS

Alder, S. *The nonverbal child.* Springfield, Ill.: Thomas, 1964.

Bereiter, C., & Engelmann, S. *Language learning activities for the disadvantaged child.* New York: Anti-Defamation League of B'nai B'rith.

Bereiter, C., & Engelmann, S. *Teaching disadvantaged children in the preschool.* Englewood Cliffs, N.J.: Prentice-Hall, 1966.

Berry, M. F. *Language disorders in children: The bases and diagnoses.* New York: Appleton-Century-Crofts, 1969.

Bryan, R. *When children speak.* San Rafael, Calif.: Academic Therapy Publications, 1971.

Bush, W. J., & Giles, M. T. *Aids to psycholinguistic teaching.* Columbus, Ohio: Charles E. Merrill, 1969.

Cheyney, A. B. *Teaching culturally disadvantaged in the elementary school.* Columbus, Ohio: Charles E. Merrill, 1967.

Eisenson, J. *Aphasia in children.* New York: Harper & Row, 1972.

Goldstein, K. *Language and language disturbances.* New York: Grune & Stratton, 1948.

Gray, G. W., & Wise, C. M. *The bases of speech.* New York: Harper & Row, 1959.

Heilman, A. *Phonics in proper perspective.* Columbus, Ohio: Charles E. Merrill, 1968.

Johnson, D. J., & Myklebust, H. R. *Learning disabilities: Educational principles and practices.* New York: Grune & Stratton, 1967.

Kaliski, L., Tankersley, R., & Iogha, R. *Structured dramatics for children with learning disabilities.* San Rafael, Calif.: Academic Therapy Publications, 1971.

Karnes, M. B. *Helping young children develop language skills.* Arlington, Va.: The Council for Exceptional Children, 1968.

Lerner, J. *Children with learning disabilities.* Boston: Houghton Mifflin, 1971.

Linn, S. H. *Teaching phonics with finger puppets.* San Rafael, Calif.: Academic Therapy Publications, 1972.

McGrady, H. J. "Language pathology and learning disabilities." In H. R. Myklebust, ed., *Progress in learning disabilities,* Vol. 1. New York: Grune & Stratton, 1968, pp. 199–233.

Mecham, M. J. *Verbal Language Development Scale.* Minneapolis: American Guidance Service, Inc., 1959.

Menyuk, P. *The development of speech.* Indianapolis: Bobbs-Merrill, 1972.

Myers, G. C. "Creative thinking activities." In *Highlights handbook.* Columbus, Ohio: Highlights for Children, Inc., 1965.

Myers, P. I., & Hammill, D. D. *Methods for learning disorders.* New York: John Wiley, 1969.

Myklebust, H. R. *Auditory disorders in children: A manual for differential diagnosis.* New York: Grune & Stratton, 1954.

Myklebust, H. R. "Childhood aphasia: An evolving concept." In L. E. Travis, ed., *Handbook of speech pathology and audiology.* New York: Appleton-Century-Crofts, 1971, pp. 1181–1202.

Myklebust, H. R. "Childhood aphasia: Identification, diagnosis, remediation." In L. E. Travis, ed., *Handbook of speech pathology and audiology.* New York: Appleton-Century-Crofts, 1971, pp. 1203–17.

Nimnicht, G., McAfee, O., & Meier, J. *The new nursery school.* New York: General Learning Corporation, 1969.

Osborn, J. Teaching a teaching language to disadvantaged children. Mimeograph paper, University of Illinois, Urbana, Ill., 1968.

Platts, M. E. *Anchor: A handbook of vocabulary discovery techniques for the classroom teacher.* Stevensville, Mich.: Educational Service, 1970.

Smith, J. A. *Creative teaching of the language arts in the elementary school.* Boston: Allyn & Bacon, 1967.

Smith, R. M. *Clinical teaching: Methods of instruction for the retarded.* New York: McGraw-Hill, 1968.

Smith, R. M., ed. *Teacher diagnosis of educational difficulties.* Columbus, Ohio: Charles E. Merrill, 1969.

Spradlin, J. "Procedures for evaluating processes associated with receptive and expressive language." In R. Schiefelbush, R. Copeland, & J. O.

Smith, eds., *Language and mental retardation.* New York: Holt, Rinehart & Winston, 1967, pp. 118–36.

Steiner, V. G., & Pond, R. E. *Finger play fun.* Columbus, Ohio: Charles E. Merrill, 1970.

Valett, R. E. *The remediation of learning disabilities.* Palo Alto, Calif.: Fearon Publishers, 1967.

Wagner, G., Hosier, M., & Blackman, M. *Listening games: Building listening skills with instructional games.* New York: Teachers Publishing, 1970.

Wedemeyer, A., & Cejka, J. *Creative ideas for teaching exceptional children.* Denver: Love Publishing Co., 1970.

Wedemeyer, A., & Cejka, J. *Learning games for exceptional children.* Denver: Love Publishing Co., 1971.

Wood, N. E. *Delayed speech and language development.* Englewood Cliffs, N. J.: Prentice-Hall, 1964.

Wood, N. E. *Verbal learning.* San Rafael, Calif.: Dimensions, 1969.

Zigmond, N. K., & Cicci, R. *Auditory learning.* San Rafael, Calif.: Dimensions, 1968.

Zimmerman, I. L., Steiner, V. G., & Evatt, R. L. *Preschool Language Manual.* Columbus, Ohio: Charles E. Merrill, 1969.

II

Arithmetic
Problems

The remediation of arithmetic problems experienced by children is an area that has, unfortunately, received relatively little attention. Arithmetic difficulties are often related to problems in other academic areas. It is frequently necessary, therefore, to investigate commonalities among learning problems for the purpose of parallel remediation. Difficulties in discrimination, memory, perception, comprehension, and handwriting can affect achievement in arithmetic as well as achievement in reading, written language, and other academic skills.

Spencer and Smith (1969) note that arithmetic skills are so complex in their interrelationships that children may have difficulty in achievement for a variety of reasons. However, three basic questions with which the classroom teacher must be concerned are:

√ 1. What deficiencies in number-readiness skills prevent the child from achieving in arithmetic?

229

2. What difficulties in computational skills and time and money concepts interfere with progress in arithmetic?
3. What specific skill difficulties prevent achievement in problem solving?

Diagnosis

Teacher Observation

The teacher should be very precise in pinpointing a child's arithmetic difficulties. Frequent observations of the child during written assignments, board work, and oral discussions will provide the teacher with useful information in specifying particular problems and planning for a remedial program. Smith (1969b) recommends the use of a checklist for recording the results of observations. He maintains that "a check sheet allows the teacher to compile a systematic collection of data, and thus helps her to focus on specific weaknesses" (p. 167). Checklists can be developed by teachers according to specific grade-level skills. Otto and McMenemy (1966) provide diagnostic arithmetic checklists that can be used by classroom teachers.

Informal Assessment

Informal teacher-made measures of arithmetic ability are well suited to the specificity of arithmetic difficulties. Various arithmetic skills may be evaluated by using items gathered from arithmetic books. The items may be placed on cards for permanent usage and administered to individual children. Separate tests should be developed for specific skills. Informal tests should be used to evaluate *one* particular task. The teacher will then be more aware of the exact difficulties being experienced by the child. The use of informal tests in arithmetic will be advantageous for the teacher in planning for individual needs within a class.

Formal Tests

Most group achievement tests include an arithmetic subtest as part of the complete battery. However, unless the test includes a profile analysis of specific arithmetic skills, the score will not be very helpful in planning an instructional program for a child. A number of good diagnostic tests in arithmetic are available for this purpose. The *Diagnostic Chart for Fundamental Processes in Arithmetic* (Buswell &

John, 1925); the *Diagnostic Tests and Self-Helps in Arithmetic* (Brueckner, 1955); the *Key Math Diagnostic Arithmetic Test* (Connolly, Nachtman, & Pritchett, 1971); the *Los Angeles Diagnostic Tests: Fundamentals of Arithmetic* (Armstrong & Clark, 1947); and the *Los Angeles Diagnostic Tests: Reasoning in Arithmetic* (Armstrong, 1926) are all very useful diagnostic instruments. These tests provide data concerning a child's strengths and weaknesses in specific arithmetic skills.

Following are a number of teaching suggestions for specific arithmetic problems. Each suggestion used should be based upon the individual needs of the child.

Arithmetic Readiness
Skills

Prior to performing adequately in basic computational skills, a child must exhibit competency in a number of skills basic to understanding other arithmetic processes. The child must:

1. Be able to discriminate among different sizes, shapes, and quantities
2. Attain an understanding of one-to-one correspondence
3. Have the ability to count meaningfully
4. Be able to order number names and sets

Diagnostic questions and teaching suggestions for remediating arithmetic readiness problems are listed below.

I. Has the Child Mastered the Skills Prerequisite for Arithmetic Achievement?

A. *Does the child discriminate different sizes, shapes, and quantities?*

1. Cut different-sized circles, squares, triangles, and rectangles from oak tag, felt, or wood. Have the child match the missing pieces to the correct spaces.
2. Provide children with different-sized buttons, pencils, nails, or paper strips. Make sure that the objects are identical except in size. Ask the children to arrange the objects by size beginning with the smallest and working toward the largest. Johnson and Myklebust (1967) suggest providing a key, such as a page of circles drawn in proper order, for children unable to arrange sizes by themselves.

3. Ask the child to find all the circular objects within the room. Contests can be held to see which child finds the greatest number of objects. Rectangular, triangular, and square shapes can be found also.

4. Provide the child with a number of different-sized containers and lids. Instruct the child to fit the lids to the containers. Stopwatches can be used to time individual children. Graphs can be kept to check progress.

5. Provide each child with a ball or a round object differing in size. Have the children line up according to the size of the ball they are holding from biggest to smallest ball. Direct the child with the smallest ball to sit down. Continue asking children to be seated, varying the directions from biggest to smallest, until all but one child is seated (Wagner, Hosier, & Gilloley, 1964).

6. Ask children to put together simple jigsaw puzzles of three to five pieces. More complex puzzles with additional pieces can be used eventually.

7. Matching index cards of various sizes to different-sized envelopes provides children with experience in relating the size of an object to an area in which it is placed (Johnson & Myklebust, 1967).

8. Give the child a set of different-sized cube blocks. Ask the child to find all the blocks that are the same size as one that you choose from the pile. Matching the cubes to an outline on paper is an extension of this activity that includes discrimination of size. This activity can be varied to teach shape discrimination by using blocks differing in form.

9. Provide the child with an assortment of different lengths of rope. Ask the child to select the rope that seems closest in size to given objects in a classroom (Behrmann & Millman, 1971).

10. Cut different shapes from felt and have children arrange them in order at the flannel board. The child is provided with the opportunity to feel and trace the outline of the shape.

B. *Does the child understand one-to-one correspondence?*

11. Provide the child with a pegboard design to duplicate. Give the child the exact number of pegs to arrange in order for his design to match the design that is provided.

12. Assign the child duties that require a one-to-one relationship, e.g., passing papers, pencils, or books to each child within a group or class.

13. Provide the child with worksheets that require finishing incomplete pictures, for example, placing a tail on each dog or a roof on each house. Be sure that all pictures are missing the same part.

14. Ask the children to make a tally mark for each time a bell is rung, a note is played on the piano, hands are clapped, or a beat is heard on a drum.

15. Provide the child with worksheets that require matching similar sets of objects on a page. Lines are drawn connecting the boxes that contain the same number of objects. Eventually the child may be asked to match a numeral, such as five, with a picture of five kites.

16. Smith (1968) suggests playing games of musical chairs, setting a table for the number of children in class or for members of a family, or checking to see if enough glasses of milk are available for the class members as practical activities that enhance one-to-one correspondence.

17. "Prepare several pieces of flannel on which there are various numbers of buttons. Prepare a second set on which there are only button holes." Ask the child to match the pieces of flannel with the same number of buttons and holes (Johnson & Myklebust, 1967, p. 258).

18. Provide individual children with a stack of chips or toothpicks. Ask the child to match a given number that you draw at the chalkboard. Large groups of children can individually participate in this activity at their desks.

19. Discuss examples of one-to-one correspondence with the children. Ask them to provide suggestions. Examples include: one person—one nose; one elephant—one trunk; one dog—one tail; one hand—one thumb, etc.

20. Wagner, Hosier, and Gilloley (1964) suggest asking children numerical questions and requiring them to provide an answer by showing the correct number of beads on a counting frame. Illustrative questions include:

"How many fingers on your hand?"
"How many windows in our room?"
"How many jars of paint on the easel?"
"How many children with glasses?"
"How many chairs in the front of the room?"

✓ C. *Does the child have difficulty in counting?*

21. Have the child make a motor response as he counts. Counting pegs as they are placed in the pegboard or beads as they are put on a string will often help the child who skips numbers while counting.

22. Let the child use an abacus. The abacus provides the child with a manipulative device and a visual image as he is counting.

23. Have the child establish the counting principle through motor activities such as clapping four times, jumping two times, or tapping on the table three times (Lerner, 1971).

24. Spitzer (1961) recommends asking one child to count the number of children in the room during morning attendance or counting aloud rather slowly and deliberately to "see how long it takes" the children to get ready for recess.

25. Provide children with worksheets having a certain quantity of objects (e.g., balls, lollipops, houses, etc.). Below each group write the numbers from one to five or one to ten. Ask children to circle the correct number. More than one group of objects may appear on each worksheet.

26. Dot-to-dot puzzles where the dots are numbered in sequence can be followed to complete a picture. The sequence of numbers can be gradually increased and pictures may become more detailed.

27. Number lines permanently attached to the top of each child's desk provide children with a constant point of reference. Longer number lines extending to larger numbers can be placed at the top of the chalkboard or on the floor. An example of a shorter number line appears below.

```
|___|___|___|___|___|___|___|___|___|___|___|
0   1   2   3   4   5   6   7   8   9   10
```

28. Provide children with worksheets having blank spaces before or after a number. Ask the child to fill in the missing numbers. For example:

    _____ 7; _____ 13; 19 _____; etc.

    Eventually a series of numbers can be used and the child is instructed to fill in the missing numbers. For example:

    23, ___, ___, 26, 27, ___, 29, ___, ___, 32.

29. Write the numbers from one to twenty on a worksheet. Include one number twice. Ask the child to circle all the numbers from one to twenty and find the extra number. Various adaptations include writing more than one number twice and extending the sequence beyond twenty (Platts, 1964).

30. Bereiter and Engelmann (1966) describe a program for teaching children to count aloud. The detailed description of their program provides teachers with basic operational skills required for this fundamental skill.

31. "Prepare a series of cards with directions for bead stringing. The number on the card indicates the number of beads to be strung for that color. At the beginning level, use actual color cues" (Wedemeyer & Cejka, 1970, p. 99).

32. Have the child close his eyes and listen to the beats of a drum as he concentrates on counting. Eventually, the child can be asked to make a mark on paper for each sound he hears (Johnson & Myklebust, 1967).

D. *Does the child understand groups or sets?*

33. Make children aware of groups by pointing out that similar things form a group. Show pictures or point out groups of animals, fruit, people, etc. Younger children can be permitted to cut and paste pictures from magazines and group them according to similarities.

34. As the child progresses in his grouping ability, ask him to group objects according to more precise criteria involving combinations of color, size, shape, quantity, etc.

35. Provide the child with a variety of simple pictures or drawings which vary in the number of objects shown.

Ask the child to match pictures or drawings according to the number of objects they contain.

36. Ask children to arrange pegs or blocks in various groupings. Instruct the child to arrange six blocks in three groups of two, for example, or twelve blocks into four groups of three. Eventually, ask the child to arrange as many groupings as possible for a certain number.

37. Prepare a series of cards which show various groupings of symbols for numbers. Ask the child to organize the cards in piles according to number. All the groupings that add up to eight would be placed in one pile, nine in another, etc. Groupings of five could include:

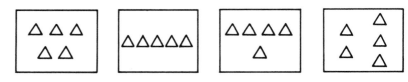

38. Cuisenaire Rods[1] serve as an excellent device for grouping work. The rods may be grouped according to size or classified according to color.

39. Platts (1964) suggests preparing a worksheet similar to the example below. Ask the children to draw circles to group the dots according to the directions.

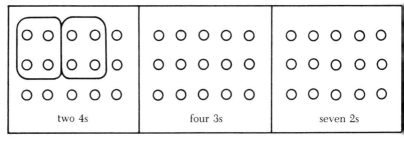

40. Play dominos with children and emphasize the various ways that a number may be grouped. Large dominos may be made on heavy cardboard and cut to appropriate size.

41. Provide the child with simple addition and subtraction statements, such as 5 + 2, and ask the child to

draw the number in each group. Children might also be provided with various groupings and asked to write the appropriate numerical statement. For example:

___ + ___ = ___

42. Johnson and Myklebust (1967) recommend cutting strips of paper into pieces one-inch wide, varying in length from one to ten inches. Ask the child which strip is the longest, the shortest, etc. Demonstrate the many ways the strips can be grouped to make an amount that is equal to a longer strip.
43. Use egg cartons to demonstrate how groups are made up of individual "members." Cut the cartons into various sections and place them together to show how a group might be visualized.
44. Have the child form various groupings using the marble board or a set of counting sticks. At first ask the child to duplicate a pattern that you provide. Gradually, verbalize directions to the child such as, "Form a group of six sticks."

Computational Skills and Time and Money Concepts

Most problems in arithmetic are due to deficiencies in basic computational skills (Otto & McMenemy, 1966). Adequate computational and conceptual skills which are fundamental to successful arithmetic achievement include:

1. An understanding of place value
2. The ability to add, subtract, multiply, and divide
3. An understanding of fractions
4. The ability to tell time
5. A knowledge of monetary values

Diagnostic questions and teaching suggestions for remediating computational difficulties are listed below.

II. Has the Child Mastered Basic Computational Skills and Time and Money Concepts?

A. *Does the child understand place value?*

45. Cut thirty squares of tagboard and number each card starting from 0 to 9, making three cards for each number. Write "ones" under each number in one set, "tens" under each number in the second set, and "hundreds" under each number in the third set. Distribute one card to each child in the room. Call out particular numbers, such as 238, and have those children holding the cards needed to form that number come to the front of the room and arrange themselves in the proper order to form that number (Platts, 1964).

46. Prepare a worksheet with three columns. The right column should be labeled "ones," the middle column "tens," and the left column "hundreds." Provide children with numbers such as 130, 28, 497, 5, 17, etc. Instruct the children to place the numbers in the correct column on the paper.

47. Ask the child questions such as, "What place does the 5 represent in 352," or "Can you write a numeral with a 7 in the hundreds place?"

48. Prepare a series of cards similar to the example below and ask the child to figure out the numbers on the card. The back of each card can correctly identify the number.

| *Front* | | *Back* |

Tens	Ones
///	/////

Back: 35

49. The abacus is an excellent aid in helping children to see that position determines the numerical value of symbols. Children can represent numbers by moving the appropriate amount of beads for numbers called by the teacher.

50. Smith (1968) suggests the use of a place-value box as part of the instruction in simple addition and subtraction. A small box with three equal-size compartments labeled "ones," "tens," and "hundreds" from right to left is used for inserting sticks, such as tongue depressors. Children add to or remove sticks from the groups located in various compartments as they add or subtract.

51. Prepare a set of cards numbered from 0 to 9. Screw three cup hooks into a board and write the words "hundreds," "tens," and "ones" over the hooks. Call out a number and have the child place the number on the correct hook corresponding to the place value (Wedemeyer & Cejka, 1970).

52. The teacher or a child makes a statement such as "I am thinking of a number that is two tens and four ones." Children are asked to write the number on the chalkboard or on a worksheet. Eventually the "hundreds" place may be added (Wagner, Hosier, & Gilloley, 1964).

53. Sticks or papers tied together and placed as "ones" or "tens" demonstrate the idea of number bases. For example, thirty-seven would be reprsented by three bundles of "tens" sticks on the left with seven "ones" sticks on the right. Children can practice with popsicle sticks in making bundles representing different numbers.

54. The "ones" and "tens" blocks of the Cuisenaire Rods can also be used to demonstrate the collective value of ten "ones" equalling one "ten." Various numbers may be represented by organizing the blocks similarly to the popsicle sticks mentioned in activity #53. To represent *place* value the blocks must be properly arranged *spatially* (i.e., ones to the right of tens, etc.).

B. *Does the child have difficulty with the fundamental operations of addition, subtraction, multiplication, and division?*

55. Use the fingers to make various addition and subtraction combinations. Hold up a certain number of fingers and add or subtract other fingers.

56. Provide the child with many concrete experiences in learning to add or subtract. Use sticks, paper clips, buttons, raisins, etc. The objects can be used to form various groupings for the more difficult combinations.

57. Give the child auditory clues by clapping out the addition or subtraction combinations. The teacher can initiate the clapping, and gradually the child can do his own clapping. Adaptations include foot tapping, jumping, or hand tapping on the desk.

58. Prepare worksheets that illustrate various number problems. Use dots, circles, lines, etc. for the groupings. Have the child fill in the correct numerals. For example:

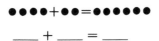

_____ + _____ = _____

59. Wagner, Hosier, and Gilloley (1964) suggest using an "addition ferris wheel" to reinforce addition facts. Draw a large circle with numbers written around it on the chalkboard. Place one number in the middle of the circle and ask children to see how quickly they can go around the "ferris wheel" by adding the middle number to the number on the outside of the circle. This activity can easily be adapted to basic subtraction, multiplication and division facts.

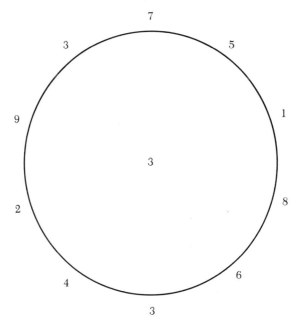

60. Flash cards of basic combinations in addition, subtraction, multiplication, and division can be used for developing quicker recognition of the combinations.

Children can work individually, in pairs, or in groups, either writing or calling out the answers.

61. Provide children with a card having a number from one to twenty written on it. Call out various combinations such as 7 + 5 or 2 X 4. The child with the correct answer holds up his card. Higher combinations can be gradually added to the cards. Eventually children may be given more than one card to hold.

62. The tachistoscope can be used to measure the recognition rate of number facts. Lerner and Vaver (1970) suggest placing number facts on transparencies, cutting them into strips, and inserting them in a filmstrip projector. The projector can then be used as a tachistoscope by exposing the facts for the desired length of time.

63. Have children use dice to practice addition, subtraction, and multiplication facts. Children may write or call out the various answers. Points can be added for each successful answer. Children may continue throwing the dice until they respond incorrectly.

64. Various games, as illustrated below, can be adapted to practicing number combinations by using addition, subtraction, multiplication, or division facts.

Hop scotch

7 −2	8 −3	4 −2
9 −5	6 −1	5 −3
8 −6	1 −0	7 −5

Climbing the ladder

8 x 5
7 x 3
2 x 4
6 x 1
5 x 5
3 x 7

Tic-tac-toe

7 + 5	9 + 4	5 + 3
8 + 3	4 + 8	3 + 7
2 + 1	5 + 6	7 + 2

65. Prepare approximately forty cards with numbers between one and ten written on each card. Place the cards face down, and have the child turn up two cards. Direct the child to add, subtract, or multiply the two cards (Wedemeyer & Cejka, 1970).

66. Prepare number-sentence worksheets leaving different frames blank. Ask children to supply the missing number. For example:

$$6 + \boxed{} = 13$$

$$\boxed{} \times 7 = 56$$

$$7 - \boxed{} = 2$$

67. Prepare a worksheet with several rows of figures. Ask the children to circle the two numbers in sequence that add up to a specific number, such as 12 (Platts, 1964).

4 5 9 ⑥ ⑥ 3 4 ⑤ ⑦

9 6 ⑤ ⑦ 3 ④ ⑧ 6 2

68. Play "Bingo" with small groups of children. Numbers appear in each of the spaces on the card. The teacher reads different combinations such as 5 + 6, 7 − 3, 6 × 2, etc. Spaces are covered if the child has the appropriate answer on his card.

69. The number line is an effective device for demonstrating the fundamental operations. The example 3 + 5 is taught by starting at three and jumping five places to eight.

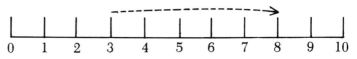

0   1   2   3   4   5   6   7   8   9   10

70. Record number combinations with answers on a tape recorder. Ask children to write or say the answer before it is played on the tape. This activity can be individually or group administered.

71. Provide children with a variety of long-division problems. Ask them to find just the *first* number in the quotient. Children can be provided with the first number and asked to show that the given number is correct.

72. Prepare a worksheet with columns of boxes. Write a number in the bottom box of each column, as illustrated below. Ask the children to fill in each box with a different combination that adds up to the number at the bottom. Subtraction facts can also be used for this activity.

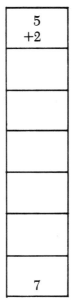

73. Spitzer (1961) suggests providing a variety of orally presented division questions such as:

   "12 can be divided into how many 4s?"
   "24 divided by 6 is how many?"
   "How many 2s equal 12?"

74. Duplicate or have each child make a multiplication chart. Explain it's usage and encourage children to use it freely. (See following page.)

1	2	3	4	5	6	7	8	9	10
2	4	6	8	10	12	14	16	18	20
3	6	9	12	15	18	21	24	27	30
4	8	12	16	20	24	28	32	36	40
5	10	15	20	25	30	35	40	45	50
6	12	18	24	30	36	42	48	54	60
7	14	21	28	35	42	49	56	63	70
8	16	24	32	40	48	56	64	72	80
9	18	27	36	45	54	63	72	81	90
10	20	30	40	50	60	70	80	90	100

75. Prepare a division worksheet where the numbers are illustrated. Have the child fill in the correct numerical statement. For example:

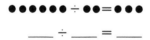

_____ ÷ _____ = _____

76. Platts (1964) suggests providing children with "preceding-fact" clues for specific combinations. For example, if 3 + 7 = 10, then what is 3 + 8? This activity can also be adapted for subtraction, multiplication, or division facts.

C. *Does the child understand fractions?*

77. Initiate fraction instruction through halves, followed by quarters and eighths. Provide children with familiar pictures that are cut in half. Ask the child to put the halves together. This procedure can also be used with foods, such as fruits, sandwiches, and cookies.

78. The importance of parts to a whole can be visually illustrated by providing children with pictures having obvious parts missing. Have them find the missing part (Behrmann & Millman, 1971).

79. Flannel board fractional cutouts and paper pie plates that are divided into different-colored fractional parts

are manipulative materials that provide children with a better understanding of fractions.

80. Prepare a worksheet with a different number of circles in each box on the page. Ask the child to split each circle in the first box into halves, each circle in the second box into thirds, etc. Younger children enjoy coloring parts of the circle.
81. Smith (1968) suggests using charts similar to those below to illustrate the relationships of fractional parts to a whole.

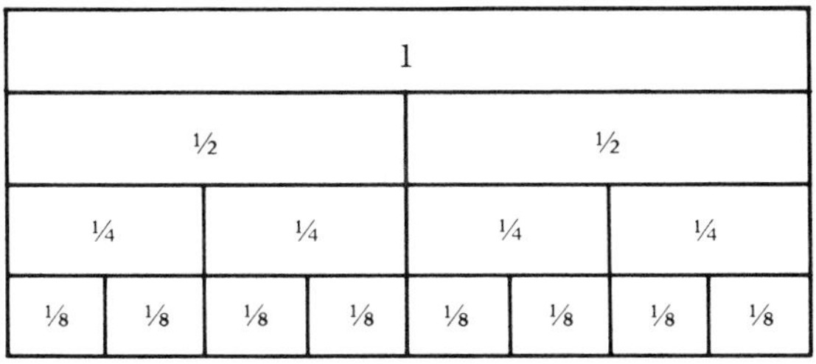
1
½
½
¼
¼
¼
¼
⅛
⅛
⅛
⅛
⅛
⅛
⅛
⅛

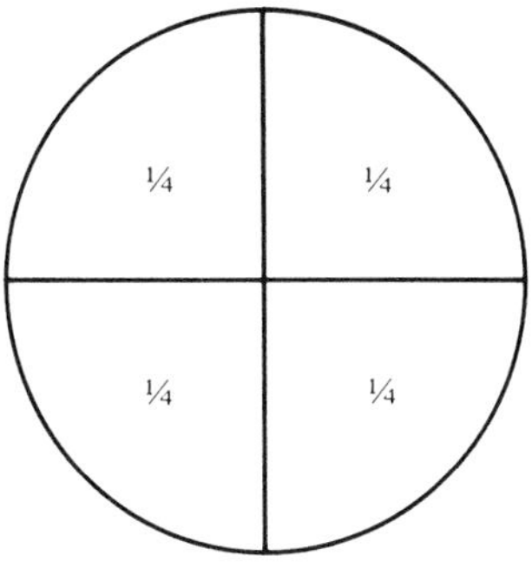
¼
¼
¼
¼

82. Provide children with a worksheet in which circles or squares are already divided and shaded. Provide a box in which the child is to write the appropriate fraction for the shaded part (Engelmann, 1969). For example:

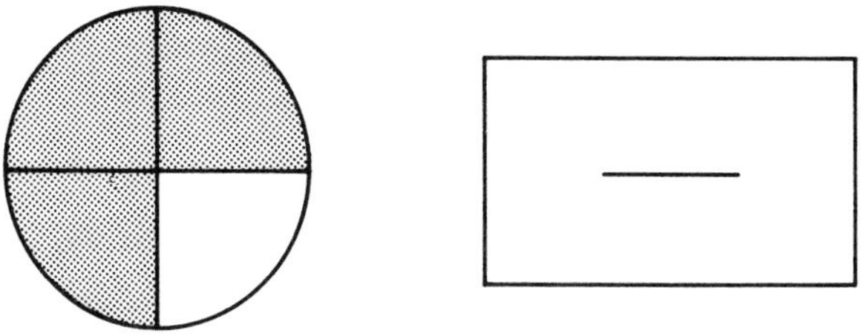

83. Gradually introduce assignments where children are working with fractions without visual clues. Have children work with fractional quantities choosing the largest and smallest quantity from a given list of fractions.

84. Prepare a worksheet comprised of a number of equivalent fractions and ask the child to circle the two equivalent fractions in each line. For example:

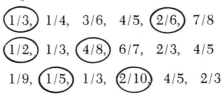

85. Use fraction number lines to introduce children to whether a fraction is equal to one whole, is greater than one whole, or is less than one whole. Counting forwards and backwards on the fraction number line may also be helpful.

86. Use the measurements in simple recipes to reinforce fractional components. Have children do the measuring for the baking of cookies, pancakes, or cakes.

D. *Does the child experience difficulty in telling time?*

87. Provide children with real clocks or teacher-made (or pupil-made) clocks to teach time telling. Clocks may be inexpensively made by attaching cardboard hands to a paper plate. Teaching clocks may also be commercially purchased through most school supply companies.

88. Use individual clocks for group activities. Ask the children a variety of time-related questions and have them set their individual clocks. For example:

The time school begins
The time we eat lunch at school
The time school ends for the day
The time you go to bed

89. Lerner (1971) suggests the following sequence for teaching time:
    a. The hour
    b. The half-hour
    c. The quarter hour
    d. Five-minute intervals
    e. Before and after the hour
    f. Minute intervals
    g. Seconds

90. Prepare a worksheet with a number of clock faces. Instruct the child to draw in the hands of the clock at certain times. Initially, the teacher should call the times aloud; eventually, they can be written under the faces.

91. Prepare a series of cards with a time written on the front of the card and a clock face showing that time on the back. Children may use the cards individually by setting their own clocks and checking their work by turning over the cards (Platts, 1964).

92. Ask children to perform activities where they can be timed.

    "How long will it take Margaret to take these papers to the office?"
    "Let's see how long it will take us to clean up our desks."
    "We may all go outside for five minutes."
    "We have three minutes to finish the arithmetic paper."
    "How long did it take you to read this story?"

93. Provide the children with TV, plane, or train schedules and ask them questions based upon the schedules. Relate the schedules to the clock and have the child find the time on the clock.

94. Have each child make up an individual time schedule or log of his day. Include activities such as the time for getting up, catching the bus, going to recess, eating lunch, going home, playing, going to bed, etc.

95. Show children various pictures (e.g., getting out of bed, eating lunch, etc.) and ask them to set their clocks at the times indicated by the pictures. Individual differences must be taken into account for slight time variations.

96. The fractions on the clock may be taught by having a child stand with his hands pointed straight up. Various times may be positioned as he lowers his hands. The teacher can call out the times as the children move their hands accordingly (Behrmann & Millman, 1971).

97. Hofmeister (1968) has developed a highly structured program to teach time telling. The programmed aspect of this material gradually introduces time-telling skills sequentially.

E. *Does the child understand monetary values?*

98. Provide children with real money whenever possible to teach money values. When real money is unavailable, authentic-looking rubber stamp reproductions of actual U.S. coins may be purchased.[2]

99. Prepare a worksheet with various coin denominations in separate boxes. Instruct the children to draw a line connecting the boxes that equal the same amount of money. For example, five pennies would equal one nickel, two dimes and one nickel would equal one quarter, etc.

100. Platts (1964) suggests preparing a worksheet with problems similar to those below and asking children to choose the greater amount and find the sum.

> Quarter + nickel + dime *OR* quarter + quarter
> Dollar *OR* nickel + three quarters
> Seven dimes *OR* three quarters
> Quarter + dime + half dollar *OR* three quarters
> Dime + dime + dime + nickel + quarter *OR* half dollar + nickel

101. Show children various combinations of coins and ask them to total the amounts. Actual coins pasted to cards should be used when possible. Otherwise, the reproduction (see activity #98) may be stamped on cards.

102. Set up a grocery store in the classroom with empty boxes and cans of food. Price each item and allow various children to be the store-keeper, cashier, and shoppers using real or play money to conduct business. Adaptations of this activity include holding several items before the entire class and asking them to add the total cost.

103. Give children a certain amount of money and ask them to purchase as many different items as possible

with the available money. The child who is able to buy the greatest number of different items without exceeding his supply of money wins the game.

104. Paste various objects (food, toys, and clothes) on cards and label each object with a price. Flash the cards individually to children and ask them to write down the change they would receive from a certain amount of money.

105. Arrange with the cafeteria manager to have certain children act as the cashier for specified periods of time. Let other children collect and total milk or bus money in school.

106. Provide children with actual or play restaurant menus. Ask the children to order a meal and total the cost. More advanced students should add tax and tip.

107. Give children newspaper grocery advertisements, if you are unable to set up a school store. Ask children to do the "weekly shopping" for their mother and total the cost of the groceries (Platts, 1964).

108. If a token reinforcement system is being used in the classroom, there are many opportunities to teach monetary concepts based on the exchange of tokens for reinforcers (see Chapter 2). Play currency may be made by the teacher and used as tokens. A currency-based token economy teaches many arithmetic skills directly, including monetary value.

Problem-Solving Skills

Some children with arithmetic difficulties are unable to operationalize number skills in story problems due to specific problem-solving deficiencies. Adequate problem-solving skills in arithmetic are based upon the child's:

1. ability to understand the language of arithmetic.
2. reasoning and analysis skills in reading story problems.

Diagnostic questions and teaching suggestions for remediating problem-solving difficulties are listed below.

III. Has the Child Developed Problem-Solving Skills?

A. *Does the child understand arithmetical terms and signs?*

109. The terms *longer* and *shorter* may be better understood if the teacher draws lines of various lengths on

the board and asks the child to make them longer or shorter. Children may also sort various objects, such as sticks, in piles of longer or shorter (Wagner, Hosier, & Gilloley, 1964).

110. The number lines may be used to develop vocabulary such as *before, after, between, larger than, smaller than,* and *the same as.* Children may refer to the number line in answering questions such as:

What number comes just *before* 7? ____
What number comes just *after* 13? ____
What number comes *between* 6 and 8? ____

111. Auditory stimulation may be used to develop the concepts of *more* and *less* by clapping the number of letters in each child's name. Ask the child if T-i-m has *more* claps than C-h-r-i-s; or M-i-s-s-y has *less* claps than J-i-m (Behrmann & Millman, 1971).

112. Provide children with different-colored beads on a string and ask them specific questions such as:

"Are there *more* blue beads than red beads?"
"Are there *fewer* yellow beads than black beads?"
"Which color has the *same* number of beads as red?"

113. Prepare a worksheet similar to the example below for use with a number line.

	(Check the correct answer)			
	Larger than	Smaller than	the Same as	
Is 2 + 2				3 + 1
Is 5 + 1				3 + 3
Is 17				71
Is 3 + 1				1 + 3
Is 6 + 2				4 + 5

114. Give children a set of cards numbered from one to ten. Instruct the child to turn up one card and ask if

the number comes *before* or *after* a number that you choose at random. *More* or *less* and *smaller than* or *larger than* can also be used for this activity.

115. Print operation signs on flash cards. Daily practice with the cards—similar to sight word flash cards—provides children with additional practice. Kinesthetic clues can be added by cutting the signs out of sandpaper and pasting them on a card.

116. Give children practice in reading arithmetic problems without working them. Have the children read $2 + 2 = 4$ or $5 - 3 = 2$ with the emphasis on the operation signs (Johnson & Myklebust, 1967).

117. Provide color cues for operation signs to call attention to the sign. Circles or boxes drawn around the signs may also enable a child to attend more closely to the sign.

118. Prepare a worksheet where the operation signs are missing. Ask the child to fill them in. For example:

$$6 \underline{\quad} 3 = 3$$
$$1 \underline{\quad} 2 = 3$$
$$2 \underline{\quad} 4 = 6$$
$$1 + 1 \underline{\quad} 2$$
$$7 \underline{\quad} 5 = 2$$

B. *Does the child have difficulty in the analysis of story problems?*

119. Have children read story problems and decide on the mathematical operation that is required to work the problem, without actually doing the computation. Encourage children to discuss why a specific mathematical operation is required for particular problems.

120. Discuss *clue words* in story problems that serve as indicators of mathematical operations. Make children more aware of these key words by underlining or circling them on seatwork papers. The clue words in the examples below are in boxes.

Michael had 9 marbles. He ⬚lost⬚ 3 of them in the park. How many does he have ⬚left⬚?
Mother baked 2 pies yesterday ⬚and⬚ 1 pie today. How many pies did Mother bake ⬚altogether⬚?

121. Ask children to write a number sentence after having read a story problem. This process helps a child to see the numerical relationships prior to working out the answer. A number sentence follows the story problem below.

> Richard has 7 cents. He owes Jackie 3 cents. How much will Richard have left after he pays Jackie?

$$7 - 3 = \underline{\quad}$$

122. Provide children with story problems that require a one-step process. The length of the sentences should be short and only essential vocabulary should be included during beginning instruction in problem solving.

123. Johnson and Myklebust (1967) suggest using sentences that emphasize "logic and rational thought" rather than rote memorization (p. 270). Practice sentences of this nature might include answering the following as True or False.

> "John, who is 38 inches tall, is shorter than Bill, who is 3 feet tall."
> "I will have to wait for 14 more days if my cousin will be visiting me in 2 weeks."
> "There are spaces for one dozen, or 14, more cars."

124. Visually represent the numerical amounts that are presented in the story problem. For examples, problems involving money can be visualized by actually providing the child with the appropriate amount of real or play money.

125. Present story problems orally and direct the child to solve the problem without the use of pencil or paper. Children are required to listen closely to the presentation. Children who successfully obtain the answer can explain the process they used to arrive at the answer.

126. Spitzer (1961) suggests using analogous problems with easier numbers to solve more difficult story problems. Numbers that may be computed more easily often simplify the solution to a more complicated problem.

127. Permit children to formulate their own story problems. Other children in the class might be required to

solve the problems, or children can also provide answers to their own problems. Direct the children to write problems involving specific operations, such as addition, subtraction, etc.

128. Orally analyze the steps that are required to solve a particular problem. Spitzer (1961) lists the following procedures to be used in problem analysis. He recommends using only one or two steps with any one problem.

(1) What is given,
(2) What is asked,
(3) What operation or operations to use,
(4) An estimate of the answer,
(5) The solution, and
(6) A check of the answer (p. 256).

129. Diagram or illustrate the story problems on the chalkboard for the child. Discuss each part of the illustration. Allow children to illustrate selected story problems.

NOTES

[1]Cuisenaire Rods may be obtained from the Cuisenaire Company of America, Inc., 12 Church St., New Rochelle, New York 10805.

[2]Stamp reproductions of coins may be purchased from Developmental Learning Materials, 7440 N. Natchez Avenue, Niles, Illinois 60648.

ADDITIONAL READINGS

Arena, J., ed. *Teaching educationally handicapped children.* San Rafael, Calif.: Academic Therapy Publications, 1967.

Behrmann, P., & Millman, J. *How many spoons make a family?* San Rafael, Calif.: Academic Therapy Publications, 1971.

Bereiter, C. *Arithmetic and mathematics.* San Rafael, Calif.: Dimensions Publishing Co., 1968.

Bereiter, C., & Engelmann, S. *Teaching disadvantaged children in the preschool.* Englewood Cliffs, N.J.: Prentice-Hall, 1966.

Feingold, A. *Teaching arithmetic to slow learners and retarded.* New York: John Day, 1965.

Hofmeister, A. *Programmed time telling.* Eugene, Ore.: Regional Special Education Instructional Materials Center, University of Oregon, 1968.

Johnson, D. J., & Myklebust, H. R. *Learning disabilities: Educational principles and practices.* New York: Grune & Stratton, 1967.

Lerner, J. W. *Children with learning disabilities.* Boston: Houghton Mifflin, 1971.

Otto, W., & McMenemy, R. A. *Corrective and remedial teaching.* Boston: Houghton Mifflin, 1966.

Platts, M. E. *Plus.* Stevensville, Mich.: Educational Service, 1964.

Sharp, F. A. *These kids don't count.* San Rafael, Calif.: Academic Therapy Publications, 1971

Smith, R. M. *Clinical teaching: Methods of instruction for the retarded.* New York: McGraw-Hill, 1968.

Smith, R. M. *Teacher diagnosis of educational difficulties.* Columbus, Ohio: Charles E. Merrill, 1969.

Spitzer, H. F. *Practical classroom procedures for enriching arithmetic.* St. Louis: Webster, 1956.

Spitzer, H. F. *The teaching of arithmetic.* Boston: Houghton Mifflin, 1961.

Swenson, E. J. *Teaching arithmetic to children.* New York: Macmillan, 1964.

Valett, R. E. *The remediation of learning disabilities.* Palo Alto, Calif.: Fearon Publishers, 1967.

Wagner, G., Hosier, M., & Gilloley, L. *Arithmetic games and activities.* Darien, Conn.: Teachers Publishing Corp., 1964.

Wedemeyer, A., & Cejka, J. *Creative ideas for teaching exceptional children.* Denver: Love Publishing Co., 1970.

Postscript

Many future developments in elementary and special education cannot be predicted with great accuracy or confidence. It seems very likely to us, however, that successful teaching of all children will continue to depend on creative, personalized instruction by individual teachers. It was not our intention in this book to present a comprehensive developmental program of instruction. Rather, our purpose was to provide teachers with a practical approach to academic and behavioral remediation and a compilation of teaching activities for specific skill deficiencies. We realize that no book alone can supply answers to all educational problems. We are successful to the extent that we have provided a workable approach to remediation and a core of useful remedial teaching techniques. Whether or not our purpose has been achieved can only be determined by feedback from our readers. If future editions of this book or similar volumes are to be of maximum value to teachers, they must be based on readers' evaluations. Consequently, we hope that you will send us your comments and suggestions. Specifically, we solicit your responses to the following:

255

1. What particular part of the book did you find most helpful?
2. How could the book or particular chapters of the book be improved?
3. What successful teaching activities have you used with children experiencing learning problems that we have not listed in this book?

Please send your responses to:

Drs. Gerald Wallace and James M. Kauffman
Department of Special Education
School of Education
University of Virginia
Charlottesville, Virginia 22901

References

Abernethy, K., Cowley, J., Gillard, H., & Whiteside, J. *Jumping up and down.* San Rafael, Calif.: Academic Therapy Publications, 1970.

Ackerman, J. M. *Operant conditioning techniques for the classroom teacher.* Glenview, Ill.: Scott, Foresman, 1972.

Adamson, G., & Van Etten, C. "Prescribing via analysis and retrieval of instructional materials in the Educational Modulation Center." *Exceptional Children* 36 (1970): 531–33.

Alder, S. *The non-verbal child.* Springfield, Ill.: Charles C. Thomas, 1964.

Allen, K. E., Hart, B. M., Buell, J. S., Harris, F. R., & Wolf, M. M. "Effects of social reinforcement on isolate behavior of a nursery school child." *Child Development* 35 (1964): 511–18.

Arena, J. I., ed. *Teaching educationally handicapped children.* San Rafael, Calif.: Academic Therapy Publications, 1967.

Arena, J. I., ed. *Building spelling skills in dyslexic children.* San Rafael, Calif.: Academic Therapy Publications, 1968.

Arena, J. I., ed. *Teaching through sensory-motor experiences.* San Rafael, Calif.: Academic Therapy Publications, 1969.

Arena, J. I., ed. *Building handwriting skills in dyslexic children.* San Rafael, Calif.: Academic Therapy Publications, 1970.

Armstrong, C. *Los Angeles diagnostic tests: Reasoning in arithmetic.* Los Angeles: California Test Bureau, 1926.

Armstrong, C., & Clark, W. W. *Los Angeles diagnostic tests: Fundamentals of arithmetic.* Los Angeles: California Test Bureau, 1947.

Armstrong, J. R. "A model for materials development and evaluation." *Exceptional Children* 38 (1971): 327–34.

Axelrod, S. "Token reinforcement programs in special classes." *Exceptional Children* 37 (1971): 371–79.

Ayres, J. A. *Southern California test battery for assessment of dysfunction (Southern California motor accuracy test, Southern California perceptual motor tests, Southern California figure-ground visual perception test, Southern California kinesthesia and tactile perception tests, Ayres space test).* Los Angeles: Western Psychological Services, 1969.

Baer, D. M., Wolf, M. M., & Risley, T. R. "Some current dimensions of applied behavior analysis." *Journal of Applied Behavior Analysis* 1 (1968): 91–97.

Bakwin, H., & Bakwin, R. M. *Clinical management of behavior disorders in children.* 2nd ed. Philadelphia: Saunders, 1960.

Bandura, A. *Principles of behavior modification.* New York: Holt, Rinehart & Winston, 1969.

Bandura, A., & Walters, R. H. *Social learning and personality development.* New York: Holt, Rinehart & Winston, 1963.

Barbe, W. B. *Creative writing activities.* Columbus, Ohio: Highlights for Children, Inc., 1965.

Barrett, H. H., Saunders, M., & Wolf, M. M. "Good behavior game: Effects of individual contingencies for group consequences on disruptive behavior in a classroom." *Journal of Applied Behavior Analysis* 2 (1969): 119–24.

Barsch, R. H. *A movigenic curriculum.* Madison, Wisc.: Department of Public Instruction, Bureau for the Handicapped, 1965.

Barsch, R. H. *Achieving perceptual-motor efficiency.* Vol. 1. Seattle: Special Child Publications, 1967.

Barsch, R. H. *Enriching perception and cognition.* Vol. 2. Seattle: Special Child Publications, 1968.

Bateman, B., ed. *Learning disorders,* Vol. 4. Seattle: Special Child Publications, 1971.

Becker, W. C. *Parents are teachers.* Champaign, Ill.: Research Press, 1971a.

Becker, W. C., ed. *An empirical basis for change in education.* Chicago: Science Research Associates, 1971b.

Becker, W. C., Engelmann, S., & Thomas, D. R. *Teaching: A course in applied psychology.* Chicago: Science Research Associates, 1971.

Becker, W. C., Thomas, D. R., & Carnine, D. *Reducing behavior problems:*

An operant conditioning guide for teachers. Urbana, Ill.: ERIC Clearing-house on Early Childhood Education, 1969.

Behrmann, P. *Activities for developing visual-perception.* San Rafael, Calif.: Academic Therapy Publications, 1970.

Behrmann, P., & Millman, J. *How many spoons make a family?* San Rafael, Calif.: Academic Therapy Publications, 1971.

Bender, L. *Visual-Motor Gestalt Test and its clinical use.* New York: American Orthopsychiatric Association, 1938.

Benson, F. A. M., ed. *Modifying deviant social behaviors in various classroom settings.* Eugene, Ore.: University of Oregon, 1969.

Benyon, S. D. "Laterality and directionality." In J. Arena, ed. *Teaching through sensory-motor experiences.* San Rafael, Calif.: Academic Therapy Publications, 1969, pp. 35–46.

Bereiter, C. *Arithmetic and mathematics.* San Rafael, Calif.: Dimensions, 1968.

Bereiter, C., & Engelmann, S. *Language learning activities for the disadvantaged child.* New York: Anti-Defamation League of B'nai B'rith.

Bereiter, C., & Engelmann, S. *Teaching disadvantaged children in the preschool.* Englewood Cliffs, N.J.: Prentice-Hall, 1966.

Bergen, J. R., & Caldwell, T. "Operant techniques in school psychology." *Psychology in the Schools* 4 (1967): 136–41.

Berkowitz, P. H., & Rothman, E. P. *The disturbed child.* New York: New York University, 1960.

Berry, K. E. *Remedial diagnosis.* San Rafael, Calif.: Dimensions, 1968.

Berry, M. F. *Language disorders in children: The bases and diagnoses.* New York: Appleton-Century-Crofts, 1969.

Bettleheim, B. "The decision to fail." *The School Review* 69 (1961): 389–412.

Bettleheim, B. Listening to children. In P. A. Gallagher & L. L. Edwards, eds., *Teaching the emotionally disturbed: Theory into practice.* Proceedings of a Symposium, Topeka, Kansas, 1970.

Bijou, S. W., & Baer, D. M. *Child development I: A systematic and empirical theory.* New York: Appleton-Century-Crofts, 1961.

Birch, H. G., & Belmont, L. "Auditory-visual integration, intelligence, and reading ability in school children." *Perceptual and Motor Skills* 20 (1965): 295–305.

Birnbrauer, J. S., Burchard, J. D., & Burchard, S. N. "Wanted: Behavior analysts." In R. H. Bradfield, ed., *Behavior modification: The human effort.* San Rafael, Calif.: Dimensions, 1970, pp. 19–71.

Blackham, G. J., & Silberman, A. *Modification of child behavior.* Belmont, Calif.: Wadsworth, 1971.

Blessing, K., ed. *The role of the resource consultant in special education.* Washington, D.C.: Council for Exceptional Children, 1969.

Bower, E. M. *Early identification of emotionally handicapped children in school.* 2nd ed. Springfield, Ill.: Charles C. Thomas, 1969.

Bower, E. M., & Lambert, N. M. *A process for in-school screening of children with emotional handicaps.* Princeton, N.J.: Educational Testing Service, 1962.

Bradfield, O. "The teacher at work." In J. Hellmuth, ed., *Learning disorders,* Vol. 1. Seattle: Special Child Publications, 1965, pp. 363–88.

Bradfield, R. H., ed. *Behavior modification: The human effort.* San Rafael, Calif.: Dimensions, 1970.

Broden, M., Hall, R. V., & Mitts, B. "The effect of self-recording on the classroom behavior of two eighth-grade students." *Journal of Applied Behavior Analysis* 4 (1971): 191–99.

Brown, P., & Elliott, R. "Control of aggression in a nursery school class." *Journal of Experimental Child Psychology* 2 (1965): 103–7.

Brueckner, L. J. *Diagnostic tests and self-helps in arithmetic.* Los Angeles: California Test Bureau, 1955.

Bryan, R. *When children speak.* San Rafael, Calif.: Academic Therapy Publications, 1971.

Buchanan, C. D. *Sullivan programmed readers.* N.Y.: Sullivan Press, 1968.

Buckley, N. K., & Walker, H. M. *Modifying classroom behavior: A manual of procedure for classroom teachers.* Champaign, Ill.: Research Press, 1970.

Buktenica, N. A. *Visual learning.* San Rafael, Calif.: Dimensions, 1968.

Bush, W. J., & Giles, M. T. *Aids to psycholinguistic teaching.* Columbus, Ohio: Charles E. Merrill, 1969.

Buswell, G. T., & John, L. *Diagnostic chart for fundamental processes in arithmetic.* Indianapolis: Bobbs-Merrill, 1925.

Bzoch, K. R., & League, R. Receptive-expressive emergent language scale. Gainesville, Fla.: Tree-of-Life Press, 1971.

Caldwell, B. M. *Preschool inventory.* revised ed. Princeton, N.J.: Educational Testing Service, 1967.

Cantrell, R. P., Cantrell, M. L., Huddleston, C. M., & Woolridge, R. L. "Contingency contracting with school problems." *Journal of Applied Behavior Analysis* 2 (1969): 215–20.

Capobianco, R. J. "Diagnostic methods used with learning disability cases." *Exceptional Children* 31 (1964): 187–93.

Carrillo, L. W. *Informal reading-readiness experiences.* New York: Noble & Noble, 1964.

Carter, R. D. *Help! These kids are driving me crazy.* Champaign, Ill.: Research Press, 1971.

Cassidy, V. M., & Stanton, J. E. *An investigation of factors involved in the educational placement of mentally retarded children: A study of differences between children in special and regular classes in Ohio.* U.S. Office of Education Cooperative Research Program, Project No. 043, Ohio State University, 1959.

Cawley, J. "Reading disability." In N. G. Haring & R. L. Schiefelbusch, eds., *Methods in special education.* New York: McGraw-Hill, 1967, pp. 209–56.

Chamberlin, R. W., & Nader, P. R. "Relationship between nursery school behavior and later school functioning." *American Journal of Orthopsychiatry* 41 (1971): 597–601.

Chaney, C. M., & Kephart, N. C. *Motoric aids to perceptual training.* Columbus, Ohio: Charles E. Merrill, 1968.

Cheyney, A. B. *Teaching culturally disadvantaged in the elementary school.* Columbus, Ohio: Charles E. Merrill, 1967.

Clarizio, H. F. *Toward positive classroom discipline.* New York: John Wiley, 1972.

Clark, G. M. "A summary of the literature on behavior disorders in brain damaged children." In H. C. Haywood, ed., *Brain damage in school-age children.* Washington, D.C.: Council for Exceptional Children, 1968, pp. 182–210.

Clark, M. M. *Left-handedness.* London: University of London Press, 1957.

Clausen, J. A. "Family structure, socialization, and personality." In L. W. Hoffman & M. L. Hoffman, eds., *Review of child development research,* Vol. 2. New York: Russel Sage Foundation, 1966, pp. 1–53.

Cohen, S. A. *Teach them all to read.* New York: Random House, 1969.

Compton, C. "Teaching in the classroom." Mimeographed lecture, San Francisco State College, San Francisco, Calif.: Summer 1965.

Connolly, A. J., Nachtman, W. & Pritchett, E. M. *Key math diagnostic arithmetic test.* Circle Pines, Minn.: American Guidance Service, Inc., 1971.

Cooper, J. O., Payne, J. S., & Edwards, C. "Food for thought: An objective approach to changing children's food preferences." *Teaching Exceptional Children* 3 (1971): 73–76.

Cratty, B. J. *Learning and playing.* Freeport, Long Island, N.Y.: Educational Activities, Inc.

Cratty, B. J. *Developmental sequences of perceptual-motor tasks.* Freeport, Long Island, N.Y.: Educational Activities, Inc., 1967.

Croutch, B. "Handwriting and correct posture." In J. I. Arena, ed., *Building handwriting skills in dyslexic children.* San Rafael, Calif.: Academic Therapy Publications, 1970.

Cruickshank, W. M. "Special education, the community and constitutional issues." In D. L. Walker & D. P. Howard, eds., *Special education: Instrument of change in education for the 70's.* Charlottesville, Va.: Department of Special Education, University of Virginia, 1972, pp. 5–22.

Cruickshank, W. M., Bentzen, F. A., Ratzeburg, F. H., & Tannhauser, M. T. *A teaching method for brain-injured and hyperactive children.* Syracuse, N.Y.: Syracuse University, 1961.

Deibert, A. N., & Harmon, A. J. *New tools for changing behavior.* Champaign, Ill.: Research Press, 1970.

De Hirsch, K., Jansky, J., & Langford, W. S. *Predicting language failure.* New York: Harper & Row, 1966.

Delacato, C. H. *The treatment and prevention of reading problems.* Springfield, Ill.: Charles C. Thomas, 1959.

Delacato, C. H. *Neurological organization and reading.* Springfield, Ill.: Charles C. Thomas, 1966.

Della-Piana, G. M. *Reading diagnosis and prescription: An introduction.* New York: Holt, Rinehart & Winston, 1968.

Denhoff, E., & Novack, H. S. "Syndromes of cerebral dysfunction; medical aspects that contribute to special education methods." In N. G. Haring & R. L. Schiefelbusch, eds., *Methods in special education.* New York: McGraw-Hill, 1967, pp. 351–83.

Dolch, E. W. *Basic sight vocabulary.* Champaign, Ill.: Garrard, 1953.

Dolch, E. W. *Better spelling.* Champaign, Ill.: Garrard, 1960.

Dunn, L. M. *Peabody picture vocabulary test.* Minneapolis: American Guidance Service, 1959.

Dunn, L. M. "Special education for the mildly retarded—Is much of it justifiable?" *Exceptional Children* 35 (1968): 5–22.

Durrell, D. D. *Durrell analysis of reading difficulty.* New York: Harcourt, Brace Jovanovich, 1955.

Eisenson, J. *Aphasia in children.* New York: Harper & Row, 1972.

Engelmann, S. *Preventing failure in the primary grades.* Chicago: Science Research Associates, 1969.

Ensminger, E. E. "A proposed model for selecting, modifying, or developing instructional materials for handicapped children." *Focus on Exceptional Children* 1 (1970): 1–9.

Ephron, B. K. *Emotional difficulties in reading.* New York: Julian Press, 1953.

Erikson, E. H. *Childhood and society.* 2nd ed. New York: W. W. Norton, 1963.

Fargo, G. A., Behrns, C., & Nolen, P., eds. *Behavior modification in the classroom.* Belmont, Calif.: Wadsworth, 1970.

Feingold, A. *Teaching arithmetic to slow learners and retarded.* New York: John Day, 1965.

Fernald, G. M. *Remedial techniques in basic school subjects.* New York: McGraw-Hill, 1943.

Ferster, C. B., & Perrott, M. C. *Behavior principles.* New York: New Century, 1968.

Ferster, C. B., & Skinner, B. F. *Schedules of reinforcement.* New York: Appleton-Century-Crofts, 1957.

Freud, A. "The relation between psychoanalysis and pedagogy." In N. J. Long, W. C. Morse, & R. G. Newman, eds. *Conflict in the classroom.* Belmont, Calif.: Wadsworth, 1965, pp. 159–63.

Freud, S. *On aphasia.* New York: International Universities Press, 1953.

Frostig, M., & Horne, D. "An approach to the treatment of children with learning disorders." In J. Hellmuth, ed., *Learning disorders,* Vol. 1. Seattle: Special Child Publications, 1965, pp. 293–305.

Frostig, M., & Horne, D. *The frostig program for the development of visual perception: teacher's guide.* Chicago: Follett, 1968.

Frostig, M., Lefever, W., & Whittlesey, J. R. *Marianne frostig developmental test of visual perception.* Palo Alto, Calif.: Consulting Psychologists Press, 1964.

Gallagher, P. A. "A synthesis of classroom scheduling techniques for emotionally disturbed children." *Focus on Exceptional Children* 5, no. 2 (1970): 1–10.

Gallagher, P. A. *Positive classroom performance: Techniques for changing behavior.* Denver, Colo.: Love Publishing Company, 1971.

Gates, A. I., & McKillop, A. S. *Gates-McKillop reading diagnostic tests.* New York: Bureau of Publications, Teachers College, Columbia University, 1962.

Getman, G. N. "The visuomotor complex in the acquisition of learning skills." In J. Hellmuth, ed., *Learning disorders,* Vol. 1. Seattle: Special Child Publications, 1965, pp. 49–76.

Getman, G. N., Kane, E. R., & McKee, G. W. *Developing learning readiness programs.* Manchester, Mo.: McGraw-Hill, 1968.

Gillingham, A., & Stillman, B. *Remedial training for reading, spelling, and penmanship.* Cambridge, Mass.: Educators Publishing Service, 1965.

Glaus, M. *From thoughts to words.* Champaign, Ill.: National Council of Teachers of English, 1965.

Glavin, J. "Persistence of behavior disorders in children." *Exceptional children* 38 (1972): 367–76.

Gnagey, W. J. *The psychology of discipline in the classroom.* New York: Macmillan, 1968.

Goldstein, H., Moss, J. W., & Jordan, L. J. *The efficacy of special class training on the development of mentally retarded children.* Summary report, U.S.O.E. Cooperative Research Project 619. Urbana, Ill.: University of Illinois, 1965.

Goldstein, K. *Language and language disturbances.* New York: Grune & Stratton, 1948.

Graubard, P. S. "The relationship between academic achievement and behavior dimensions." *Exceptional Children,* 1971, 755–57.

Gray, G. W., & Wise, C. M. *The bases of speech.* 3rd ed. New York: Harper & Row, 1959.

Green, R. L., & Stachnik, T. J. "Money, motivation, and academic achievement." *Phi Delta Kappan* 50 (1968): 228–30.

Hackett, L. C., & Jensen, R. C. *A guide to movement exploration.* Palo Alto, Calif.: Peek Publications, 1967.

Hainsworth, P. K., & Siqueland, M. L. *Early identification of children with learning disabilities: The Meeting Street School Screening Test.* Providence, R.I.: Crippled Children and Adults of Rhode Island, Inc., 1969.

Hall, N. A. *A handbook of remedial reading techniques for the classroom teacher.* Stevensville, Mich.: Educational Service, 1969.

Hall, R. V. *Managing behavior.* Lawrence, Kan.: H. & H. Enterprises, 1971a.

Hall, R. V. "Training teachers in classroom use of contingency management." *Educational Technology* 11, no. 4 (1971b): 33–38.

Hall, R. V. Axelrod, S., Foundopulos, M., Shellman, J., Campbell, R. A., & Cranston, S. S. "The effective use of punishment to modify behavior in the classroom." *Educational Technology* 11, no. 4 (1971): 24–26.

Hall, R. V., Cristler, C., Cranston, S., & Tucker, B. "Teachers and parents as researchers using multiple baseline designs." *Journal of Applied Behavior Analysis* 3 (1970): 247–55.

Hall, R. V., Fox, R., Willard, D., Goldsmith, L., Emerson, M., Owen, M., Davis, F., & Porcia, E. "The teacher as observer and experimenter in the modification of disputing and talking-out behavior." *Journal of Applied Behavior Analysis* 4 (1971): 141–49.

Hammill, D. D. "Evaluating children for instructional purposes." *Academic Therapy* 6 (1971): 341–53.

Haring, N. G. *Attending and responding.* San Rafael, Calif.: Dimensions, 1968.

Haring, N. G., Hayden, A. H., & Allen, K. E. "Intervention in early childhood." *Educational Technology* 11, no. 2 (1971): 52–61.

Haring, N. G., & Lovitt, T. C. "Operant methodology and educational technology in special education." In N. G. Haring & R. L. Schiefelbusch, eds., *Methods in special education.* New York: McGraw-Hill, 1967, pp. 12–48.

Haring, N. G., & Phillips, E. L. *Educating emotionally disturbed children.* New York: McGraw-Hill, 1962.

Haring, N. G., & Phillips, E. L. *Analysis and modification of classroom behavior.* Englewood Cliffs, N. J.: Prentice-Hall, 1972.

Haring, N. G., & Whelan, R. J. "Experimental methods in education and management." In N. J. Long, W. C. Morse, & R. G. Newman, eds., *Conflict in the classroom.* Belmont, Calif.: Wadsworth, 1965, pp. 389–405.

Harris, A. S. "Visual and auditory modalities: How important are they? Con-challenger." In N. B. Smith, ed., *Current issues in reading.* Newark, Delaware: International Reading Association, 1969, pp. 184–90.

Harris, M. B., ed. *Classroom uses of behavior modification.* Columbus, Ohio: Charles E. Merrill, 1972.

Hegge, T. G., Kirk, S. A., & Kirk, W. D. *Remedial reading drills.* Ann Arbor, Mich.: George Wahr Publishing Company, 1940.

Heilman, A. W. *Phonics in proper perspective.* Columbus, Ohio: Charles E. Merrill, 1968.

Heilman, A. W. *Principles and practices of teaching reading.* 3rd ed. Columbus, Ohio: Charles E. Merrill, 1972.

Hernandez, D. E. *Writing behavioral objectives: A programmed exercise for beginners.* New York: Barnes & Noble, 1971.

Hewett, F. M. *The emotionally disturbed child in the classroom.* Boston: Allyn & Bacon, 1968.

Hofmeister, A. *Programmed time telling.* Eugene, Ore.: Regional Special Education Instructional Materials Center, University of Oregon, 1968.

Homme, L. E. "Human motivation and environment." In N. G. Haring & R. J. Whelan, eds., *The learning environment: Relationship to behavior modification and implications for special education.* Kansas Studies in Education 16, no. 2 (1966): 30–39.

Homme, L. E. *How to use contingency contracting in the classroom.* Champaign, Ill.: Research Press, 1969.

Homme, L. E. "Using behavioral technology to alter children's behavior." In P. A. Gallagher & L. L. Edwards, eds., *Educating the emotionally disturbed: Theory into practice.* Proceedings of a Symposium, Topeka, Kansas, 1970.

Hopkins, B. L., Schutte, R. C., & Garton, K. L. "The effects of access to a playroom on the rate and quality of printing and writing of first and second-grade students." *Journal of Applied Behavior Analysis* 4 (1971): 77–87.

Jastak, J. F., & Jastak, S. R. *The wide range achievement test manual.* Wilmington, Del.: Guidance Associates, 1965.

Johnson, D. J., & Myklebust, H. R. *Learning disabilities: Educational principles and practices.* New York: Grune & Stratton, 1967.

Jordan, T. E., & DeCharms, R. "The achievement motive in normal and mentally retarded children." *American Journal of Mental Deficiency* 64, (1959): 457–66.

Kaliski, L., Tankersley, R., & Iogha, R. *Structured dramatics for children with learning disabilities.* San Rafael, Calif.: Academic Therapy Publications, 1971.

Kaluger, G., & Kolson, C. J. *Reading and learning disabilities.* Columbus, Ohio: Charles E. Merrill, 1969.

Karnes, M. B. *Helping young children develop language skills.* Arlington, Va.: The Council for Exceptional Children, 1968.

Katz, P. "Verbal discrimination performance of disadvantaged children: Stimulus and subject variables." *Child Development* 38 (1967): 233–42.

Kauffman, J. M. "Psychoeducational technology: Criteria for evaluation and control in special education." *Focus on Exceptional Children,* in press.

Kauffman, J. M., Cullinan, D., Scranton, T. R., & Wallace, G. *An inexpensive device for programming ratio reinforcement. The Psychological Record* 22 (1972): 543–44.

Kauffman, J. M., & Scranton, T. R. *Parent control of thumbsucking in the home: A case study.* Unpublished manuscript, University of Virginia, Charlottesville, Va., 1972.

Kauffman, J. M., & Vicente, A. R. "Bringing in the sheaves: Observations on harvesting behavioral change in the field." *Journal of School Psychology* 10 (1972): 263–268

Kaufhold, S., & Kauffman, J. M. *Reducing operant crying.* Unpublished manuscript, University of Virginia, Charlottesville, Va., 1972.

Kephart, N. C. *The brain-injured child in the classroom.* Chicago: National Society for Crippled Children and Adults, 1963.

Kephart, N. C. "Perceptual-motor aspects of learning disabilities." In E. Frierson & W. Barbe, eds., *Educating children with learning disabilities.* New York: Appleton-Century-Crofts, 1967, pp. 405–13.

Kephart, N. C. *Learning disability: An educational adventure.* West Lafayette, Ind.: Kappa Delta Pi Press, 1968.

Kephart, N. C. *The slow learner in the classroom.* 2nd ed. Columbus, Ohio: Charles E. Merrill, 1971.

Kern, W. H., & Pfaeffle, H. "A comparison of social adjustment of mentally retarded children in various educational settings." *American Journal of Mental Deficiency* 67 (1962): 407–13.

Kirby, F. D., & Toler, H. C. "Modification of preschool isolate behavior: A case study." *Journal of Applied Behavior Analysis* 3 (1970): 309–14.

Kirk, S. A. *Educating exceptional children.* 2nd ed. Boston: Houghton Mifflin, 1972.

Kirk, S. A., McCarthy, J. J., & Kirk, W. D. *Illinois test of psycholinguistic abilities.* revised ed. Urbana: University of Illinois Press, 1968.

Kirshner, A. J. *Training that makes sense.* San Rafael, Calif.: Academic Therapy Publications, 1972.

Koppitz, E. *Bender-Gestalt test for young children.* New York: Grune & Stratton, 1964.

Krasner, L. "Behavior modification—values and training: The perspective of a psychologist." In C. M. Franks, ed., *Behavior therapy: Appraisal and status.* New York: McGraw-Hill, 1969.

Kugel, R. B., & Parsons, M. H. *Children of deprivation: Changing the course of familial retardation.* Washington, D.C.: Department of Health, Education and Welfare, 1967.

Kuypers, D. S., Becker, W. C., & O'Leary, K. D. "How to make a token system fail." *Exceptional Children* 35 (1968): 101–9.

Landsman, M., & Dillard, H. *Evanston early identification scale manual* (Field Research ed.). Chicago: Follett Educational Corporation, 1967.

Langstaff, A. L., & Volkmor, C. B. "A method for creating and continuing individualized instruction." In J. Arena, ed., *Selected papers in learning disabilities. Progress in parent information, professional growth, and public policy.* Sixth Annual International Conference on Learning Disabilities. Pittsburgh: Association for Children with Learning Disabilities, 1969, pp. 59–65.

Lazarus, P. W. "The medium is not the method." *Academic Therapy* 6 (1971): 229–32.

Lerner, J. W. *Children with learning disabilities.* Boston: Houghton Mifflin, 1971.

Lerner, J. W., & Vaver, G. "Filmstrips in learning." *Academic Therapy* 5 (1970): 320–24.

Lichtenberg, P., & Norton, D. G. *Cognitive and mental development in the first five years of life.* Rockville, Md.: National Institute of Mental Health, 1970.

Lincoln-Oseretsky tests of motor proficiency. Los Angeles: Western Psychological Services, 1965.

Linder, R. "Diagnosis: Description or perscription? A case study in the psychology of diagnosis." *Perceptual & Motor Skills* 20 (1965): 1081–92.

Linn, S. H. *Teaching phonics with finger puppets.* San Rafael, Calif.: Academic Therapy Publications, 1972.

Long, N. J., Morse, W. C., & Newman, R. G., eds. *Conflict in the classroom.* 2nd ed. Belmont, Calif.: Wadsworth, 1971.

Lovitt, T. C. "Assessment of children with learning disabilities." *Exceptional Children* 34 (1967): 233–39.

Lovitt, T. C., & Curtiss, K. A. "Effects of manipulating an antecedent event on mathematics response rate." *Journal of Applied Behavior Analysis* 1 (1968): 329–33.

Lovitt, T. C., & Esveldt, K. A. "The relative effects on math performance of single *versus* multiple-ratio schedules: A case study." *Journal of Applied Behavior Analysis* 4 (1970): 261–70.

Lovitt, T. C., & Smith, J. O. "Effects of instructions on an individual's verbal behavior." *Exceptional Children* 38 (1972): 685–93.

Lowell, E. L., & Stoner, M. *Play it by ear.* Los Angeles: John Tracy Clinic, 1960.

McCarthy, J. J., & McCarthy, J. F. *Learning disabilities.* Boston: Allyn & Bacon, 1969.

McCarthy, J. M., & Paraskevopoulos, J. "Behavior patterns of learning disabled, emotionally disturbed, and average children." *Exceptional Children* 35 (1969): 69–74.

McClearn, G. E. "Genetics and behavior development." In M. L. Hoffman & L. W. Hoffman, eds., *Review of child development research,* Vol. 1. New York: Russel Sage Foundation, 1964, pp. 433–80.

McGrady, H. J. "Language pathology and learning disabilities." In H. R. Myklebust, ed., *Progress in learning disabilities,* Vol. 1. New York: Grune & Stratton, 1968, pp. 199-233.

McIntyre, R. B. "Evaluation of instructional materials and programs: Applications of a systems approach." *Exceptional Children* 37 (1970): 213–20.

McKenna, A. R. "Some notes on the teaching of handwriting." In J. I. Arena, ed., *Building handwriting skills in dyslexic children.* San Rafael, Calif.: Academic Therapy Publications, 1970.

MacMillan, D. L., & Forness, S. R. "Behavior modification: Limitations and liabilities." *Exceptional Children* 37 (1970): 291–97.

Madsen, C. H., Becker, W. C., & Thomas, D. R. "Rules, praise, and ignoring: Elements of elementary classroom control." *Journal of Applied Behavior Analysis* 1 (1968): 139–50.

Madsen, C. H., & Madsen, C. K. *Teaching/discipline.* Boston: Allyn & Bacon, 1970.

Magdol, M. S. *Perceptual training in the kindergarten.* San Rafael, Calif.: Academic Therapy Publications, 1971.

Mager, R. F. *Preparing instructional objectives.* Palo Alto, Calif.: Fearon, 1962.

Mager, R. F. *Developing attitude toward learning.* Palo Alto, Calif.: Fearon, 1968.

Meacham, M. L., & Wiesen, A. E. *Changing classroom behavior: A manual for precision teaching.* Scranton, Pa.: International Textbook Company, 1969.

Mecham, M. J. *Verbal language development scale.* Minneapolis: American Guidance Service, Inc.: 1959.

Medlin, V. L., & Warnock, H. H. *Word making methods book.* Salt Lake City, Utah: Word Making Publications, 1958.

Menninger, K. *The vital balance.* New York: Viking Press, 1963.

Menyuk, P. *The development of speech.* Indianapolis: Bobbs-Merrill, 1972.

Meyen, E. L. *Developing units of instruction: For the mentally retarded and other children with learning problems.* Dubuque, Iowa: Wm. C. Brown, 1972.

Mikulas, W. L. *Behavior modification: An overview.* New York: Harper & Row, 1972.

Miller, M. B. "Behavioral research: A modest primer for teachers." In P. S. Graubard, ed., *Children against schools.* Chicago: Follett, 1969, pp. 217–51.

Minde, K., Lewin, D., Weiss, G., Laviguer, H., Douglas, V., & Sykes, E. "The hyperactive child in elementary school: A 5 year, controlled, followup." *Exceptional Children* 38 (1971): 215–21.

Monroe, M. *Children who cannot read.* Chicago: University of Chicago Press, 1932.

Morse, W. C. "The crisis teacher." In N. J. Long, W. C. Morse, & R. G. Newman, eds., *Conflict in the classroom.* Belmont, Calif.: Wadsworth, 1965, pp. 251-54.

Morse, W. C., Cutler, R. L., & Fink, A. H. *Public school classes for the emotionally handicapped: A research analysis.* Washington, D.C.: Council for Exceptional Children, 1964.

Murphy, P. *A special way for the special child in the regular classroom.* San Rafael, Calif.: Academic Therapy Publications, 1971.

Myers, G. C. "Creative thinking activities." In *Highlights handbook.* Columbus, Ohio: Highlights for children, Inc., 1965.

Myers, P. I., & Hammill, D. D. *Methods for learning disorders.* New York: John Wiley, 1969.

Myklebust, H. R. *Auditory disorders in children: A manual for differential diagnosis.* New York: Grune & Stratton, 1954.

Myklebust, H. R. *Picture Story Language Test: The development and disorders of written language,* Vol. 1. New York: Grune & Stratton, 1965.

Myklebust, H. R. "Childhood aphasia: An evolving concept." In L. E. Travis, ed., *Handbook of speech pathology and audiology.* New York: Appleton-Century-Crofts, 1971, pp. 1181-1202.

Myklebust, H. R. "Childhood aphasia: Identification, diagnosis, remediation." In L. E. Travis, ed., *Handbook of speech pathology and audiology.* New York: Appleton-Century-Crofts, 1971, pp. 1203-17.

Neilson, N. P. *Physical education for elementary schools.* New York: Ronald Press, 1956.

Neisworth, J. T., Deno, S. L., & Jenkins, J. R. *Student motivation and classroom management.* Lamont, Pa.: Behavior Technics, 1969.

Nimnicht, G., McAfee, O., & Meier, J. *The new nursery school.* New York: General Learning Corporation, 1969.

O'Leary, K. D., Becker, W. C., Evans, W. C., & Saudargas, R. A. "A token program in a public school: A replication and systematic analysis." *Journal of Applied Behavior Analysis* 2 (1969): 3-13.

Orton, J. L. *A guide for teaching phonics.* Winston-Salem, N.C.: The Orton Reading Center, 1964.

Osborn, J. *Teaching a teaching language to disadvantaged children.* Mimeographed paper, University of Illinois, Urbana, Ill., 1968.

Otto, W., & McMenemy, R. A. *Corrective and remedial teaching.* Boston: Houghton Mifflin, 1966.

Paraskevopoulos, J., & McCarthy, J. M. "Behavior patterns of children with special learning disabilities." *Psychology in the Schools* 7 (1969): 42-46.

Pate, J. E., & Webb, W. W. *First grade screening test manual.* Circle Pines, Minn.: American Guidance Service, 1969.

Patterson, G. R. "An application of conditioning techniques to the control of a hyperactive child." In L. P. Ullmann & L. Krasner, eds., *Case studies in behavior modification.* New York: Holt, Rinehart & Winston, 1965, pp. 370-75.

Patterson, G. R. *Families: Applications of social learning to family life.* Champaign, Ill.: Research Press, 1971.

Patterson, G. R., & Gullion, M. E. *Living with children: New methods for parents and teachers.* Champaign, Ill.: Research Press, 1968.

Payne, J. S., Finegold, I., & Cooper, J. O. "Transportation for the betterment of children." Paper presented at Conference on the Education of Mentally Retarded Persons, St. Louis, Missouri, September 1971.

Pearson, G. H. J. *Psychoanalysis and the education of the child.* New York: W. W. Norton, 1954.

Perry, H. W., & Morris, T. E. "The role of the educational diagnostician." In J. Arena, ed., *Selected papers on learning disabilities. Successful programming—many points of view.* Fifth annual conference of the Association of Children with Learning Disabilities. Pittsburgh: Association for Children with Learning Disabilities, 1969, pp. 128-30.

Peter, L. J. *Prescriptive teaching.* New York: McGraw-Hill, 1965.

Peterson, D. R. "Behavior problems of middle childhood." *Journal of Consulting Psychology* 25 (1961): 205–9.

Peterson, R. F., & Whitehurst, G. J. "A variable influencing the performance of generalized imitative behaviors." *Journal of Applied Behavior Analysis* 4 (1971): 1–9.

Peterson, W. "Children with specific learning disabilities." In N. G. Haring & R. L. Schiefelbusch, eds., *Methods in special education.* New York: McGraw-Hill, 1967, pp. 159–208.

Phillips, E. L. "Problems in educating emotionally disturbed children." In N. G. Haring & R. L. Schiefelbusch, eds., *Methods in special education.* New York: McGraw-Hill, 1967, pp. 137-58.

Phillips, E. L., Phillips, E. A., Fixen, D. L., & Wolf, M. M. "Achievement place: Modification of the behaviors of pre-delinquent boys within a token economy." *Journal of Applied Behavior Analysis* 4 (1971): 45–59.

Phillips, E. L., Wiener, D. N., & Haring, N. G. *Discipline, achievement, and mental health.* Englewood Cliffs, N.J.: Prentice-Hall, 1960.

Piaget, J. *The origins of intelligence in children.* New York: International Universities Press, 1952.

Platts, M. E. *Plus.* Stevensville, Mich.: Educational Service, 1964.

Platts, M. E. *Anchor: A handbook of vocabulary discovery techniques for the classroom teacher.* Stevensville, Mich.: Educational Service, 1970.

Platts, M. E., Marguerite, S. R., & Shumaker, E. *Suggested activities to motivate the teaching of the language arts.* Stevensville, Mich.: Educational Service, 1960.

Popham, W. J., & Baker, E. L. *Establishing instructional goals.* Englewood Cliffs, N.J.: Prentice-Hall, 1970.

Premack, D. "Toward empirical behavior Laws I. Positive reinforcement." *Psychological Review* 66 (1959): 219–33.

President's Council on Physical Fitness, *AAHPER youth fitness test manual.* Washington, D.C.: President's Council on Physical Fitness, 1967.

Quay, H. C., Morse, W. C., & Cutler, R. L. "Personality patterns of pupils in special classes for the emotionally disturbed." *Exceptional Children* 32 (1966): 297–301.

Reed, J. C., Rabe, E. F., & Mankinen, M. "Teaching reading to brain-damaged children: A review." In D. D. Hammill & N. R. Bartel, eds., *Educational perspectives in learning disabilities.* New York: John Wiley, 1971, pp. 94–114.

Reynolds, G. S. *A primer of operant conditioning.* Glenview, Ill.: Scott, Foresman, 1968.

Roach, C., & Kephart, N. *The purdue perceptual-motor survey test.* Columbus, Ohio: Charles E. Merrill, 1966.

Robbins, L. N. *Deviant children grown up.* Baltimore: Williams & Wilkins, 1966.

Ross, S. L., DeYoung, H. G., & Cohen, J. S. "Confrontation: Special education placement and the law." *Exceptional Children* 38 (1971): 5–12.

Rubin, R., & Balow, B. "Learning and behavior disorders: A longitudinal study." *Exceptional Children* 38, (1971): 293–99.

Russell, D. H., & Karp, E. E. *Reading aids through the grades.* New York: Teachers College Press, 1938.

Salzberg, B. H., Wheeler, A. J., Devar, L. T., & Hopkins, B. L. "The effect of intermittent feedback and intermittent contingent access to play on printing of kindergarten children." *Journal of Applied Behavior Analysis* 4 (1971): 163–71.

Schiefelbusch, R. L. "Introduction." In N. G. Haring & R. L. Schiefelbusch, eds., *Methods in special education.* New York: McGraw-Hill, 1967, pp. 1–11.

Schubert, D. G., & Torgerson, T. L. *Improving reading through individualized correction.* Debuque, Iowa: William C. Brown, 1968.

Schurr, E. *Movement experiences for children.* New York: Appleton-Century-Crofts, 1967.

Sharp, F. A. *These kids don't count.* San Rafael, Calif.: Academic Therapy Publications, 1971.

Sherman, J. A., & Baer, D. M. "Appraisal of operant therapy techniques with children and adults." In C. M. Franks, ed., *Behavior therapy: Appraisal and status.* New York: McGraw-Hill, 1969.

Short, J. F. "Juvenile delinquency: The sociocultural context." In L. W. Hoffman & M. L. Hoffman, eds., *Review of child development research,* Vol. 2. New York: Russell Sage Foundation, 1966, pp. 423–68.

Simon, K. A., & Grant, W. V., eds. *Digest of educational statistics.* Washington, D.C.: U. S. Office of Education, 1968.

Skiba, E. A., Pettigrew, L. E., & Alden, S. E. "A behavioral approach to the control of thumbsucking in the classroom." *Journal of Applied Behavior Analysis* 4 (1971): 121–25.

Skinner, B. F. *Science and human behavior.* New York: Free Press, 1953.

Skinner, B. F. *Verbal behavior.* New York: Appleton-Century-Crofts, 1957.

Skinner, B. F. *Beyond freedom and dignity.* New York: Alfred A. Knopf, 1971.

Slingerland, B. H. *Screening tests for identifying children with specific language disability.* Cambridge, Mass.: Educators Publishing Service, 1962.

Sluyter, D. J., & Hawkins, R. P. Delayed reinforcement of classroom behavior by parents. *Journal of Learning Disabilities* 5 (1972): 20–28.

Smith, J. A. *Creative teaching of the language arts in the elementary school.* Boston: Allyn & Bacon, 1967.

Smith, J. M., & Smith, D. E. P. *Child management: A program for parents.* Ann Arbor, Mich.: Ann Arbor Publishers, 1966.

Smith, R. M. *Clinical teaching: Methods of instruction for the retarded.* New York: McGraw-Hill, 1968.

Smith, R. M. "Collecting diagnostic data in the classroom." *Teaching Exceptional Children* 1 (1969a): 128–33.

Smith, R. M., ed. *Teacher diagnosis of educational difficulties.* Columbus, Ohio: Charles E. Merrill, 1969b.

Spache, G. D. *Diagnostic reading scales.* Monterey, Calif.: Del Monte Research Park, California Test Bureau, 1963.

Spache, G. D. *The teaching of reading.* Bloomington, Ind.: Phi Delta Kappa, 1972.

Spache, G. D., & Spache, E. B. *Reading in the elementary school.* Boston: Allyn & Bacon, 1969.

Spalding, R. B., & Spalding, W. T. *The writing road to reading.* New York: Morrow, 1957.

Spencer, E. F., & Smith, R. M. "Arithmetic skills." In R. M. Smith, ed., *Teacher diagnosis of educational difficulties.* Columbus, Ohio: Charles E. Merrill, 1969, pp. 152–70.

Spitzer, H. F. *Practical classroom procedures for enriching arithmetic.* St. Louis: Webster, 1956.

Spitzer, H. F. *The teaching of arithmetic.* 3rd ed. Boston: Houghton Mifflin, 1961.

Spradlin, J. "Procedures for evaluating processes associated with receptive and expressive language." In R. Schiefelbusch, R. Copeland, & J. O. Smith, eds., *Language and mental retardation.* New York: Holt, Rinehart & Winston, 1967, pp. 118–36.

Staats, A. W. "Reinforcer systems in the solution of human problems." In G. A. Fargo, C. Behrns, & P. Nolen, eds., *Behavior modification in the classroom.* Belmont, Calif.: Wadsworth, 1970.

Stainback, W. C., Payne, J. S., Stainback, S. B., & Payne, R. A. *Establishing a token economy in the classroom.* Columbus, Ohio: Charles E. Merrill (1973).

Stanton, J. E., & Cassidy, V. M. Effectiveness of special classes for educable mentally retarded. *Mental Retardation* 2, no. 1 (1964): 8–13.

Steiner, V. G., & Pond, R. E. *Finger play fun.* Columbus, Ohio: Charles E. Merrill, 1970.

Stephens, T. M. *Directive teaching of children with learning and behavioral disorders.* Columbus, Ohio: Charles E. Merrill, 1970.

Strang, R. *Diagnostic teaching of reading.* 2nd ed. New York: McGraw-Hill, 1969.

Strauss, A., & Lehtinen, L. *Psychopathology and education of the brain-injured child,* Vol. 1. New York: Grune & Stratton, 1947.

Stuart, R. B. *Trick or treatment: How and when pyschotherapy fails.* Champaign, Ill.: Research Press, 1970.

Sulzbacher, S. I., & Houser, J. E. "A tactic to eliminate disruptive behaviors in the classroom: Group contingent consequences." *American Journal of Mental Deficiency* 73 (1968): 88–90.

Sulzer, B., & Mayer, G. R. *Behavior-modification procedures for school personnel.* Hinsdale, Ill.: Dryden Press, 1972.

Swenson, E. J. *Teaching arithmetic to children.* New York: Macmillan, 1964.

Tharp, R. G., & Wetzel, R. J. *Behavior modification in the natural environment.* New York: Academic Press, 1969.

Thomas, A., Chess, S., & Birch, H. G. *Temperament and behavior disorders in children.* New York: New York University, 1968.

Tompkins, J. "Preface." In N. J. Long, W. C. Morse, and R. G. Newman, eds., *Conflict in the classroom.* 2nd ed. Belmont, Calif.: Wadsworth, 1971.

Trembly, D. "Should your child write with the left hand?" In J. I. Arena, ed., *Building handwriting skills in dyslexic children.* San Rafael, Calif.: Academic Therapy Publications, 1970.

Ullmann, L. P. "Behavior therapy as social movement." In C. M. Franks, ed., *Behavior therapy: Appraisal and status.* New York: McGraw-Hill, 1969.

Ullmann, L. P., & Krasner, L., eds. *Case studies in behavior modification.* Holt, Rinehart & Winston, 1965.

Valett, R. E. *The remediation of learning disabilities.* Palo Alto, Calif.: Fearon, 1967.

Valett, R. E. *A psychoeducational inventory of basic learning abilities.* Palo Alto, Calif.: Fearon, 1968.

Valett, R. E. *Modifying children's behavior: A guide for parents and professionals.* Palo Alto, Calif.: Fearon, 1969.

Van Riper, C. *Speech correction: Principles and methods.* 4th ed. Englewood Cliffs, N.J.: Prentice-Hall, 1963.

Van Witsen, B. *Perceptual training activities handbook.* New York: Columbia University Press, 1967.

Wagner, G., Hosier, M., & Blackman, M. *Listening games: Building listening skills with instructional games.* New York: Teachers Publishing, 1970.

Wagner, G., Hosier, M., & Gilloley, L. *Arithmetic games and activities.* Darien, Conn.: Teachers Publishing Corp., 1964.

Wahl, J. "Two approaches to spelling problems: Self-discovery and phonics." In J. I. Arena, ed., *Building spelling skills in dyslexic children.* San Rafael, Calif.: Academic Therapy Publications, 1968.

Wahler, R. G. "Setting generality: Some specific and general effects of child behavior therapy." *Journal of Applied Behavior Analysis* 2 (1969): 239–46.

Walker, H. M. "Empirical assessment of deviant behavior in children." *Psychology in the Schools* 6 (1969): 93–97.

Wallen, C. J. *Competency in teaching reading.* Chicago: Science Research Associates, 1972.

Webster, S. W., ed. *The disadvantaged learner.* San Francisco: Chandler, 1966.

Wedemeyer, A., & Cejka, J. *Creative ideas for teaching exceptional children.* Denver: Love Publishing Co., 1970.

Wedemeyer, A., & Cejka, J. *Learning games for exceptional children.* Denver: Love Publishing Co., 1971.

Weinthaler, J., & Rotberg, J. M. "The systematic selection of instructional materials based on an inventory of learning abilities and skills." *Exceptional Children* 36 (1970): 615–19.

Wepman, J. M. *Auditory discrimination test.* Chicago: Joseph M. Wepman, 1958.

Westman, J., Rice, D., & Berman, E. "Relationship between nursery school behavior and later school adjustment." *American Journal of Orthopsychiatry* 37 (1967): 725–31.

Whaley, D. L., & Malott, R. W. *Elementary principles of behavior.* New York: Appleton-Century-Crofts, 1971.

Whelan, R. J. "Educating emotionally disturbed children: Reflections upon educational methods and therapeutic processes manifested in the classroom." Paper presented at the Council for Exceptional Children, West Central Regional Conference, Oklahoma City, November, 1960.

Whelan, R. J. "The relevance of behavior-modification procedures for teachers of emotionally disturbed children." In P. Knoblock, ed. *Intervention approaches in educating emotionally disturbed children.* Syracuse, N. Y.: Syracuse University, 1966, pp. 35–78.

White, M. A., & Charry, J. eds. *School disorder, intelligence, and social class.* New York: Teachers College Press, 1966.

Williams, R. J. "The biological approach to the study of personality." In T. Millon, ed., *Theories of psychopathology.* Philadelphia: W. B. Saunders, 1967, pp. 19–31.

Wilson, R. M. *Diagnostic and remedial reading for classroom and clinic.* Columbus, Ohio: Charles E. Merrill, 1967.

Wolf, M. M., Giles, D. K., & Hall, R. V. "Experiments with token reinforcement in a remedial classroom." *Behaviour Research and Therapy* 6 (1968): 51–64.

Wolf, M. M., Hanley, E. L., King, L. A. Lachowicz, J., & Giles, D. K. "The timer game: A variable interval contingency for the management of out-of-seat behavior." *Exceptional Children* 37 (1970): 113–17.

Wood, N. E. *Delayed speech and language development.* Englewood Cliffs, N.J.: Prentice-Hall, 1964.

Wood, N. E. *Verbal learning.* San Rafael, Calif.: Dimensions, 1969.

Woolbright, W. J. Test results and what they mean. *Academic Therapy* 6 (1971): 429–31.

Zifferblatt, S. M. *You can help your child improve study and homework behaviors.* Champaign, Ill.: Research Press, 1970.

Zigmond, N. K., & Cicci, R. *Auditory learning.* San Rafael, Calif.: Dimensions, 1968.

Zimmerman, I. L., Steiner, V. G., & Evatt, R. L. *Preschool language manual.* Columbus, Ohio: Charles E. Merrill, 1969.

Zimmerman, J., Zimmerman, E., Rider, S. L., Smith, A. F., & Dinn, R. "Doing your own thing with precision: The essence of behavior management in the classroom." *Educational Technology* 11, no. 4 (1971): 26–32.

Index

Name Index